Mary and Archie Tisdall acquired their great love of travel during Archie's service in the Royal Air Force, when they were in such diverse countries as Singapore, Jordan, Libya, Tunisia and Malta. After returning to live in England, they bought a motorcaravan and started to explore Europe. Gradually they began to write of their experiences for magazines.

They have travelled extensively in Spain, spending many winters in the Canary Islands. This resulted, in 1984, in the publication of two guide books: *Gran Canaria and the Eastern Canary Islands* (which is now published in two volumes, *Gran Canaria* and *Lanzarote and Fuerteventura*) and *Tenerife and the Western Canary Islands* of which this book is a completely revised new edition with an expanded section for La Palma, La Gomera and El Hierro. Their affection for Spain has also taken them to the Balearic Islands and the outcome is a three title series: *Majorca*, *Menorca* and *Ibiza and Formentera*. Other books include *The Algarve* and *Madeira and Porto Santo*.The need to update and revise their books, and to look for new material, now keeps Mary and Archie Tisdall happily on the move for a large part of the year. They have two sons and two daughters, and when not travelling live in Salisbury, Wiltshire.

Acknowledgements

We wish to thank the following individuals and organisations:
Tenerife: The Director Patronato de Turismo and Gloria Salgado, and also Marion at the Officino de Turismo, Santa Cruz; Tim Wise, Concay Inmobiliaras, Puerto de la Cruz; Viajes Insular.
La Palma: The Director Patronato de Turismo and Gilberto Duque Lugo, also the Director of Sol Hotels.
La Gomera: The Director Patronato de Turismo and Lourdes Garcia, also David Diaz Herrera and Cecilia.
El Hierro: The Director Patronato de Turismo and Luis Espinosa Krawany.
London: The Director of the Spanish National Tourist Office; Thomson Holidays and Gloria Ward.
Salisbury: Lunn Poly and Jerry Dell.
Worthing: Classic Collection Holidays, Arthur Thomson.
Madrid: The Trasmediterranea Shipping Company, Angel Mato Adrover and Carlos Rodriguez Copete, ships' captains and crews; and Maria Eugenie, Santa Cruz de Tenerife.

Our grateful thanks to all our family and friends; to our patient editor Yvonne Messenger, and Vanessa Charles; Kelso Graphics, Scotland; and finally our publisher, Roger Lascelles.

Canary Island Series

TENERIFE

La Palma   La Gomera   El Hierro

Mary & Archie Tisdall

Roger Lascelles, Cartographic and Travel Publisher

47 York Road, Brentford, (Middx) TW8 0QP. Tel: 081 847 0935 Fax: 081 568 3886

Publication Data

Title	Tenerife, La Palma, La Gomera, El Hierro
Printing	Kelso Graphics, Kelso, Scotland
Photographs	By the authors
ISBN	1 858790 50 6
Maps	John Gill, Chessington
Edition	Fourth, Apr 1993
Publisher	Roger Lascelles
	47 York Road, Brentford, Middlesex, TW8 0QP
Copyright	Mary & Archie Tisdall

Distribution

Africa:	South Africa	Faradawn, Box 17161, Hillbrow 2038
Americas:	Canada	International Travel Maps & Books, P.O. Box 2290, Vancouver BC V6B 3W5.
	U.S.A.	Available through major booksellers with good foreign travel sections
Asia:	India	English Book Store, 17-L Connaught Circus, P.O. Box 328, New Delhi 110 001
Australasia:	Australia	Rex Publications, 15 Huntingdon Street, Crows Nest, N.S.W.
Europe:	Belgium	Brussels – Peuples et Continents
	Germany	Available through major booksellers with good foreign travel sections
	GB/Ireland	Available through all booksellers with good foreign travel sections.
	Italy	Libreria dell'Automobile, Milano
	Netherlands	Nilsson & Lamm BV, Weesp
	Denmark	Copenhagen – Arnold Busck, G.E.C. Gad, Boghallen
	Finland	Helsinki – Akateeminen Kirjakauppa
	Norway	Oslo – Arne Gimnes/J.G. Tanum
	Sweden	Stockholm/Esselte, Akademi Bokhandel, Fritzes, Hedengrens. Gothenburg/Gumperts, Esselte. Lund/Gleerupska.
	Switzerland	Basel/Bider: Berne/Atlas; Geneve/Artou; Lausanne/Artou: Zurich/Travel Bookshop

Contents

Part II: Tenerife

Part III: La Palma

Part IV: La Gomera

Part V: El Hierro

Foreword

'Across the seas we beheld Seven Islands, each with its own
special delight'

With a wonderful climate all year, sandy beaches, exotic landscapes,
a range of accommodation to suit all tastes, and shops stocked with a
wide selection of low priced goods, the Canary Islands are a paradise
for the holidaymaker.

This book explains how to get there, costs, where and when to
travel, with plenty of information about accommodation, attractions
and local life. Facts and information are as accurate as possible at the
time of going to press. The exchange rate quoted is 178 pesetas to £1.
These are free trade islands and you get good value for your money
as many items are subject only to local taxes.

The Canaries consist of seven main islands which lie in the
Atlantic, some seventy miles (112km) west of North Africa. They are
divided into Western and Eastern Provinces. This guide describes the
Western islands: Tenerife, La Palma, La Gomera and El Hierro. The
Eastern Islands of Gran Canaria, Lanzarote and Fuerteventura are
described in companion volumes.

Most of all we hope that these books will help you to know, visit
and enjoy the many delights of the golden Canary Islands, as we have
done.

ONE

About the Canary Islands

The charm of the Canaries

When you go to the Canary Islands you will find a sunny archipelago of seven islands in the Atlantic, lying just west of Morocco on the same parallel as the Bahamas. They are happy islands, peaceful yet full of life and cheerful colour. They are Lands of Eternal Spring, where sun-drenched days are refreshed by gentle breezes, and the blue seas are warm and invitingly clear.

The Canary Islands, easily accessible by sea and air, offer a wide range of accommodation from luxury resorts to casual island comfort to suit any need, taste and budget. You can sit in the sunshine for breakfast, lunch and tea, and dine by moonlight under a warm, starry sky.

Fresh fish, meats and tropical fruits will tempt your palate, while island rums, wines and liqueurs refresh the spirit.

The diversity of landscapes in the Canary Islands is unique: sand dunes in Maspalomas, Gran Canaria; black volcanic mountains in Lanzarote; lush green pine forests in La Palma; simple fishing villages in La Gomera and El Hierro, and tranquil beaches in Fuerteventura. There are many different places to enjoy: bright spots like Puerto de la Cruz in Tenerife or Playa del Ingles in Gran Canaria; historic buildings in Las Palmas; the mighty mountain of Teide; the splendour of Gomera's Valle Gran Rey.

There is a great range of activities: shopping for low-priced goods; refreshing swims in a warm Atlantic; fishing and wind surfing in ideal conditions; exploring hidden valleys, volcanic craters, tropical parks; wandering down ancient narrow streets and wondering at prehistoric caves; experiencing the lively night clubs and elegant casinos. The islands also offer some unfamiliar enjoyments: participating in charming folk dancing and flamenco; watching a wild west show; finding out how bananas grow; seeking out the little

A typical Canarian courtyard, with gracious fountain and luxuriant potted plants. The stairway leads to the carved pinewood balcony.

blind white crabs; riding a camel; sailing on a real windjammer; looking for the famous Canary song bird in its natural habitat.

Best of all, perhaps, you can soak up the sunshine and relax, warm and happy in the fresh clear air of the Canary Islands, at any time of year.

Their situation

The Canary Islands are an archipelago of seven major islands, Tenerife, La Gomera, La Palma, El Hierro, Gran Canaria, Lanzarote and Fuerteventura, and six small islets, Isla de los Lobos, Isla Graciosa, Isla de Montana Clara, Isla de Alegranza, Roque del Oeste and Roque del Este. The islands are situated in the Atlantic Ocean 112 km west of Morocco and 1120 km south of Spain, at a latitude of 28°. They are south of the islands of Madeira. The area of the archipelago is in the region of 7500 sq km. The Tropic of Cancer lies 480 km to the south.

The appearance of the Canary Islands indicates that they were formed by a number of violent volcanic eruptions many years ago so there is much evidence of volcanic cones and lava. The highest point of eruption was Mount Teide, in Tenerife.

Generally speaking the five most westerly islands, Gran Canaria, Tenerife, La Palma, La Gomera and El Hierro, are more mountainous and green. Lanzarote and Fuerteventura, being dry desert, are immensely interesting and similar to parts of North Africa. The islands tend to have steep coastal cliffs in the north while the southern coasts are more level. Except for Lanzarote all have central high mountains.

The islands' features are rocky mountains, thick forests, deeply wooded ravines, fertile plains, volcanic wasteland and stretches of sand dunes. The best beaches are mainly on the east and south coasts. Some are golden or white, others are volcanic black sand.

Five small islets lie off the north of Lanzarote – La Graciosa Alegranza, Montana Clara, Roque del Oeste and Roque del Este.

The islet of La Graciosa is 42 sq km in area and can be clearly seen from Lanzarote, just a kilometre away. The population of 800 reside mainly at Caleta del Sebo, living by fishing and visits from tourists. Lovely golden beaches have been earmarked for future development. The other four islets are uninhabited, except for sea birds.

Between Lanzarote and Fuerteventura is the islet of Los Lobos, just 6.5 sq km. The only village is El Puertito, where the fishermen supplement their income from the holidaymakers who visit from Corralejo, the port in the north of Fuerteventura. Day trips can be made only when the sea is calm. The channel between Fuerteventura and Los Lobos, called La Bocaina, is noted for its strong currents and huge Atlantic rollers. It is also a plentiful fishing ground.

Climate

The Canary Islands are warm and fresh with spring-like weather. The mean temperature varies between 25°C and 18°C, with many days of brilliant sunshine; midday temperatures can reach 32°C, or more. The average sea temperature in winter is 18°C and in summer 22°C, making all year round swimming possible.

The small amount of rain falls mainly in the north of the islands, where it is more green with a humidity of between 60% and 69%. The rainfall is governed by the mountains on each island and varies accordingly. Tenerife and Gran Canaria have more rainfall than Lanzarote and Fuerteventura. Rain is heaviest between November and February–June, July and August being the driest months.

Winds are predominantly northwesterly (*Los Alisos*) occasionally veering to easterly when they bring hot air and dusty sand from North Africa. The latter wind is called *sirocco* and usually lasts three to four days. Because of the light breezes that blow most days, the climate is invigorating and gives a sense of well being.

Because of the mountains and the fact that the islands are small land masses, there can be considerable change in the weather on the same day. The north can be cloudy while the south remains sunny. There is a saying that somewhere on every island there is sunshine every day.

The sun sinks quickly in these latitudes giving short evenings so often spectacular sunsets are seen. The nights can be very clear and conducive to star gazing. Because of the clear air an Astro-Physical Observatory has been built on the island of La Palma.

Sufferers from bronchitis, influenza and asthma find much relief when staying in the Canary Islands, especially during the winter months. However those suffering from respiratory ailments should not settle in the city of Las Palmas, Gran Canaria, because of the acknowledged pollution problem caused by traffic congestion, dust from building projects and the occasional *sirocco* dust storm from the Sahara Desert.

Thus one of the biggest incentives to visit the Canary Islands is its

Climatic Chart

Average temperature	Jan	Feb	Mar	Apr	May	Jun	Jul	Aug	Sep	Oct	Nov	Dec	Yearly
°C	17.8	17.9	18.5	19.3	20.4	22.0	23.6	24.2	24.0	23.5	21.5	18.8	21.7
°F	64.0	64.2	65.3	66.7	68.7	71.6	74.4	75.5	75.2	74.3	70.7	65.8	71.0
Humidity%	67	67	66	64	63	63	59	60	65	68	69	67	65
Cloudy Days	2	1	0	0	1	0	0	0	0	0	1	2	7
Clear Days	6	6	6	8	7	8	11	12	9	6	3	4	86
Sunny Days	18	16	20	18	18	16	13	12	17	18	17	16	199
Rainy Days	7.5	6	4.9	4	2	1	1	1	2	6	10	9	54

predictable climate. With so little variation during the year and from one year to another, visitors can be assured of sunshine practically every day. Even if there is cloud, it will not be cold. The few rainy days do not last for long, then the sun shines again.

Los Cristianos beach has yellow sand which is swept clean every day. There are plenty of shops, bars and restaurants close by.

When to go

The Canary Islands are ideal for all-the-year-round holidays. During the summer months a high proportion of Spanish nationals visit the islands. During the period October to May, the majority of visitors come from the cooler climates of Germany, Scandinavia, Holland and France. Many local shop keepers and restaurant owners take their holidays during the month of June, which (they say) can be a slack month. It is also the cheapest travel period for package tours. The peak period is from November to February when a high percentage of the accommodation is booked in advance; this is the time of the year when most tourists from the UK arrive. Christmas and New Year is the most expensive period but good value. During the winter months there can be some low cloud and a little rain, which falls mainly in the north. Puerto de la Cruz has a moister and cooler climate than

Playa de las Americas, consequently the north has more vegetation than the drier south. If you wish to see the flora of Tenerife at its best go in March to July. Almond blossom time is early February.

Because of the constant demand in the most popular tourist areas of Playa de Las Americas and Puerto de la Cruz in Tenerife, it is advisable to plan one's visit well in advance, especially over the Christmas period.

Some hotels and apartments have tariff variation as follows:

Low season – 1 May to 30 June
Mid season – 1 July to 31 October
High season – 1 November to 30 April

Tourist information

Visitors to the Canary Islands require a valid passport. You do not need a visa for a stay of up to 90 days, but after this it may be necessary. Information can be obtained from: The Spanish Consulate, 20 Draycott Place, London SW3 2SB. Tel: 071 581 5921.

Up to date tourist information can be obtained from: The Spanish National Tourist Office, 57/58 St. James's Street, London SW1A 1LD. Tel: 071 499 0901.

Vaccinations are not normally needed for the Canary Islands. Only in the case of an epidemic would they be required.

Visitors are allowed to bring in any amount of foreign or local currency in notes or travellers cheques. You may take out 100,000 pesetas and foreign currency equivalent to 500,000 pesetas (£2,525).

Spanish Tourist Offices

The Spanish Tourist Industry is organised through the Secretaria de Estado, part of the Ministerio de Transportes, Turismo and Communicaciones and funded by the State. The Secretaria has a delegation in the capital of each province and public information offices are also there.

Oficinas Municipales de Turismo are situated in towns and villages of particular tourist interest and are there to provide information, free of charge. It is recommended that use be made of these tourist offices in the Canary Islands; they can supply lists of accommodation, island and town maps, literature often with good pictures. Although in some offices the staff may have only limited knowledge of English, much effort is made to assist tourists. They can be found in:

Western Province

Tenerife	Palacio Insular, Santa Cruz de Tenerife. Tel: 24 22 27.
La Palma	Calle O'Daly, Santa Cruz de la Palma. Tel: 41 16 41.
La Gomera	Calle Medio 4, San Sebastian. Tel: 87 01 55.
El Hierro	Cabildo Insular del Hierro, Valverde. Tel: 55 03 02.

Eastern Province

Gran Canaria	Parque Santa Catalina, Las Palmas. Tel: 26 46 23.
Lanzarote	Parque Municipale, Arrecife.
Fuerteventura	Ministero de Trabajo, Avenida General Franco, Puerto del Rosario.

TWO

Getting to the Canary Islands

Arrival by air

Of the seven islands, La Gomera is the only one that does not have an airport but one is being built near Playa de Santiago in the south of the island. (However there are ferries from Los Cristianos in the south of Tenerife to San Sebastian de la Gomera – see page 25.)

The airports of the Canaries

Tenerife	– Aeropuerto Los Rodeos (Inter Island) Tel: 25 79 40.
Aeropuerto	– Reina Sofia (International) Tel: 77 00 50.
Gran Canaria	– Aeropuerto de Gando
Fuerteventura	– Aeropuerto Los Estancas (Puerto del Rosario)
Lanzarote	– Aeropuerto de Lanzarote (Arrecife)
El Hierro	– Aeropuerto de Hierro (Valverde) – Tel: 44 01 15
La Palma	– Aeropuerto de la Palma. Tel: 44 01 15.

The airport at El Hierro is virtually a landing strip, but it is of good size and sufficient for the three return flights each day between Tenerife and El Hierro.

On all the other islands the airports are modern and efficient and well able to cope with the traffic, which is sometimes very heavy.

The system for handling passengers and their luggage is the same as for all international airports and the Spanish have no wish to slow the flow of tourists. The airports are well served with taxis and buses. Booking arrangements for hotels, apartments and car rental at Tenerife, Gran Canaria and Lanzarote can be made from the airport. But late arrivals may find the hotel booking desks closed, if so it is likely that a taxi driver will assist.

Further airport information is given in the chapters dealing with individual islands.

Air services
The only scheduled air service direct to the Canaries is provided by the Spanish state airline: Iberia, 169 Regent Street, London W1 RBE. Tel: 071 437 5622.

There are scheduled flights from London, via Madrid, to the Canary Islands, the return fare being about £200.

There are several charter flights used by package operators, which fly direct between the UK and the Canary Islands. Seats on these aircraft are sometimes available, without accommodation. Travel agents are able to supply details. Prices vary according to the season but can be lower than those of Iberia. The flight time between London/Gatwick and Reina Sophia, Tenerife is 4 hours.

There are no direct flights to La Palma or El Hierro but there are inter-island air services from Tenerife.

Inter island flight times

Reina Sophia or Los Rodeos (Tenerife)	to	Las Palmas (Gran Canaria) – 35 mins
	to	Los Estancos (Fuerteventura) – 55 mins
	to	Valverde (El Hierro) – 40 mins
	to	La Palma (La Palma) – 30 mins
	to	Arrecife (Lanzarote) – 40 mins

Arrival by sea (from Cadiz)

The only car and passenger ferry service operating from Spain to the Canary Islands is from Cadiz (southern Spain) to Tenerife, Gran Canaria, Fuerteventura and Lanzarote, and it is operated by the Trasmediterranea Shipping Company. It is not possible to go directly to the other islands, though there are ferries to La Palma, El Hierro and La Gomera from Tenerife, and to Lanzarote and Fuerteventura from Gran Canaria. But first you have to get to Cadiz ...

By rail to Cadiz

Rail tickets for travel from UK to Cadiz, Spain, can be obtained from: **European Rail Travel Centre**, Victoria Station, London SW1 1JY. Tel: 071 834 2345; or through a travel agent. There are no Spanish Railway agents in the UK.

By road to Cadiz

The most direct way is to cross from Plymouth (Devon) to Santander in northern Spain and then drive south to Cadiz (see section Driving in Spain – page 38).

Brittany Ferries operate a regular car and passenger ferry (from Millbay Docks, Plymouth) throughout the year. The crossing takes twenty-four hours in fully stabilised ships. Driving into the car deck is a simple operation. The ships are comfortable with air-conditioned de luxe, two- and four-berth cabins, some with showers and toilets. There is a wide promenade, sun deck, lounges with bars and dance floor, restaurant, duty free shop, cinema, games and children's room.

Arriving in Santander, there are many routes across Spain, the most direct being via Burgos, Madrid, Cordoba and Sevilla to Cadiz. Distance on this route is 1165 km.

One can cross to France by using any of the Channel ports and travel overland to Spain, thence down to Cadiz in the south. However, during the winter months the mountain passes in northern Spain and Andorra can be closed by snow. An alternative route is to drive down to the French Mediterranean and continue along the east coast line of Spain to reach Cadiz.

Yet another variation is to reach Spain and drive along the north coast, then down the western coast in Portugal and along the Algarve to Spain and Cadiz. The latter route, though much longer, gives a very scenic drive.

Ferry costs vary with type of accommodation and length of vehicle but examples of tourist one-way costs with **Brittany Ferries** are:

	High	Low Season
Plymouth to Santander		
Car and 2 persons with cabin	£336	£249
Portsmouth to St Malo		
Car and two persons	£199	£124

Brittany Ferries Millbay Docks, Plymouth PL1 3EF. Tel: 0752 221321
The Brittany Centre Wharf Road, Portsmouth, PO7 8RU. Tel: 0705 827701.
P. & O. Ferries Freepost, Southampton, SO9 1BG.
Sealink Travel Ltd. PO Box 29, Victoria Station, London SW1V 1JX. Tel: 071 834 8122.

The ferry from Cadiz

During the winter months Trasmediterranea run one ferry a week between Cadiz (in southern Spain) and the Canary Islands. During the summer (2 June to 6 October) it crosses every two days. The ferry calls at Santa Cruz de Tenerife, Las Palmas de Gran Canaria, Fuerteventura and Lanzarote on every voyage, taking nearly two days for the full trip. This is the only ferry service operating between the Spanish peninsula and the Canaries. It is advisable to book well in advance.

There are two ferry ships operating the service at present. They are similar, of about 10,000 tons, each carrying 743 passengers and 250 vehicles. Described as floating hotels, they have a swimming pool, à la carte restaurant, self-service cafeteria, bars, sport facilities, reading room, dance floor, television, shop, hairdresser, children's playroom and lifts. First and Tourist Class, two, three and four berth cabin accommodation is provided.

The Trasmediterranea ferry ships operating between the islands are smaller but services are adequate considering that the voyages are of shorter duration: about seven hours and usually overnight. First and Tourist Class accommodation is provided. All Trasmediterranea ferries have vehicle space, which is drive-on/drive-off. On occasions it may be necessary to reverse on to the car deck.

Trasmediterranea also provide a Jetfoil service between Las Palmas de Gran Canaria and Santa Cruz de Tenerife. It is very fast, taking only eighty minutes, and there are four services a day. Popular with business people and day trippers. Foot passengers only. U.K. Agent for Trasmediterranea is:

Melia Travel Agencies 273 Regent Street, London W1R 7PB. Tel: 071 499 6493.

Reservations can also be made in Spain through travel agents. Trasmediterranea have offices in a number of towns in Spain.

In Cadiz: Avenida de Carranza, 26. Tel: 28 43 11. Telex 76028.

In Madrid: (Head Office) Plaza Manuel Gomez Moreno. Tel: 456 00 07. Telex 27731.

In Las Palmas: Muelle Santa Catalina. Tel: 26 00 70.

In Santa Cruz de Tenerife: (Administration Offices), Marina 59. Tel: 28 78 50. For reservations and tickets: Muelle Norte.

Ports in the Canary Islands

The location of the ports on each island where ferries, car ferries, jetfoil and cruise liners arrive and depart are:

Tenerife
Santa Cruz: All services.
Los Cristianos: Gomera Ferry (to La Gomera). Trasmediterranea to La Gomera.

La Palma
Santa Cruz: Trasmediterranea to Santa Cruz de Tenerife

La Gomera
San Sebastian: Trasmediterranea to Los Cristianos, Tenerife. Gomera Ferry to Los Cristianos, Tenerife.

El Hierro
Puerto de la Estaca: Trasmediterranea to Santa Cruz de Tenerife and La Gomera.

Gran Canaria
Las Palmas: All services.

Lanzarote
Arrecife: Trasmediterranea to Las Palmas, Gran Canaria.
Playa Blanca: Alisur Ferry to Corralejo, Fuerteventura.

Fuerteventura
Puerto del Rosario: Trasmediterranea to Las Palmas, Gran Canaria; Arrecife, Lanzarote.
Corralejo: Alisur Ferry to Playa Blanca, Lanzarote.
Morrojable: Trasmediterranea to Santa Cruz de Tenerife and Las Palmas, Gran Canaria.

Inter island ferry services

Trasmediterranea Shipping Company
Santa Cruz de Tenerife to las Palmas, Gran Canaria;
* Departs Tuesday, Thursday, Saturday, Sunday 1800 hrs.
  Santa Cruz de Tenerife to Santa Cruz de la Palma:
* Departs Wednesday, Friday 2345 hrs.
Santa Cruz de Tenerife to El Hierro:
* Departs Monday, Wednesday, Friday 2345 hrs.
  Santa Cruz de Tenerife to Feurteventura:
* Departs Monday, Thursday 1800 hrs.

Jetfoil service
Santa Cruz de Tenerife to Las Palmas de Gran Canaria:
* Departs daily except Sunday 0730, 0915, 1600 hrs. Sunday 1915, 1600 hrs.
  Single fare 4,650 pesetas. Tel: 277570.
Santa Cruz de Tenerife to Morrojable, Fuerteventura.
  Departs daily except Sunday at 0915 hrs.
  Single fare 6,700 pesetas

The inter island ferry m/v Ciudad de La Laguna departs from Santa Cruz de Tenerife for La Palma and El Hierro.

Hydrofoil service
Los Cristianos to San Sebastián de la Gomera:
* Departs daily 0800, 1000, 1500 and 1700. Crossing time 35 minutes.
  Single fare 2,100 pesetas. Tel: 796178

Gomera ferry service
The Gomera Ferry operates one ship, the 'Benchijugua', between Los Cristianos, Tenerife and San Sebastián de la Gomera. Tel: 21 90 33. A modern car and passenger ferry, it takes one and a half hours for the journey. There is a connecting bus service between Los Cristianos and Santa Cruz de Tenerife.

San Sebastián de la Gomera – 0800, 1330 and 1800 hrs.

Los Cristianos – 1000, 1530 and 2000 hrs.

Fares:

Passenger, single – 1450 pesetas

Vehicle and two passengers, return – 10,800 pesetas.

Cruises

The following companies operate inclusive luxury liner cruises to the Canary Islands:

Fred Olsen Travel Ltd. Crown House, Crown Street, Ipswich, Suffolk 1P1 3HB. Tel: 081 780 1040.

P & O 77 New Oxford Street, London WC1A 1PP. Tel: 071 831 1331 (P & O Cruises), 071 831 1881 (Princess Cruises).

CTC Lines 1 Regent Street, London, SW1Y 4NN. Tel: 071 930 5833.

Cunard 8 Berkeley Street, London W1. Tel: 071 491 3930.

Arrival by yacht

For those who have the necessary skills and a suitable yacht, it is possible to reach the Canary Islands, though it is well to realise they are in the Atlantic Ocean, not the Mediterranean. For up to date details write to:

National Assembly of Yacht Captains Muelle España, Zona Deportiva, Barcelona, Spain; or

The Spanish Sailing Federation Juan Vigon 23, Madrid, Spain.

Yacht and boat facilities

The Canary Islands are ideally situated for yachts and motor vessels, having many suitable marinas and moorings, natural sheltered bays and harbours. Many boats moor there for the winter season, some waiting, as Christopher Columbus did, for the trade winds to take them to the West Indies. There are yacht marinas in:

Tenerife: Real Club Náutico, Carretera de San Andres, Santa Cruz de Tenerife. Tel: 27 37 00.

Gran Canaria: Real Club Náutico, Leon y Castillo, Las Palmas. Tel: 23 45 66.

Lanzarote: Casino Club Náutico, Calle Blas Cabrera Felipe, Arrecife.

Fuerteventura: Club Náutico Mar Azul, Puerto Azul Tarajalejo, Tuinje.

La Palma: New Royal Yacht Club, General Mola 6, Santa Cruz de la Palma. Tel: 41 11 84.

La Gomera: Yacht Club, Calle del Conde, San Sebastián de la Gomera. Tel: 87 10 53.

The following ports in the Western Province have yacht moorings or anchorages:

Tenerife: Candelaria, Las Galletas, Los Cristianos, Los Gigantes, Puerto Colon and Radazul.

La Palma: Santa Cruz de la Palma, Tazacorte, Puerto Naos.

La Gomera: San Sebastián, Playa de Santiago, Valle Gran Rey.

El Hierro: Puerto de las Estaca, La Restinga.

It should be noted that this list is by no means comprehensive. Further information should be obtained. A useful book is *The Canary Island Cruising Guide* (Guia Nautica de Canarias) ISBN 0 9517486 02. World Cruising Publications, PO Box 165, London WC1 5LA.

THREE

Where to stay

The range of accommodation

Once, the most popular holiday destination in Tenerife was Puerto de La Cruz in the north, where the climate is moist and the scenery luxuriant. Of recent years, there has been a vast increase of tourist accommodation in the dry south, and Playa de las Americas, with its higher sunshine rate and holiday fun atmosphere, has overtaken its rival in the north. Los Cristianos, too, is next in favour, having a lively port, sandy beach and long promenade.

In the south-west Los Gigantes has kept its upmarket image. However this resort is hilly and can be difficult for the elderly. More suitable is the small southern town of El Medano where the now limited accommodation is being increased. Because of high winds and strong seas on either side of the sheltered town beach many windsurfers holiday here.

In the north of Tenerife, Punta Hidalgo, Bajamar, Los Silos and San Marcos are all small quiet seaside resorts where it is advisable to rent a car. There is little tourist accommodation in the mountainous centre of the island.

In the past accommodation in La Palma, La Gomera and El Hierro has been sparse apart from the Paradors, but recently there has been an improvement in the tourist industry of these islands and all are welcoming holidaymakers. Classic Collection Holidays of Worthing offer holidays there.

Accommodation ranges from luxury hotels to simple guesthouses and camping. An up-to-date list of all types of accommodation currently available in Tenerife, La Palma, La Gomera and El Hierro can be obtained from: The Tourist Office (Palacio Insular), Plaza España, Santa Cruz de Tenerife. Tel: 24 22 27.

It is recommended that you choose accommodation that has been inspected by the Tourist Board and that you book through property or travel agents. It is unwise to seek unlisted places, especially in the cities where some proprietors may not observe security regulations nor maintain hygiene standards.

Hotels and guesthouses

Hotels
Hotels (*Hoteles* – H) are classified from 1 to 5 stars. The rating is always displayed outside as H plus the number of stars. Hotels provide rooms and meals as required in their own restaurant. The larger hotels usually have outdoor swimming pools, tennis courts, shops and entertainment. Many have courtesy buses to take visitors to the beach. Those with three stars or more provide rooms with private bathrooms and toilets. Most have balconies often with sea views. Maid service and laundry should be available.

Hotel Apartments
Hotel Apartments (*Apartamentos Hoteles* – HA) are similar to hotels but have flats, bungalows or chalets. The star rating is shown after HA.

Residential Hotels
The hotels (*Hoteles Residencia* – HR) supply rooms but without restaurant facilities. They usually have less luxurious furnishings though often have private bathrooms and toilets.

Guesthouses
Modest hotels and guesthouses (*Hostales* – HS) with a star rating of one to three. They provide accommodation with or without meals. They do not have dormitories.

Pensions
Guesthouses (*Pensiones* – P) with a small number of rooms, providing full board.

Residences
These establishments (*Residencias* – R) provide accommodation with a shared bathroom. Only breakfast available.

Inns

Inns (*pousadas, tabernas*) are usually in country districts; the standard is mostly good, but can vary. It is best to view rooms before booking. Often in beautiful surroundings with local atmosphere.

The star rating

Below is a brief description of the star rating with approximate cost of a double room (non package and excluding the 4% tax) per night, with breakfast.

Five-star hotel – 24,000 pesetas. Air conditioning in public rooms and bedrooms. All bedrooms have bathrooms, hot and cold water, telephone. Laundry and ironing service. Some suites have sitting rooms. Garage, lift and bar. Hairdresser.

Four-star hotel – 13,000 pesetas. Air conditioning in public rooms and bedrooms. Seventy-five per cent of bedrooms have bathrooms with hot and cold water, telephone. Laundry and ironing service. Garage, lift and bar.

One of the luxury hotels in the south. This one has the unusual feature of gold coloured lifts which run externally up and down the modern facade.

Three-star hotel – 9,000 pesetas. Fifty per cent of bedrooms have bathrooms with bath. Fifty per cent have showers, washbasin, WC, telephone. Laundry and ironing service. Full central heating.

Two-star hotel – 7,000 pesetas. Fifteen per cent of bedrooms have bathrooms with baths, Forty-seven per cent have showers, washbasins and WC, one common bathroom to six bedrooms, telephone. Lift in buildings of more than four storeys. Full central heating.

One-star hotels – 5,500 pesetas. Twenty-five per cent of bedrooms have washbasin, shower and WC. Twenty-five per cent with shower and washbasin. One common bathroom to every seven bedrooms. Laundry and ironing service. Telephone on every floor. Lift in buildings of more than five storeys. Full central heating.

Three-star guesthouses – 5,000 pesetas. Five per cent of bedrooms with bathrooms with bath. Ten per cent with shower, washbasin and WC, one common bathroom to every eight rooms, telephone. Laundry and ironing service. Lounge.

Two-star guesthouses – 4,500 pesetas. All bedrooms have washbasin, one common bathroom to every ten bedrooms. Public telephone. Lounge and lobby. Lift in five storey buildings.

One-star guesthouse 3,500 pesetas. All bedrooms have washbasins with cold water. One bathroom for twelve rooms. Public telephone.

It is advisable to book accommodation in advance, particularly at the time of festivals and at tourist resorts. Reservations in writing can be sent direct to hotels. Letters sent to five, four and three-star hotels can be written in English. For lower categories it is advisable to write in Spanish. More details of hotels are given in the island chapters.

Paradors

A *parador* is the name given to hotels (Paradors Nacionales de Turismo) run by the Secretary of State for Tourism in Spain and the Canary Islands. Ususally they are in converted historic castles, palaces, convents and monasteries and generally in a location of special scenic beauty or interest. Internal decor is of a luxurious standard, often containing antiques and works of art. They offer every comfort as well as an excellent cuisine. The restaurants are open to non-residents. Sometimes paradors can be more expensive than equivalent hotels but they provide a unique tourist experience. It is advisable to book in advance.

The Spanish Tourist Office publishes an informative brochure called 'Paradores', which is given free on request. In the Western Canaries there are *paradors* in Tenerife (Parador Nacional Canadas del Teide), La Palma (Parador Nacional de Santa Cruz de la Palma) and El Hierro (Parador Nacional Isla del Hierro).

Apartments, bungalows and villas

Self-catering accommodation is available on all the main islands. In the big resorts purpose-built blocks are of enormous size, having their own restaurants, public rooms, swimming pools, sports facilities, supermarket, hairdressing salon and boutique. Some have evening entertainments, such as flamenco shows and music groups.

In the apartments (*apartamentos*) provisions will include bed linen, towels, kitchen equipment and cooking facilities, with cutlery, crockery and glasses. The majority have balconies, often with sea views. High rise blocks have lifts. Most provide maid service but in some cases only once a week. At the reception, details will be found of local entertainment, coach excursions and car hire.

Often built around a swimming pool, bungalows and villas are more attractive as they usually have gardens and shrubs close by. There are always restaurants, bars and supermarkets in the vicinity.

Some (approximate) non-package tour accommodation prices are:

Los Cristianos, Tenerife – One bedroom apartment, can sleep four, 25,000 pesetas per week.

Ten Bel, Tenerife – Seaside bungalow in holiday complex, swimming pools, sports facilities, entertainments, transfer from airport. Sleeps four to six. 29,000 pesetas per week.

Camping

Camping rules that apply in mainland Spain also apply in the Canary Islands. A copy of the camping regulations should be obtained by anyone intending to camp in the Canaries. This can be obtained from:

The Spanish National Tourist Office 57-58 St. James's Street, London SW1A 1LD. Tel: 071 499 0901.

The official Spanish camp site list shows only one site in Tenerife and none in La Gomera, La Palma and El Hierro. However, in all the islands there are Parques Recreativo in forests where camping is permitted at certain times. Usually only water, toilets and barbecue fires are provided. These sites can become very busy with students

Modern facilities and level pitches, with fine views of the Teide Mountains makes Camping Nauta popular with Canarians and international campers.

and Canarians. But Europeans have been known to have used these places, though permission from the Tourist Office or Town Hall should be obtained. See island chapters for more details of camping parks. Because of the lack of camp sites, off site camping is tolerated in the islands, but care is required in conforming with the regulations.

It is not necessary to have a Camping Carnet, but it is an advantage, particularly for those who camp outside sites, as third party insurance is included. Camping Carnets can be obtained from camping and motoring organisations such as the AA, RAC and Caravan Club, and cost approximately £3. A passport-size photo is required.

Camping on site

You will be required to present your passport at the camp site reception. Persons under the age of 16 may not be admitted unless accompanied by an adult. Silence must be respected between 2300 and 0800 hours. Fires are not permitted except in allocated places. Campers are not allowed to carry offensive weapons. Valuables may be left with the camp manager for safe keeping. Most sites have their own post boxes and supermarkets. Every reception office has an official complaints book.

Camping off site

Camping is allowed outside official camp sites provided one has the permission of the owner of the land. Areas where most campers tend to congregate are in the south of Tenerife but, generally speaking, campers are accepted on all the islands (although Canarians would prefer that visitors used the hotels, villas and apartments). We advise campers to seek the advice of the local police when they wish to camp in this way.

No more than three units may camp together for more than three days outside a site and the number must not exceed ten persons. In the case where campers wish to stay longer, special permission must be obtained, giving at least 15 days notice, from:

Provincial Delegado de Turismo Calle de la Marina 5, Santa Cruz de Tenerife.

Camping is not allowed in the following places: on dry river beds, seasonal flooding areas; within military, industrial or tourist areas; within a radius of 150 metres from the source of a town's water supply; within urban areas or unreasonably near the roadside; within one kilometre of an official camp site.

Backpackers

As we have said, although there are many beaches, camping is not permitted in most tourist areas. In the past, the 'hippy' type of backpacker has caused the authorities much trouble, hence the reluctance to let groups of campers forgather. However, back-packers do visit the islands, using simple hostels with the odd night camping; but care is required in conforming with the regulations.

Caravans

The terrain of the Canary Islands is not conducive to touring with a towed caravan. After using them to cross Europe, caravanners then stay in rented accommodation. Now that Camping Nauta (Las Galletas, Tenerife) is open, caravans park there for long periods and people tour with their cars. Some reduction is made for long stays. A few hardy caravanners may find quiet places which are suitable for a short stay, having obtained permission from the police or the owner: these sites, usually on waste ground, are few and far between.

Motorcaravans

Certainly the most suitable way to camp in the Canary Islands is to use a motorcaravan. The diversity of scenery and regions makes travelling interesting and varied. Provided one parks with consideration to the regulations there should be few problems.

Hints for campers

One of the main requirements of all campers is water, which in the Canary Islands is in short supply. Therefore it is necessary to conserve and plan ahead. Most petrol filling stations will allow containers to be filled but make sure that it is drinking water (*agua potable*) or buy bottled water from a supermarket. Camping 'Gaz' is available in towns and some villages.

Further information on camping in the Canary Islands can be obtained from periodicals such as *Caravan*; *Camping; Motorcaravan, Motorhome Monthly and Motorcaravan World*.

A new club for caravan and motorcaravanners has recently been formed in Tenerife called Caravanning Club Tinerfe Canarias. One of its aims is to improve camping conditions and amenities on the islands. Further information can be obtained from: Tim Wise, Calle Enrique Talg, Apartado 670, Puerto de la Cruz. Tel: 37 14 52 and 37 21 06.

If you are taking a trailer caravan or motorcaravan to Tenerife it is necessary to travel to the Spanish port of Cadiz to embark on the Trasmediterranea ferry for Santa Cruz (see Chapter One). The voyage takes two days. From Santa Cruz it's an easy drive of about an hour south along the fast autopista to Nauta Camping, which will be signposted at the turn seawards for Las Galletas. The address for making your booking is: Nauta Camping, Canada Blanca, Las Galletas, Tenerife. Two camps are soon to open in the north.

Travel agents' services

There are numerous travel agents (*viajes*) in the tourist parts of the Canary Islands. Their services are varied: agents for hotels, apartments, ferry and flight bookings; car hire, coach tours and currency exchange. Open from 0900 to 1300 and 1630 to 1900 hrs, Monday to Friday. 0900 to 1300 on Saturday and closed on Sundays and Public Holidays.

British-run Viajes Blandy, Fernando Poo and Wagonlit Cooks have branches in Tenerife, as do Melia, Solymar, Macari, Barcelo and Phileas Fogg. Other well established firms are Viajes Cyrasa, Insular and Ultramar Express. The latter two firms have English-speaking staff and excursions throughout the islands with coaches that are modern and comfortable.

Ultramar Express La Hoya 26, Puerto de la Cruz. Tel: 38 17 50. Avenida de Sol, Bajamar, La Laguna. Tel: 54 11 04. Complejo Comercial, Playa de las Americas. Tel: 79 12 51.

Viajes Insular Avenida del Generalisimo 15, Puerto de la Cruz. Tel: 38 02 62. Playa de las Americas. Tel: 79 01 54.

The Travel Shop Parque Margarita, Los Cristianos. Tel: 79 37 22 or 79 35 64. In addition to all the usual touristic services and money exchange etc. this English owned and English speaking agency specialises in very competitively priced flights to England from Tenerife.

Package holidays

There are many UK firms operating package holidays to the Canary Islands. These provide a wide choice of selection and offer good value to holidaymakers with a limited amount of time. They also enable customers to budget in advance for most of their holiday expenses.

When you book a package holiday, the price of the air fare is included, plus transport to and from your destination, unless otherwise stated. Tour operators' brochures will give details of flight arrangements, type of resort, entertainments and the star rating of the accommodation. These vary from five-star luxury hotels to modest guesthouses, self-catering apartments and villas. In some instances it is possible to visit more than one island during your holiday.

At present the islands of Tenerife and Gran Canaria have the most package tours available, with Lanzarote a very popular third choice. Fuerteventura has recently entered the tourist market and now has hotels in both north and south. Thomson Holidays and Select go to Gomera.

In the larger resorts and holiday complexes like Puerto de la Cruz and Playa de las Americas entire hotels and apartment blocks are taken over by the tour operator and prove so popular that they are full for most of the year. The cheaper high season packages are to simple self-catering apartments and cost about £225 per person sharing a double room or apartment for two weeks. Hotels will cost about £275 to £350 for the same period but can increase to £500. (One has to remember that the Canary Islands are a 4-hour flight from London, which makes it more expensive than going to the Mediterranean.)

Amongst the tour operators offering Canary Island packages are: Airlink, Aspro, Airtour, Cambrian, Carousel, Cosmos, Ellerman,

Enterprise, Horizon, Martyn, Palmair, Select, Sovereign, Student Travel, Thomson Holidays, Tjaereborg and Travel Club.

Saga Holidays offer package holidays to Tenerife for the over-sixties during 'off-peak' periods. Thomson Holidays 'Young at Heart' brochure has extended winter holidays.

An independent specialist operator who gives a very personal service on a high level is Classic Collection Holidays, Wiston House, 1 Wiston Avenue, Worthing, West Sussex BN14 7QL. Tel: 0903 823088. Their package holidays are based on using scheduled flights, so holidays are totally flexible to meet individual requirements. With stays from three nights to three months they offer Two Centre holidays and Explorer Tours which can include taxi or self-drive. In some instances their high class accommodation is exclusive to the UK market, especially in the smaller Canary Islands.

Timeshare

Time share is the ownership of a property (apartment or bungalow) for any period you care to purchase, such as a week, a month or more in a year. There is a once only payment, and then an annual fee to cover maintenance, electricity and water. It is a modern way to own a holiday home for the purchased period and you are free to use it as you wish. For example the Club Tenerife, Los Cristianos offer properties. The purchase cost for a one-bedroom apartment for one week a year cost from £1,695 (tel: 75 08 12). You are advised to seek qualified advice before signing any documents.

Property and real estate agents

The Canary Islands present an appealing location for purchasers to invest in property, but it is advisable to get specialist advice on the subject.

Selling apartments, bungalows and villas, the administration of properties, letting, legal advice, repairs, technical services and insurance, are all transactions carried out by real estate companies in the Canary Islands, and most of the firms employ multi-lingual staff, trained to assist clients.

'Time-sharing' is on the increase and firms like Wimpey have recently entered the market. *Urbanizaciones*, as property developments are called, tend to group in nationalities in particular areas. For instance, Scandinavians seem not to mix a great deal with Germans.

The British appear to favour Puerto de la Cruz and Playa de las Americas in Tenerife.

Real estate companies and agents in Tenerife where English is spoken are:

Santa Cruz de Tenerife: Felix Morales Ruiz , Villalba Hervas 1. Tel: 27 63 63.

Los Cristianos: Ocean Properties, Avenida Suecia 50. Tel: 79 12 62.

Puerto de la Cruz: Tim Wise, Inmobiliaria Concay, Edificio Iguazu, Calle Enrique Talg, Apartado 670. Tel: 37 14 52 and 37 21 06. Advice given for booking apartments. English resident (18 years). Highly recommended.

FOUR

Getting about in the Canaries

There are no trains in the Canary Islands so you have to get about by road. Fortunately the main roads and motorways are good, and *autopistas* (motorways) are free of tolls. Traffic is heavy only in cities and towns but the driving is well disciplined. However roads in the country are sometimes little more than rough tracks across desert land and progress can be slow.

A good road map of the Canary Islands is therefore essential. Recommended is the series published by Firestone Hispania available in the Canary Islands from petrol filling stations and bookshops. In Great Britain and Ireland they can be obtained from bookshops with a strong foreign map section or direct, by post, from the agent, Roger Lascelles (Dept Firestone) 47 York Road, Brentford, Middlesex, TW8 0QP. Tel: 081-847 0935. Map T-32 covers all the Canary Islands. Map E-50 is of Tenerife only, with several useful town plans. Map V-1 details the four islands of the Western Province covered by this book.

Driving in Spain and the Canary Islands

If you are taking a car to the Canary Islands, driving through Spain and taking the car ferry from Cadiz to either Tenerife or Gran Canaria you will require the following:
1   Driving Licence
2   International Driving Permit
3   Green Card Insurance (issued by your insurance company)
4   Bail Bond (from AA, RAC or insurance company – this is an indemnity if you are involved in an accident)
5   Vehicle Registration Document
6   Passport

  7   A spare set of light bulbs (Spanish law requirement)
  8   A red triangle, for warning of breakdown obstruction
  9   Means of changing direction of headlight dip
10   GB sticker

Up to date information on this subject is best obtained from the AA, RAC or the Spanish Tourist Office. However, the following points are worthy of note:

- Drive on the right-hand side of the road.
- Sound your horn when overtaking.
- Stop for pedestrians on crossings.
- Wear seatbelts.
- Only sidelights required in built up areas.
- Do not cross the single white line, it is equivalent to the double white line in the UK.
- Observe the no overtaking signs, and speed limits.
- Give way to traffic coming from the right, particularly at roundabouts.

There is an on-the-spot fine for failing to use seat belts and for other offences, so it is advisable to carry about 25,000 pesetas with you. Maximum speed in towns and villages is 40 kph, elsewhere 90 kph. Police patrol on motor cycles especially on the Carretera General (main road).

Road signs

Most road signs are international. One important traffic control is the *cambio de sentido* (direction change), generally controlled by traffic lights, which prevents vehicles turning across oncoming traffic or from doing a U-turn. Here are some road sign translations:

Aduana   customs post
Aparcamiento   parking
Atencion   caution
Blandones   soft verges
Cedo el paso   give way
Despacio   slow
Desvio   diversion
Derecha   right
Escuela   school
Estacionamiento prohibido   no parking
Izquierda   left
Obras   workmen
Pare   stop
Peligro   danger

Peligroso   dangerous
Paso prohibido   no thoroughfare
Peatones   pedestrians
Salidas   exit

Petrol filling stations

In the Canary Islands some petrol filling stations are closed all day Sundays and public holidays. They do not provide car repair services; this is a separate service (*taller mechanico*). Good toilets and drinking water can be found at filling stations. Auto shops sell spares and sweets. Car wash services are similar to those in the UK.

Petrol comes in three grades: Extra – 98 octane, Super – 96 octane, Normal – 92 octane. At the time of writing super is 63 pesetas per litre. Do not confuse petrol (*gasolina*) with diesel (*gasoil*) which is 49 pesetas per litre. Some lead free (*sin plombo*) is available at 61 pesetas per litre.

Car servicing and repairs

There are plenty of places for servicing and repairing cars. The cities of Tenerife and Gran Canaria have agents for most well-known British and foreign cars. There could be some delay in obtaining a particular spare part required from abroad.

In country places a small workshop (*taller mechanico*), which deals with local vehicles, will assist. The standard is good and repairs are promptly effected. Costs are usually more reasonable than in the UK. Facilities for tyre fitting, battery charging and car washing are available.

Car hire

Self-drive car hire agencies in the Canary Islands include international names like Hertz and Avis, Organizacion Canaria Coches Aquiler (abbreviation OCCA) and local firms. Prices vary, so it is worth shopping around if you are in a large resort such as Puerto de la Cruz.

The type of cars range from a luxury Mercedes to a safari jeep. Motorcycles, scooters and bicycles can also be rented. (Crash helmets have to be worn on motorcycles.) Some idea of price is given below (clients pay for petrol):

Seat Marbella, 3450 pesetas per day. 22,150 pesetas per week.
Opel Corsa, 3800 pesetas per day. 23,500 pesetas per week.

Ford Fiesta, 3900 pesetas per day. 24,000 pesetas per week.
Seat Ibiza, 4600 pesetas per day. 26,500 pesetas per week.
Ford Escort, 5500 pesetas per day. 28,000 pesetas per week.
Jeep Suzuki, 6500 pesetas per day. 35,000 pesetas per week.
Minibus 9 places, 9000 pesetas per day. 47900 pesetas per week.

Avis UK can arrange to have a car for you at the Aeropuerto Reina Sofia, Tenerife, on your arrival. If you book in the UK it will cost you less. Telephone 081 848 8733 for details.

In some instances the minimum age for drivers is 21. Passport, driving licence and a deposit of about 7000 pesetas are required. Confirm that vehicle insurance is included in the hire cost – this is usually about 1000 pesetas per day and personal insurance 400 pesetas per day. It is advisable to book in advance.

Getting about by bus

Tenerife is well provided with public bus services; in the other islands the service is adequate. Bus stops are marked, sometimes by *parada* (stopping place). You always enter a bus from the front and buy your ticket from the conductor or driver; only single journey (*ida*) tickets are issued. Remember to retain your ticket as inspectors cover all routes. Canary bus queues are usually orderly and line up facing the direction which the bus will travel. For long distances there are fast buses having limited stops, sometimes marked *Expres* or *Directo*. Buses run every day including public holidays. Timetables can be obtained from Tourist Offices and some bus terminals. Further information is given in the sections describing individual islands.

The Canarians call their buses *guaguas* (pronounced 'wah wah') but *autobus* is generally understood. Vehicles range from comfortable long distance coaches to ancient bone-shakers on the smaller islands. A *Titsa* bus is a long distance public transport bus, which is a green *guagua*. If you speak a little of the language and enjoy mixing in with the locals, it can be an interesting experience to travel on one of these buses. Bus stations are listed in the island chapters.

Taxis

Taxis are a pleasure to use on the Canary Islands and give a good but not always cheap service. Generally they are large Mercedes and kept very clean by their Canarian drivers. You may have to listen to taped Canarian music and some drivers do not allow smoking. At night most display a green light as being available for hire, also there is a sign indicating 'free' (*libre*). Taxis in the larger towns have meters and the drivers are very good at giving change, though they expect a tip (*propina*) of about ten per cent. Minimum fare is about 225 pesetas.

For those taxis that do not have meters, or if you wish to go beyond the city or town limits, it is necessary to arrange the price beforehand. Misunderstandings usually occur because of lack of communication; some drivers will write down the price and place, which is helpful. Baggage may require a surcharge of about 30 pesetas per item. More details are given in island chapters.

The central meeting place in Santa Cruz de la Palma is the Plaza de España. This view shows the imposing facade of the Ayuntamiento (town hall), 1569, and statue of Philip II of Spain.

Excursions by coach

There is no doubt that one of the easiest ways of enjoying the sights of the Canary Islands is to take a coach tour. All the islands offer this facility, though the choice is far wider in the more visited islands. Half-day, whole-day and evening trips are well advertised in travel agents, hotels and local papers.

Make sure that you book on an excursion that has an English speaking guide and check whether the cost includes a meal. Remember to take your sunglasses, camera and cardigan, possibly flat shoes and a towel, if it includes a beach trip. Your tour is sure to stop at an *artesania* (souvenir shop), so extra cash may be required. It is normal practice to tip the coach driver at the end of the tour (100 pesetas). You will feel it is worth it having seen some of the twists and turns on the mountain roads.

Amongst the places you can expect to see are volcanoes, forests, saltpans, orange groves, banana plantations, caves, ancient ruins, historic buildings, botanical gardens, leisure parks, vineyards, flamenco and folk dancing. You can experience camel rides, taste wine, watch potters at work, see cigars being hand rolled, visit night clubs, *son et lumières* and wild west shows.

From Tenerife it is possible to visit La Gomera by coach: this includes a one-and-a-half hour sea crossing on the car ferry from Los Cristianos, a tour of the island and return the same day. Also from Tenerife, there is an excursion to La Palma: by coach to the airport, a thirty-minute flight, tour of the island and return the same day.

More details of coach excursions are given in the island chapters.

FIVE

Food and drinks

Buying food

The Canary Islands, because of their free trade ports, have a great variety of food and drink. The tourist areas, especially, are full of exotic foodstuffs from all over the world. Ports like Santa Cruz de Tenerife, with international traffic, offer an enormous selection of gourmet and epicure foods.

Prices of imported foods from Spain tend to be higher than on the mainland. Most other food prices are comparable with, if not cheaper than, Europe. Of course, if you buy a tin of baked beans with an English brand name, then it will be more expensive than a similar product bearing a Canarian or Spanish brand name.

Meat (*carne*) is plentiful. Local Canarian pork (*cerdo*) is excellent: pork chops (*chuleta de cerdo*) are on every menu. Beef (*carne de vacca*) is of good quality and imported from Brazil. There is no problem with getting it minced (*carne picada*). Lamb (*cordero*) and mutton (*carne de carnero*) are rather more expensive. Liver (*higado*) and kidneys (*rinon*) are cheap and tasty. Chickens (*pollo*) are plentiful, fresh or frozen. Very succulent is young goat or kid (*cabrito*) which is roasted on special festive occasions. Rabbit (*conejo*) is much used for stews.

Fish (*pescado*) is found in all towns and villages, though sometimes supplies run out early in the day. Prices are high owing to the demand. Varieties include, tuna (*atun*), cod (*bacalad*), hake (*merluza*), swordfish (*espada*), mackerel (*caballa*) and sardines (*sardinas*). It is possible to go to the fishing villages and buy fish straight off the boats but the prices remain high.

Cheese (*queso*) is imported from many countries and Dutch cheese can be bought more cheaply here than in Holland. Goat's cheese, (*queso blanco de cabra*) mainly from the smaller islands, is particularly flavoursome.

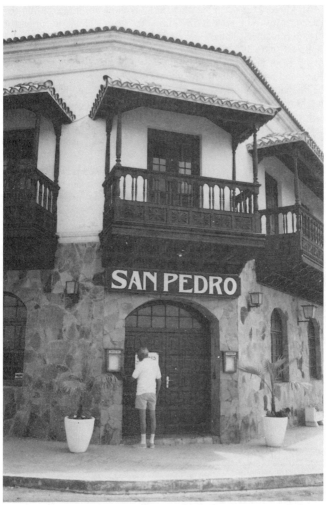

A fine old mansion now turned into a high class restaurant. It has a super sea view eastwards towards Puerto de la Cruz.

Milk (*leche*) is not often sold fresh, as there are few cows on the islands. Most milk is 'long-life', imported from Holland in cartons or plastic containers. Tinned and powdered milk are also available.

Bread (*pan*) is sold in most supermarkets, but the place to buy really fresh bread, including brown, is a baker's shop (*panaderia*). Rolls and bread are light but not crusty as French bread. Cakes may be bought from a *pasteleria*. These do not usually sell bread as well, but have a selection of sweets and chocolates (*confites y bombón*).

Various brands of tea and coffee are on sale, including ground coffee and Nescafé, the latter a little dearer than in the UK. Excellent local and Spanish honey (*miel*) can be bought; the date palm honey (*miel de palma*) has an unusual flavour.

There is plenty of fresh fruit and vegetables. This is best bought in the open markets but supermarkets in the tourist centres are well supplied. The selection is wide, so enjoy fresh strawberries and pineapples at Christmas time!

Mojo picon and mojo verde

To make your own red *mojo* sauce use the following ingredients:

> 2 or more cloves of garlic
> 1 chilli pepper
> 1 teaspoon paprika
> half teaspoon of cummin
> half teaspoon of oregano
> 3 tablespoons of olive oil
> 2 tablespoons of vinegar
> 100 ml water
> pinch of salt and pepper

Crush garlic and chilli, then mix thoroughly with all other ingredients. The sauce will store well in an airtight jar.

To make green *mojo* sauce use the milder ingredients above but substitute chopped coriander and parsley for the paprika and chilli pepper. This *mojo verde* is especially good with fish.

Local dishes

It is possible to have typical British meals in the Canaries. 'Real English Breakfast' signs are displayed in all tourist resorts. Most hotel restaurants serve food that tends to be bland; trying to please all their customers, they refrain from too much flavour.

Local dishes often include *papas arrugadas* (wrinkled potatoes) – quite delicious little new potatoes cooked in their skins in sea- or salt-water; these should be eaten with their skins on. Served with chops or fish, they will be accompanied by a Canarian piquant sauce called *mojo*, made of oil, vinegar, salt, pimento and spices. *Mojo picon* is red and hot, *mojo verde* is green and milder; often the sauces vary according to the cook. The sauces can be obtained in supermarkets, a small bottle costing about 150 pesetas.

Familiar Spanish dishes include gazpacho a tasty cold soup made from tomatoes, onions, pimentos, olive oil and sherry; and *paella* – rice cooked with saffron to which is added meats, fish and vegetables. *Tortilla* can be a simple omelette or *tortilla española* when potatoes, onions and vegetables are added.

Canarian soups (*sopa*) are tasty and almost a complete meal, so many good things are included. The one that is recommended to tourists is *sopa de berros*, watercress soup with herbs.

Stews (*puchero* or *estofado*) are considered a main dish; often made with rabbit (*estofado de conejo*), they are eaten with *gofio*, a meal made from wheat or maize which is toasted before being ground, and then made into a sort of dumpling, or sometimes eaten as bread.

Fish stew (*cazuela canaria*) is a fish casserole, with potatoes, onions, tomatoes, peppers and saffron. Sometimes the fish is cooked whole, the vegetable juices being served first as a soup, then the fish and vegetables are eaten. Try some *pulpo* – better forget that it is octopus, then you will enjoy it!

Chicken (*pollo*) is usually roast (*pollo asada*) on a spit and will be served with chipped potatoes, these can often be offered as 'Take away' meals.

Desserts (*postre*) are usually fresh fruit (*fruta*), ice cream (*helados*) or flan which is a creme caramel. Mouth watering *gateaux* are filled with strawberries (*fresas*) and cream (*nata*).

Other island specialities are *quesadilias* – cheesecakes from El Hierro, and *rapaduras* – an almond and honey sweet from La Palma.

Our special favourite Canarian foods are:

Cabrito al horno	– roast young goat
Cochinillo asado	– roast suckling pig
Cocido canario	– Canarian stew
Cordonices rellenas	– stuffed quail
Jamón canario	– local ham
Parillada criolli	– charcoal steak

Salmonetes fritos	– fried red mullet
Atun con salsa de tomate	– tunny fish in tomato sauce
Zarzuela	– fish stew
Platanos a la canaria	– banana fried in brandy sauce
Galletas de almendra	– almond biscuits

Drinks

All the islands produce their own wine but in such small amounts that there is little for the visitor to buy. The best is said to be *vino del monte* from Gran Canaria. Lanzarote's *Malvasia* or malmsey wine is in better supply; it can be bought sweet (*dulce*) or dry (*seco*). Tenerife produces a *malvasia* and a *moscatel*, El Hierro has a *vino dulce*, a sweet wine. La Palma's wine is also a *malvasia* and can be purchased sweet or dry. The latter is pleasant when chilled and served as an aperitif.

Plenty of wine is imported from mainland Spain and sells from 140 pesetas a litre. Good Spanish wines come from Rioja, Valdepenas and Jumilla. Spanish champagne costs from 500 pesetas per bottle.

The local drink is rum (*ron*) which is distilled throughout the islands and sold in every bar and supermarket. It is a fiery spirit which needs to be tasted with caution. *Ron miel* is a honey rum, similar to a liqueur. As you would expect there is a drink made from bananas: this is a yellow liqueur called *cobana*. Other liqueurs are produced from oranges, pineapples, cherries, almonds and coconuts; assorted bottles of these liqueurs make attractive souvenirs.

As liquor is duty-free it is cheap; even whisky is less expensive than in Europe or at duty-free shops in airports or ships. It is possible to buy English beer from a keg; however the local beer (*cerveza*) is a light cool drink which is very refreshing at all times. Mineral waters and soft drinks such as Coca-cola and Seven-up are plentiful. The latter drink can be helpful if you have a queasy tummy.

Spanish brandy (*coñac*) is said to have a less delicate flavour than French brandy. 'Soberano' and 'Fundador' are two Spanish brandies that are 37° proof, costing about 800 pesetas per litre, and worth tasting. *Sangria* is a Spanish drink, popular with tourists, that is usually served in a jug for two or more people. It is a mixture of red wine, orange juice, brandy, mineral water, slices of fruit and plenty of ice – refreshingly cool, it can be more potent than it tastes.

Bars and restaurants

In bars it is not necessary to pay for your drinks until you leave, even if you are there all day or night. They never close until the last party leaves. Tipping (called *propina*) is usual. The Spanish eat canapés or appetisers (called *tapas*) when they have a drink; sometimes these are quite elaborate, almost a meal. Lunch is served in restaurants between 1300 and 1500 hrs and dinner from 1930 to 2230 hrs.

It is quite in order for unaccompanied females to use cafés, bars and restaurants. Girl students often sit in a café with a coffee for an hour or so studying their books. Friends will meet at a table in the sunshine for an aperitif, drink a glass of wine, eat some olives or peanuts, and no one will hasten their departure. The end of the afternoon is the time when women take a cup of chocolate and *churros* – delicious sweet fritters, freshly cooked. Black coffee is *café solo*, white coffee is *café con leche*.

Tourist offices have lists of recommended restaurants and local newspapers have plenty of advertisements. The choice of type of restaurant or bar is enormous, nowhere could a greater variety of cuisine be enjoyed. The larger islands have establishments of the very highest international standard. The range goes down to the very sleezy bars in the red light districts of the cities.

All restaurants in the Canary Islands must display a tourist menu of the day (*menu del dia*), at an average price of 800 pesetas; sometimes this includes wine. The menu might be a substantial soup, grilled steak or pork chop, salad, fried potatoes, bread, ice cream or cake. Coffee is always extra. As on the continent, in the Canary Islands food and drink consumed at the bar is cheaper than when ordered from a waiter (*camarero*) and served at a table.

Restaurants are graded into four categories, denoted by the number of forks (*tendores*) shown. The grading reflects the price rather than the quality of the food, with four forks being the highest grade.

The best way to sample local food is to eat where the Canarians gather. Do not be shy of entering, the islanders are well used to seeing tourists about, mostly they take little notice and just get on with their own lives.

Out of town the bars and shops can be unobtrusive, often having half closed doors with maybe a faded Coca-cola sign. Once inside the service will be friendly but not inquisitive. Incidentally, because drinks are inexpensive you will find that your measure will be more than generous, so you have been warned! Street bars have tables and chairs on the pavement.

In tourist areas special half portions of dishes are available, and children are always welcome in all bars and restaurants. In some places there are high chairs for younger children.

The choice of eating places is vast ranging from the simple tapas bar and British style pub to a selection of international cafés and restaurants that specialise in national dishes. Prices vary from a few pesetas for a sandwich (*bocadillo* 150 pesetas), egg and chips (*huevo y patatas* 290 pesetas), chicken and chips (*pollo y patatas* 700 pesetas) and steak at about 1,000 pesetas. Obviously the ambience of the place makes a difference to your bill (*la cuenta*).

It is well to remember that eating out at night starts late, 2000 hrs onwards, with some restaurants serving meals until 0200 hrs. A number of restaurants provide music with dancing continuously throughout the evening. Often entertainments such as flamenco and folk groups have star appearances. An average price of a meal without drinks in such an establishment could be 1350 pesetas. Because of the warm nights the general trend is to stay out of doors much later than in the UK. Eating, drinking and dancing under the stars are very much part of Canarian night life.

Restaurants are listed in the island chapters. The authors emphasise that with a change of chef or management the standard might alter.

Nightlife

There is plenty to do in the evenings if you are in any of the big holiday resorts and especially the capital cities. You will find night clubs, casinos, discos, theatres, cinemas, bingo halls, bowling alleys and flamenco shows.

It is well known that the term night club (*sala de fiesta*) means a place where a wife or girl friend can be taken; often it includes more than one show, flamenco and folk dancing included. The shows in a cabaret are usually of a less innocent character. Orquidea Surprise (tel: 75 13 86) is a floorshow located a kilometre from Los Cristianos (near the zoo), a well presented lively entertainment with topless showgirls. Dinner available.

Discoteca are the usual discos with flashing lights, modern music and a small dance floor. A few have free entrance but generally it costs about 500 to 800 pesetas and includes the first drink; further drinks will cost the same price. Discos open about 2200 hrs and last until 0500 hrs.

In Puerto de la Cruz look for Joy, Qatar, Dania Park, Can Can and Botanico.

In Playa de las Americas, Acapulco, Castilla, Club Dolar, Kabuga and Tiffany.

Other forms of evening entertainment are the many night excursions by coach. Often these start from one of the hotels and journey into the mountains to a *ranchero* for a barbecue. The inclusive price will allow for some free drinks and a generous dinner, entertainment and dancing to a live band. Singing on the coach ride home is not compulsory! Other evening excursions include visits to night clubs with tables being reserved, a free first drink and dancing between shows.

Excursions from Los Cristianos and Playa de las Americas providing popular fun for the family are: A Medieval Night; Excursion to nearby castle of San Miguel; Jousting exhibition and Banquet followed by Drifter's Show.

SIX

Practical information for visitors

Budgeting for your holiday

The cost of living should not prove higher in the Canary Islands than Europe or the UK. Generally speaking, package tour holidaymakers require spending money for entertainments, drinks and possibly additional meals, unless the package includes full board. You must allow for extra costs such as taking part in sports and excursions, the hire of chairs and sun umbrellas, laundry, and tips (*propina*) for waiters, taxi drivers and porters (about 10%); and maybe some extra film for the camera and souvenirs.

Prices in tourist areas will probably be a few pesetas higher than elsewhere but if one takes into account the extra cost of travelling to a non-tourist area to do one's shopping, it will probably work out much about the same. For the independent traveller, it is possible to live quite cheaply especially by buying local foods. Chicken, tomatoes, cucumbers, eggs, bread and many drinks are less expensive than in the UK. Bars and restaurants are less costly and give cheerful and good service.

Chemists

The Spanish for chemist is *farmacia* and these are marked by a green Maltese cross. Unlike the UK, the chemists in Spain sell only medications, and they are able to give you medical advice and render First Aid. They do not sell toilet requirements. For these you must go to a *drogeria* or *perfumeria*. In the Canary Islands chemists are found in all towns and resorts and in some villages, too. Generally they open from 0900 to 1300 and 1630 to 2000 hrs Monday to Friday, Saturday 0900 to 1200 hrs. As in the UK there will be a chemist open on Sundays. The rota should be displayed on the door and given in local newspapers.

Church services

The Canarians are mostly Roman Catholics and have churches in all towns and villages. Visitors are always welcomed with courtesy.

Anglican and Evangelical Churches are to be found in the main tourist resort. Lists of addresses with times of church services can be obtained from Tourist Offices and large hotels. There are no synagogues in the Canary Islands. Protestant churches in Tenerife are:

St George's Church Plaza 25 de Julio, Santa Cruz. (Anglican)

All Saints Parque Taoro, Puerto de la Cruz.

Tenerife Christian Centre In Swedish Church, Calle del Pozo. (Evangelical)

San Eugenio Church Pueblo Canaria, Playa de las Americas. (Church of England)

South Tenerife Christian Fellowship First Floor, Apolo Centre, Los Cristianos.

Clothes

You will need lightweight clothes for the Canary Islands. A heavy top coat is not necessary but windcheaters, anoraks and woollen jumpers are essential when visiting high mountain areas. A lightweight raincoat may prove useful.

Generally speaking, loose-fitting cotton and drip-dry garments are the most comfortable. For walking in the hills take stout flat-heeled shoes, as the terrain can be very hard and stony. On the beach rubber flip-flop sandals are useful. Remember that one's feet tend to swell in warm weather so take light footwear.

Sunhats and sunglasses should be used, for the sun in the Canaries is strong and care must be taken to avoid sunstroke.

Evening wear is mostly casual. Some hotels and restaurants require men to wear ties and jackets. When visiting churches it is not essential to wear a hat or scarf but it is expected that you will not be wearing beach clothes. Skimpy clothing is frowned on in towns. Some banks and petrol stations will refuse to serve you if you are not adequately covered.

Only in the early morning are the streets in Los Cristianos deserted. Note the attractive patterned tiles and the striped sunshades, very necessary at mid-day.

On beaches bikinis are permitted and topless sunbathing is seen. Notices are displayed in the few places where naturists may take off their clothes.

Buying clothes locally

When in Tenerife you will be able to purchase any clothes you may require from a good selection of shops. The main tourist resorts have plenty of boutiques with modern styles. Men's and children's clothes are available, too, in all styles and sizes.

Prices cover a wide range. Many of the Paris fashion houses have shops here and the big stores have whole floors full of all types of clothing including sportswear. Bargain counters with cheaper goods will be marked *rebaja* which means a reduction in price. Sometimes the open air village markets have good bargains but examine the goods to see that they are not shop-soiled. It is possible to find oriental silks, furs and leather goods at advantageous prices. When possible it is a good idea to check on the equivalent UK price first.

The range of clothes in the shops of La Gomera, La Palma and El Hierro is more restricted. However it is possible to buy various materials and have clothes made up. In Tenerife a gentleman's suit can be tailored in 24 hours.

Clothes imported from Spain can be a little more expensive than in the UK. Most of the hotels have a boutique nearby; the local supermarket will probably stock beachware, sportswear, lightweight shoes and hats.

The local hand-embroidered blouses, skirts and shawls make attractive souvenirs. Prices vary little between the various islands.

Communications

Post

Post offices (*Correos*) similar to those in the UK are in all towns and some villages. Open from 0900 to 1300 hrs Monday to Saturday, closed on Sunday and public holidays.

In Tenerife the post offices are:

Santa Cruz: Plaza España (main square)
Puerto de la Cruz: Calle Jon del Pozo (opposite bus station)
Playa de las Americas: Pueblo Canario (next to church)
Los Cristianos: Edificio Arenal (behind Mobil petrol station)
Los Gigantes: Avenida Maritima.

You may have letters and parcels sent to a local post office for you

The tall white buildings against the blue sky are a striking feature. They house the telescopes of the Astro Physical Observatory, built along the mountainous dorsal fin of Tenerife.

to collect. They should be addressed to you (surname first, then initials) at Lista de Correos, in the appropriate town (e.g. Lista de Correos, Puerto de la Cruz, Tenerife, Canary Islands, Spain). There is no charge for this service. When you collect your mail from the post office you will be required to show your passport.

In shops where you purchase postcards, stamps are usually sold as well. At the time of writing postage to EC countries costs 45 pesetas for letters (20 grm) and postcards. Local letters and postcards 15 pesetas. Spain letters and postcards 27 pesetas. Letters and postcards to Europe outside the EC, 55 pesetas. All mail goes by air; parcels can be registered.

The Canary Island post boxes are painted yellow, similar in shape to those in the UK. The exception is at main post offices where posting boxes are in the wall of the building. Sometimes they are marked *extranjero* (for destinations abroad) and *insular* (for local islands). Small yellow post boxes, square in shape, may be attached to houses in remote country villages.

Telephones

Telephoning from the Canary Islands to the UK or other countries is simple, provided the coin box is not too full to accept further coins. This happens quite frequently in busy tourist centres. Look for a telephone kiosk which says *international*; those marked *urbano* are for local calls only.

You can use 200, 100, 25 or 5 peseta coins (15 pesetas is the minimum to make a local call; 200 pesetas the minimum to make an international call) and the directions for use are displayed in several languages near the telephone. In hotels, the switchboard operator will dial your number for you and call you back as soon as the call is through. Some hotels have telephones in the bedroom. A small charge is made for this service.

When using the public telephone, first dial 07 for international calls. Wait for a high pitched continuous sound then dial the code of the country required (for UK this is 44) followed by the subscriber's code and number. In cases where the code starts with 0 it is omitted. For example, for London (071), just dial 71.

International country code numbers from the Canary Islands:

Austria	–	43
Denmark	–	45
Germany	–	49
Holland	–	31
Italy	–	39

Portugal	–	351
Sweden	–	46
UK	–	44

By dialling 9198, it is possible to arrange personal calls. *Cobro revertido* means the recipient of the call pays the cost.

For general information concerning telephones, telegrams, cables and telex, dial 003. In Puerto de la Cruz, Playa de las Americas and Los Cristianos, public kiosks called *Telefonica* have telephone booths where you can make local or international calls. You pay the telephonist after your call (they take Visa) and she will assist if you have a problem. Open daily from 0900 to 1300 and 1600 to 2100 hrs.

Telegraph

Cable messages can be passed, day or night, by way of the main telephone exchange. Dial 362000.

Telex/fax

For teleprinter service, dial 363717. For emergency remittances, one's own bank at home can send money by teleprinter to a Spanish bank. This service can be granted very quickly. If necessary, ask permission to use a travel agent's telex. Fax is now widely used.

Consulates

In case anything untoward should happen, like losing your passport, it is useful to know the whereabouts of the nearest Consul.

Police Headquarters and the Town Hall (*Ayuntamiento*) will also assist. Information notices and books in hotels are handy places for finding such addresses.

Passports can only be issued by the British Consulate in Madrid. Forms for this purpose are obtainable from the Santa Cruz Consulate. There is now an optional courier service costing 500 pesetas which speeds up the process.

British Consulate in Tenerife Consulado Britanico, Plaza Weyler 8 (1st Floor), Santa Cruz. Tel: 28 68 63. Open Monday to Friday 0900 to 1200

American Consulate in Tenerife Consulado de los Estados Unidos de America, Alvarez de Lugo 10, Santa Cruz de Tenerife. Tel: 28 69 50.

Irish Consulate La Marina 7, Santa Cruz. Tel: 24 56 71.

Dentists

Dentists (*estomatologista* or *odontologo*) are fully qualified, similar to doctors. Those called *dentista* may have adequate qualification for simple surgery. The service is good and not over expensive. Generally one can call at the surgery, without an appointment, and take one's turn.

Doctors

Doctors (*médicos*) have clinics which are run in a business-like manner. In tourist resorts, there would be an English-speaking receptionist. You usually get immediate attention and pay a fee of about 2000 pesetas for a visit or consultation. They will give you a receipt for insurance purposes. If you are given a prescription you take it to a chemist (*farmacia*) whose sign is a green Maltese cross. Unlike in the UK, chemists in Spain sell only medications, not toilet requirements, but they are able to give you advice and first aid.

There are also First Aid Posts (*Casa de Socorro*), which is a national service. These posts are often in the country and the buildings are marked with a red cross and a road sign.

Duty free allowance into the UK

200 cigarettes or 50 cigars or 250 grms of tobacco
2 litres of still wine
1 litre of spirits over 38%
or 2 litres of fortified wine (ie sherry, vermouth, etc.)
50 grms perfume
or 0.25 litres toilet water

At present the Canary Islands, although part of Spain, are not in the EC.

Electricity, radio, television and video

Electric current voltage is 220 to 225 AC, occasionally 110 to 125 AC. Plugs are the two round-pin variety.

There are local radio stations in the Canaries. News in English and other languages is broadcast daily during the summer. The World Service of the BBC is on short wave. Frequencies include 12095, 9410, 15070 and 9915 Khz. It is possible to hear Radio 4 on long wave, when atmospheric conditions are good.

British television sets are not suitable in the Canary Islands. (Spanish television uses Norma G for black and white and Pall for colour.) Most hotels and many bars have black and white or colour television, and nearly all the programmes are in Spanish and relayed from mainland Spain. There are few videos in English that can be rented at present but it is possible to rent a video camera in order that you can record your holiday. Tele Video Canarias, Obispo Perez Caceres, 5. Puerto de la Cruz. Tel: 38 77 61.

Fire precautions

Fire precautions are observed in the Canary Islands, with public buildings and hotels being inspected for adequate fire escape equipment. Details of emergency exits are shown in each hotel room. Modern fire fighting equipment is located in all buildings used by the public.

Hairdressing

Men's barbers are called *Barberia* and ladies' salons *Peluqueria*. In tourist areas prices are higher than in towns. Most large hotels have their own salons and the standard is generally very good. The Canarians have particularly well groomed hair and frequently use hairdressers.

Health

There are no dangerous animals or poisonous reptiles in the Canaries, not many flies and only a few mosquitoes. The spring-like weather is healthy and invigorating. Over-indulgence with food and drink can cause discomfort and an upset tummy. It is wise to wash all fruits and salads before eating.

There is no shortage of medications in the Canary Islands, but if you prefer a particular British brand it is wise to take a supply with you. Tap water should not be drunk by visitors unless it is first boiled. Water considered fit for drinking is *agua potable* and unsuitable is *agua non potable*. Bottled water is quite cheap and available at supermarkets. Called *agua mineral* it is either aerated (*con gas*) or still (*sin gas*).

Canary tummy is a form of sickness and diarrhoea which may last for a few days. Take 'Salvacolina', a suitable Spanish medication for this, available from chemists. Should the complaint persist it is advisable to consult a doctor. However cases of upset tummy are not to be expected and most people find the Canary climate will make them feel years younger.

Care should be taken to avoid too much initial exposure to the sun. The wearing of sun hats and sun glasses can be helpful. Remember that the sun's rays are very much stronger here than in the UK, so allow periods of fifteen minutes exposure to direct sunlight, at first, to parts of the body not usually exposed. Make sure that plenty of sun lotion is applied. Do not wait until the skin is turning red, that may be too late.

Sunstroke can be very distressing. Symptoms are a severe headache, vomiting and much discomfort. Mild cases require a cool shaded room with plenty of liquid. ('Seven Up' is a helpful drink.) Apply calamine or similar cream to affected parts. If the skin is blistered or the symptoms are not improving, do not hesitate to consult a chemist or doctor. Hotels have the addresses and telephone numbers of the nearest doctor or clinic. Some chemists are open all night.

Laundry and dry cleaning

If you wish to have clothes cleaned or laundered, it is probably easier to use the services of your hotel or apartment. Maids will collect laundry and return it clean the same day, lists of charges are usually put in each room. Dry cleaners are more rare and very busy. Launderettes are only just beginning to appear in the major tourist resorts. With the warm sunshine clothes dry very quickly so drip-dry garments are practical. There are all the usual washing powders and detergents available.

Medical services

Spain is part of the EEC and there are reciprocal medical arrangements. If you wish to take advantage of these you will need a Form E111, Certificate of Entitlement to Benefits in the EEC, obtainable from your local DHSS office. However, it is advised that you take out personal insurance to cover the holiday period. This will include arrangements for emergency repatriation; your Travel Agent can advise you.

Money and banks

Currency

The Canary Islands are a part of Spain and therefore the currency is the *peseta*. The coins in use are: 1, 5, 25, 50, 100, 200 and 500 pesetas. Notes are: 1000, 2000, 5000 and 10,000 pesetas.

The 'high street' banks there are the same as in Spain and have names like, Banco de Bilbao, Banco Hispano Americano, Banco de Santander and Banco Central. Opening hours do vary slightly but generally are 0830 to 1400 hrs daily, closing at 1300 on Saturdays. Closed on Sundays and public holidays. Most Spanish banks accept Eurocheque cards or equivalent, displaying the sign. Be sure to check with your own bank whether your cheque card is valid for use in Spain (the Canary Islands). When you go to the bank you will need to take your cheque book or travellers' cheques, and your passport, they will probably wish to know where you are staying. One can also cash travellers' cheques and exchange currency in travel agents and hotels. The currency exchange rate is displayed in most banks and travel agents. A small commission is charged for the transaction. Our experience is that the Banco de Bilbao gives very favourable rates of exchange, accepts Eurocheque cards and has English speaking staff.

The larger hotels will have deposit boxes or small safes for guests to lock up their valuables. The Canarians generally are law abiding but in busy plazas, markets and at fiesta time it is sensible to take precautions against pickpockets.

Newspapers and books

English daily and Sunday newspapers can be purchased in cities, tourist complexes and at airports, usually a day after publication. Newspapers are about twice the UK price. English books and paperbacks are also available in these places.

In Tenerife an English language newspaper *Here and Now*, is published on the 14th and 28th of each month. It contains lively information on hotels, eating places, news of events, topical subjects and advertisements, useful for the tourist as well as residents. Price 75 pesetas. There is also a free monthly magazine in the south of the island: *Tenerife Holiday* is available in shops, hotels and travel agents. It features local news, events and sports and includes maps of tourist locations and health centres.

Opticians

Opticians (*optica*) provide a very good service. In towns and tourist centres they are able to test your vision, without charge, and supply the required spectacles in about 48 hours. Generally charges are lower than in the UK, with a very good choice of frames.

Police

There are several types of police in the Canary Islands and Spain. The *Guardia Civil* who wear a green uniform are armed law enforcement officers. It is advisable not to get involved in a misunderstanding with them, they rarely admit to speaking English and have a great deal of power. The Municipal Police are the local town and village police, either in brown or dark blue uniforms. The Traffic Police, besides controlling traffic, give assistance with breakdowns and other problems. Their patrol cars are marked *Trafico Policia*. All types of police are approachable and helpful, especially the Traffic Police.

To call police tel: 091. Santa Cruz Police HQ: tel: 21 25 11. Municipal Police, Los Cristianos, Arona: tel: 76 63 62. Playa de Las Americas, Adeje: tel: 78 04 29. Puerto de la Cruz: tel: 35 04 28.

Security

Although the Spanish police have increased their vigilance, as elsewhere, petty crime is still prevalent, especially in the tourist resorts.

It is always wise to use the hotel safe deposit boxes provided for your passport, jewellery and traveller's cheques. Lock your room door or the door leading to the balcony or terrace. Avoid carrying large sums of money. Your handbag should be carried away from the road side to avoid it being snatched by a motorcyclist. Do not put your wallet in your back trouser pocket, and be alert when leaving a bank. Cameras are a prime target, crowded markets and fiestas are places to be extra careful. Never leave valuables in a car.

It is suggested that you have a photocopy of the relevant information on your passport and that you record details of credit cards, driving licence and airline tickets, to facilitate replacement in the event of loss.

Always report incidents of loss to the police: you will need evidence of having done this if you are going to make a claim on your insurance. It is helpful to have a witness. There is a Lost Property Office in all major Spanish towns; stolen items have turned up in this way if not of marketable value.

If the worst comes, do not offer resistance. It is not worth being heroic. Your safety is surely more important than possessions.

Problems and complaints

Complaints about accommodation should be made on official complaints forms (*hojas de reclamaciones*); tourist establishments should have these or the Tourist Office will supply them, but usually the receptionist or the public relations person (*relacions publico*) will sort out any problem you may have; they mostly speak English.

(Opposite) Top: *The floral clock in Parque Garcia Sanabrit is much admired by both* Tinerfenõs *and visitors, especially as it does give the correct time.*

(Opposite) Bottom: *The Camel Safari Park is a popular outing for the family, who can enjoy a touch of adventure amongst the cacti.*

In extreme cases it may be necessary to go to the police (*policia municipal*) or the Town Hall (*Ayuntamiento*). You will find officials pleased to assist, but be patient, the Canarian way of life is not to hurry.

Public conveniences

Public conveniences are few and far between in the Canary Islands. They are marked *aeso* or *servicio*, or *señoras* (ladies) and *caballeros* (gentlemen). Pictographs are also used. Toilets are available at petrol filling stations. It is quite permissible to use the cloakrooms of a hotel, bar or café and it is not necessary to be a customer.

Public conveniences will be found in market places (*mercado*) but they are sometimes austere. Payment for the use of a toilet is not required but it is usual to tip the attendant.

Shopping

Shopping in the Canary Islands is very much like shopping in the UK and Europe. Even in the smaller islands there are the supermarket-type shops with prices marked on all goods. In the tourist areas the shop assistants will understand English but their knowledge of German will be even better, owing to the higher percentage of tourists coming from Germany.

Shopping baskets and trolleys are available, any personal parcels of shopping may have to be deposited at the entrance, and a numbered tag is given as a receipt. In some shops you are expected to select your own vegetables. Sometimes meat is prepacked but usually at the meats, fish, cheese and delicatessen counters you are served. It may be necessary to take a numbered ticket for your order of service.

(Opposite) Top: *This striking rock upthrust, familiar to generations of visitors to Tenerife, stands in an area known as Los Roques, situated a few kilometres south of Mt Teide, the high point of the island.*
(Opposite) Bottom: *Many types of lava can be seen in the Teide National Park.*

Amongst the many good buys in the Canary Islands are embroidery, ceramics, palm leaf baskets, wood carvings, colourful costume dolls and cigars. Because local taxes are low, certain goods can be cheaper here than in the country of origin. Tobacco, liquor, cameras, radios and watches can be purchased with a saving in cost.

All the big towns and many villages have open air markets, where the atmosphere is friendly and informal. The markets are a good place to start a conversation with the Canarians, who are outgoing friendly people. When Canarians go shopping they like to socialise; rarely do they expect to be served without having a chat.

Taking children to the Canary Islands

Taking young children to the Canary Islands presents no real problems. The Canarians are always interested in children, and indeed look after their own with much love and care.

Hotels, apartments and bungalows have cots and high chairs, sometimes at a small extra charge. Play rooms and paddling pools, plus babysitting services, help to make life pleasant for all. There are plenty of toy and clothes shops, baby foods and toilet requirements.

Amusements, train rides, playgrounds, ice creams, beach equipment, all are reasonably priced. Young children are allowed into bars and cafes, restaurants and hotel lounges until late at night. Hotels have courtesy buses to convey you to the nearest beach.

However, care should be taken not to overtire young children, who easily become excited and possibly restless with the change of surroundings. New foods may not appeal but usually staff are understanding and helpful. Do not overdo the amount of fresh fruits or salads at first. Plenty of liquid to drink is sensible.

Young children often go on coach excursions and have a happy time. Do take some toys or games to amuse a toddler, for sitting in a coach will become tedious without some diversion. Use the toilet when the coach makes a stop for this purpose; drivers have to work to a schedule and it is not always possible to make emergency halts on narrow mountain roads.

With plenty of beaches and warm sea water most youngsters are completely happy. Please do not force your child into the sea, use a little encouragement to paddle or sit at the edge, it is not sensible to be 'tough' when a child is nervous of water. Making a sand castle and fetching a bucket of sea water will do a lot towards gaining confidence. Be sure to provide the child with a sun hat and protection

---

Picnic sites

On all the Western Canary Islands, ICONA, Spain's National Nature Conservancy Agency, has set up useful recreational zones. At these picnic sites there are playgrounds for children, also wooden tables and benches, often a toilet and drinking water taps.

Outside stone built barbecues have free firewood as the chopping of live trees is forbidden and other fires must not be lit. Open all the year, they are usually busy at weekends with Canarian families.

---

for the skin, and do not leave him to play in the sun for too long at a time. Guard carefully against sunburn and sunstroke (see Health section).

Time

Time is the same throughout the Canary Islands. From April to September Summer Time is in force, the same as in the UK. In winter the Canaries observe Greenwich Mean Time, one hour earlier than mainland Spain.

Tipping

Tipping (the *propina*) is expected, as in the UK and the Continent. In bars, cafés and restaurants, even though a service charge may be added, a tip in the region of ten per cent is generally given, perhaps less for a drink in the bar. The Spanish are proud and well-mannered and do not make much of the subject.

Porters, maids and cloak room attendants should also be tipped 100 pesetas, though porters at airports may have a fixed charge per piece of luggage. Taxi drivers expect a ten per cent tip.

Water

Water is generally scarce in the Canary Islands, particularly where there is little in the way of natural water supplies. There is much reliance on private wells and reservoir catchments, there are desalination plants, and some of the larger hotels have their own installations. Never waste water here. Tenerife is better off for water because it has the 3718m Mount Teide, which is generally snow covered in winter. La Palma is the greenest and wettest island of the group; being situated on the north west it is affected by moisture-carrying trade winds. Tap water is considered suitable to drink, but it does contain minerals. To be on the safe side it is recommended that visitors buy the bottled water which is sold in all supermarkets and bars. *Agua sin gas* is still water, *agua con gas* is aerated.

Torre de Conde, San Sebastián, La Gomera. This fortress was built in 1447 by Fernan Peraza, Conde de Gomera. It is now a national monument and holds a collection of weapons and native artefacts.

SEVEN

The Canary Islands and the islanders

History of the Canary Islands

The Canary Islands were known to the Ancient World under various names; the Greek called them 'The Isles of the Blessed' and Homer described them as the location of the 'Elysian Fields'. Later Herodotus, writing in the fifth century BC, referred to them as 'The Garden of Hesperides' and the archipelago was generally known to the Romans as 'The Fortunate Islands'. Much of the early history of the Canary Islands is uncertain and is only partly explained in the myths and legends that tell of the first inhabitants' experiences.

It seems likely the Canarians were known to seafarers well before the Spanish colonised the islands in the fifteenth century. The Phoenicians are reputed to have collected *orchilla*, a purple dye, from the islands during their explorations along the coast of North West Africa; they used the dye to colour carpets and clothes. The Roman writer Pliny the Elder (AD 23 to 79) writes of an expedition sent by King Juba II of Mauretania (Morocco) to 'The Fortunate Islands' about 30 BC. Pliny tells how Juba's troops found the islands deserted but with many ruins of great buildings. The soldiers saw enormous wild dogs roaming the islands, and they brought two of the animals back to the King. Afterwards the lands became known as the 'Canis Islands', *canis* being the Latin for 'dog', and in later years the 'Islands of Dogs' was corrupted to 'Canaria'. The collective name, therefore, of the Canary Islands has nothing to do with the native bird of that name but refers to these wild dogs.

The Guanches

When the Spaniards arrived in the fifteenth century they found a primitive race, akin to Stone Age people, occupying the islands. How they got there and their origins still remain something of a mystery.

The Encyclopaedia Britannica records that the aboriginal inhabitants of the Canary Islands were called Guanches (*Guan* person, *Chinet* Tenerife, thus 'Man of Tenerife').

The Guanches, now extinct, appear from their skulls and bones to have resembled the Cro-Magnon race of the Quaternary age. It seems that they may have come from central and southern Europe via North Africa in some distant age. The characteristics of grey-blue eyes and blondish hair still persist in some of the present inhabitants. In the two islands of Tenerife and Gomera the Guanche type has been retained with more purity than in the others. No inscriptions have been found in these islands so it would seem that the Guanches did not know how to write. In all the islands, except these two, Semitic

Red stone statues of ten ancient Guanche kings stand guard along the seafront at Candelaria, close to the Basilica de Nuestra Señora de la Candelaria. These very large, rough hewn statues conjure up the story of the heroic resistance of the earliest inhabitants against the Spanish Conquistadores.

inscriptions and rock signs have been discovered. From these facts it would seem that people from the neighbourhood of Carthage and the Semitic races landed in the Canary Islands.

The Guanches lived in natural caves; they used to paint their bodies and wear garments of goatskin and vegetable fibres, some of which have been found in tombs in Gran Canaria. Necklaces of wood, bone and shells, polished battle axes, lances and clubs are to be seen on display in the various museums in the Canary Islands. Many cave dwellings still exist today in the mountains and remain in daily use, being handed down by each generation and much sought after as part of their heritage.

In Guanche times, many very old people, after bidding farewell to their families, were carried to a sepulchral cave, given a bowl of milk and left to die. Guanches embalmed their bodies and 'mummies' have been found wrapped in goat and sheep skins. In districts where cave dwelling was impossible they built small round houses; their communities were ruled by a king or chief.

They worshipped gods and goddesses, the sun and moon, believed in evil spirits and venerated the rocks and the mountains. Religious festivals took precedence over wars and personal quarrels.

When the Spanish conquered the islands during the fifteenth century, the Guanches are said to have put up heroic resistance against the invaders and many folk tales tell of the bravery of the doomed defenders, who in some instances preferred honourable suicide rather than ignominious defeat.

During the year 999 AD the Arabs landed and traded on Gran Canaria. In the thirteenth and fourteenth centuries Genoese, Majorcan, Portuguese and French navigators visited the islands and had a friendly welcome from the Guanches.

Early in the fourteenth century, Lancellotto Malocello, an Italian nobleman from Genoa, discovered Lanzarote and gave his name to the island when charting a map. Although he exploited the natives for labour he made no attempt to take over the island.

Spanish Conquest 1402-96

The conquest of the Canary Islands by the Spanish lasted nearly a century, starting in 1402. The French nobleman, Jean de Bethancourt, under the commission of the King of Spain, together with another nobleman, Gadifer de Salle, invaded Lanzarote and Fuerteventura. After a hard struggle they managed to subdue the islands and to a lesser extent also La Gomera and El Hierro.

Ostensibly the Spanish invasion was to spread Christianity but they also took slaves and killed many of the inhabitants who put up a noble resistance. There was much intrigue and fighting amongst the invaders themselves when taking over the islands. This included an interim Portuguese ownership of Lanzarote and Gomera but in 1470 the Portuguese ceded their rights to the Catholic Kings of Spain. Captain Juan Rejon was sent to claim the lands for Spain and stop the fighting. In 1478 Juan Rejon landed in Gran Canaria with Castilian troops; after many cruel battles he was replaced by Pedro de Vera who in April 1483 took over the island for Spain.

Alfonso de Lugo and his forces also fought many battles against the Guanches before their resistance was broken. The majority were killed in battle, some taken as slaves, a few were assimilated amongst the invaders. In 1492 La Palma fell, then in 1496 the final battle was fought at La Victoria de Acentejo in Tenerife, so at last the conquest was over and the entire archipelago was incorporated into the Crown of Castile.

Columbus

When in 1492 Christopher Columbus began his search for the New World, he put into Las Palmas, Gran Canaria for repairs to his ships. Later he sailed on to La Gomera for water and victuals. On future voyages he returned several times to the islands, especially La Gomera, where it is reputed he was enamoured with the beautiful widow Beatriz de Bobadilla, whom he had met previously at the Spanish court.

International trade

The Canaries became a useful staging post between Europe and the Americas, but were subject to attacks by pirates from many countries, including the English, Dutch and the Moors who were looking for slaves and timber. During the sixteenth and seventeenth centuries the islands began to prosper with the cultivation of the vine, the production of sugar, and ship repairs. Canary 'sack' or 'malmsey' wine was much sought after by Elizabethan sailors such as Raleigh and Drake. Records show that Thomas Nichols, a 'factor' of an English company which traded in sugar, lived in Tenerife from 1556 to 1571. He wrote a book, *The Fortunate Islands*, published in London in 1583.

In 1589 Philip II of Spain created the post of Captain General of the Canaries. Fortifications were built as a means of defence and protection from raiding pirates and other invaders. Many of these fortresses remain to this day and form museums of interest to the tourist. During the following years the islands developed and prospered, but a serious challenge to Spanish sovereignty was made

Concrete replica of the Santa Maria, Christopher Columbus's sailing ship. Inside it is a naval museum which houses historic naval documents, old flags and many sea objects of interest to the tourist.

by the British under Lord Nelson in 1797. They were repulsed in the Battle of Santa Cruz de Tenerife, where Nelson lost an arm, one hundred and twenty-three British sailors were wounded and two hundred and twenty-six killed.

The Paisley and Little Company of London carried out a thriving business between 1770 and 1834. They exported Canarian wine and in return imported to the Canaries textiles, flour, tobacco and English manufactured goods. Major business houses were established by the late eighteenth century and firms like Yeowards from Liverpool and Elders and Fyffes from London both had banana and shipping trade based on the islands.

Province of Spain

In 1823 the Canary Islands were united to become a single province of Spain with its capital at Santa Cruz de Tenerife, this caused much annoyance to Gran Canaria, who thought that Las Palmas was of equal importance and deserved the title. The Law of Free Ports was passed in 1852, turning the archipelago into a duty-free area and allowing the Canarians to trade with the whole world. Although Spain remained neutral during the First World War, the drop in maritime traffic had a harmful effect on the islands.

In 1927 the archipelago was declared two provinces of Spain, each with its own capital and council. The provinces are:

Western Province
Tenerife (capital: Santa Cruz de Tenerife), La Gomera, El Hierro and La Palma.

Eastern Province
Gran Canaria (capital: Las Palmas), Fuerteventura, Lanzarote with the islets of Los Lobos, Graciosa, Montana Clara, Alegranza, Roque del Oeste and Roque del Este.

There is still friendly rivalry between the two provinces.

It was while serving as Military Governor of the Canary Islands that, in 1936, General Franco plotted then led the anti-Socialist revolt that sparked off the Spanish Civil War, and the Canary Islands were used as a base for training the revolutionary troops.

During the Second World War, Spain and the Canaries remained neutral. After the war, as a result of the development of modern refrigeration and commercial air transport, the agricultural industries of the islands improved. Ports were enlarged to cope with modern shipping, airports were built or enlarged.

Tourism, which started with a great boom at the beginning of the 1970s, is now a major industry and an all-the-year-round influx of sun-seeking visitors has taken people away from the land to work in hotels and shops. The Canary Islands today with a population of 1,500,000 are peaceful, progressive and working hard for a stable economy.

The Canarian way of life

The Canarian way of life is like that in Spain – out-going and friendly. The Canarians like to sing, play music and dance whenever possible. For no reason at all they may greet you and shake hands. To pass a Canarian you know and not greet him is an insult. It is impossible to rush Canarians into taking a decision, but given time they will be pleased to help you, particularly if you are in trouble. Should you ask the way to a place, it is quite likely that you will be taken there, or someone else will be asked to assist you.

They are a proud people who dress well, with hair neatly groomed. They do not like tourists wearing scanty clothing other than on the beaches.

Although the bars and cafés are open all day and not closed until late at night, drunkenness is very rare indeed. Thankfully, there are few cripples or beggars in the streets. Disabled people are employed to sell lottery tickets at street corners in the towns. Old people are cared for by their families.

The visitor will notice the pace of life will seem slower, people do not rush about frantically as in North European countries. The Spanish word *mañana* meaning tomorrow, often applies – why hurry?

Communal activities are ritualised. The evening gossip, called the *paseo*, is still enjoyed in every town or village, especially in the *plaza mayor* (main square). As the sun begins to set, people walk slowly up and down the streets, the air is filled with lively chatter. Children play in the plazas, young girls giggle and smile at the boys. Families sit outside cafés talking with friends while at the corners stand patient lottery ticket sellers and gipsies displaying embroidered tablecloths and souvenirs. The *Guardia Civil* (police) pace slowly about, always in pairs, their revolvers hanging at the ready. They, too, will stop for a coffee and a chat. Young children are allowed to stay up late so that the whole family get together in a restaurant or on a park bench. Canarians love their children very much, and are always pleased to talk about them. It is a good form of introduction if you make a pleasant remark about a child.

The islanders consider themselves to be *Canarios*, not Spaniards, whom they talk of as *Peninsulares*. The people of Tenerife are known as *Tinerfenos*, those from La Palma as *Palmeros*; and those from La Gomera as *Gomeros* and El Hierro as *Herrenos*.

Although the Spanish culture naturally has predominating influence, there are also South American, Portuguese and British undertones. The British community, now numbering about 6,000, has for many years contributed to the business way of life. It is only comparatively recently with the growth of tourism that German and Scandinavian entrepreneurs have infiltrated.

The cheerful Canarians realise that tourism is an economic necessity for them, and their good-natured acceptance of hordes of foreigners is to be admired.

Language

The Canarians speak Spanish. The accent and pronunciation is slightly different in each island but for Spanish speakers there is not much problem with comprehension. Canarians generally make an effort to communicate, and many also speak English, German and French.

Nowadays English is taught as a second language in the higher grade schools. So if you have a query you are more likely to get an answer from a student than from an older person. In the smaller country villages it may be hard to find someone who understands English at all. Thus it is sensible to carry an English/Spanish dictionary and phrase book, also a local map, when seeking directions and information. (See also Appendix A.)

Flora and fauna

A botanist's paradise

The Canary Islands have been called a botanist's paradise: the physical characteristics of the islands and their climate, with little variation between the seasons, combine to produce a diversity of environments for a variety of flora, within a relatively small area. The islands are a true Garden of Eden where dark, dense forests give way to heathers, gorses and bracken. Steep green valleys are terraced with eucalyptus, mimosa, cork trees and broom. Lush meadows harbour butterflies, dragonflies and ladybirds amongst the wild marigolds and buttercups. Oases of palm trees give shade for the cultivation of alfalfa, while cineraria and honeysuckle mingle in the hedgerows.

In the populated areas of the island in parks and gardens, geraniums, rosy hibiscus, carnations, marigolds, nasturtiums and bougainvillea bring a riot of colour, somtimes growing wild along the verges. The poinsettia, often in double form and of various hues from deep red to pale lemon, grows into thick hedges as high as trees. The exotic strelitzia, the bird of paradise flower with its waxen blue, white and orange blossom, and birdlike shape, has now become established as the Canary Islands symbolic flower. And one of the greatest delights of the islands is the sweet perfume of their wild aromatic plants and exotic flowers. Laburnums, honeysuckle, broom, eucalyptus, pine, many more, blend together to create a wonderful nosegay from nature.

About 1,800 different species of plants grow wild. Some have been here since the late Tertiary period: fossilised plants have been discovered, similar to those found in Mediterranean areas dating from that time. One of the last surviving trees of the Tertiary era is the *Dracaena draco*, which may be called a living fossil. The tree is known as the dragon tree, or dragon's blood tree because of the resinous secretions which, when exposed to the air, turn a dark, blood red. The one at **Icod de los Vinos** in Tenerife is reputed to be at least

3,000 years old. It is a weird sight, with its main thick trunk branching out into many more trunks, and a massive ridged top with spiky green leaves. The Guanches attributed magical powers to the sap of the dragon tree and thought it a cure for various ailments.

Botanical Gardens and National Parks

Each wave of newcomers has introduced new varieties of plants to the Canaries, and since the Middle Ages the islands have been used for acclimatising tropical plant species before taking them to colder climates. The Botanical Gardens in Tenerife contain thousands of rare exotic plants from all over the world, as well as endemic species, and are well worth a visit. There is much to be seen, also, in the National Parks.

In the hot dusty south of Tenerife more than half a million cacti are grown annually. Here at Casa Cactus visitors are welcome to admire a weird and wonderful display – rather prickly souvenirs!

Teide National Park (Tenerife) is famous for a small violet (*viola cheiranthifolio*) adapted to the strong sun and dry conditions the only living plant found 3,000 m above sea level. Another plant growing in this area is the red Tajinaste or Tiede Viper's Bugloss (Pride of

Tenerife). It is one of the most admired plants in the park: with its single stem growing up to two metres high, it is densely covered with reddish blossoms and makes a striking picture against the dry volcanic soil. Other species include the laburnum with its bright yellow flowers and the Teide Broom or Broom of the Peak *(Retama del Pico)*. At the end of April a profusion of highly fragrant pink and white blossoms sprout from its stiff twigs, presenting a unique sight for, in the whole world, it is only in the stony and lofty regions of the Tiede National Park and La Palma that this plant survives.

Caldera de Taburiente National Park (La Palma) is very different from the Teide National Park because of the abundance of water in the region; numerous fountains spring from the earth becoming streams and waterfalls. The landscape of the park is shaped by the Canary pine *(pinus Canariensis)*. This species constitutes nature's important defence against erosion. Others growing in profusion are the Faya or La Haya, an arborescent shrub which has oblong and pointed leaves related to the tree heath, small hollies like *ilex platyphylla* and the big *Barbusano* trees.

Garajonay National Park (Gomera), situated in the centre of the island, is a mixture of crags, hills, slopes and gorges. More than half the area is covered with Laurisilva forest (Laurisilva is a sub tropical formation dating from the Tertiary era). The principal trees that make up the Laurisilva are the laurel, the linden, heather and the small holly. A characteristic of the forest of Garajonay is that trees have trunks and branches which are covered with age-old lichen and moss. Hanging down in fairy-like gossamer, they give an eerie and bewitched air of mystery.

Apart from the National Parks, the islands have numerous places where wild flowers, ferns and trees grow in great profusion. In many ways it is unfortunate that the majority of popular tourist resorts are situated in the drier and more desert-like areas. With such a variety of entertainment and golden beaches nearby, some visitors never find the time to visit the less populated, verdant areas, and they come away with a one-sided impression of the beauty of the Canary Islands.

Wildlife

The islands' fauna are less numerous than the plants, the most famous being the giant lizards of El Hierro *(lacerta simonyi)* which grow to a length of one metre. Recently thought to be extinct they have again been discovered, but their whereabouts is a guarded secret. Smaller versions of these lizards, the Tizon, can sometimes be observed in the drier regions; they are quite harmless. There are no poisonous snakes and only a few scorpions, mosquitoes and flies.

Rabbits, hares, goats, camels, donkeys and similar animals have been introduced by man.

Bird life is varied. There are over two hundred species, some so well adapted to life on the islands that they can fly only short distances. There are many pigeons, partridge, quail, blackbirds, robins and sparrows. Birds of prey such as crows, vultures, buzzards, white eagles and sparrow hawks are seen frequently. Perhaps disappointingly the native Canary bird (*sarinus Canaria*), which is completely yellow when domesticated, is a brownish colour with only touches of yellow in the wild; but its song is still sweet. The Tenerife chaffinch has an iridescent black and blue plumage.

But perhaps the most striking bird seen is the hoopoe, whose bold black and white wing pattern, erectile crest, pink-brown plumage and long curved bill, make it instantly recognisable; its 'hoo poo poo' call carries far.

The melody of the bird song can be heard in many parks and gardens all over the islands. The National Parks, too, provide ornithologists with much to observe and note.

Migrant birds use the Canary Islands, especially seabirds crossing the Atlantic. Birds from North Africa, too, visit Fuerteventura and the sandy Jandia beaches: little egrets, sandpipers and curlews search the inland saltwater pools for food.

Brilliant butterflies, dragonflies, moths and other small insects breed the green vegetal areas of the Canaries. The cochineal insect (*coccus cacti*) is bred on the Nopal, a prickly pear type cactus, mainly in Lanzarote; it is used to make the cochineal dye which gives a red colouring to edibles like sweets, toothpaste and lipstick. Transparent-winged cicadas with their shrill chirping, fill the air with the sounds of a tropical night.

Agriculture

Two important factors influencing climate and consequently agriculture in the Canaries are the winds, which blow in from the Atlantic and the north-east (trade winds), and the Gulf Stream, which flows in to warm the colder Canaries currents. The winds bring clouds which, when they hit the high mountainous areas, condense to give rain. Thus, in those islands which have a central mountainous zone, we find that the northern and western parts are humid and verdant, while the southern parts, beyond the mountains, are drier and less fertile. Much less rain falls on the islands of Lanzarote and Fuerteventura because these are much flatter; besides they are nearer to the coast of Africa and are subject to hot winds blowing from the Sahara.

At one time the economy of the islands rested on the cultivation of sugar cane, but it became unprofitable; then the vine took over – Canary sack and Malvasia were as popular as Madeira but this too failed. Sugar and wine are still produced but today the main crop is bananas. These are exported all over the world but for economic reasons the main market is Spain. Tomatoes, potatoes and cucumbers are also important exports, and various other vegetables – such as peppers, aubergines and onions – are produced for overseas markets. In recent years the export of flowers, by air, has increased: these are mainly roses, carnations and the islands' brilliant strelitzias. Cereals, salads, greens, beans, apples and pears are cultivated mostly for the local market.

Tobacco is grown, mainly in La Palma, where factories produce cigars which have a high reputation. The cigarette industry is still important in Tenerife.

The little Canary banana, *musa cavendishii,* is deliciously sweet, to be enjoyed when there. Sometimes, as with the tomato, it is difficult to purchase the ripe fruit because they are cropped when very green. One frequently encounters huge lorries carrying enormous loads of the heavy 'hands' of green bananas along narrow country roads; they can make travelling very slow.

On all the islands the country people work long and hard, often with hand tools, sometimes assisted by donkeys and camels – an incongruous sight. Modern machinery is gradually being introduced both in the field and packing shed.

Fishing industry

Fish is part of the staple diet of the islanders particularly those who live by the sea. They will often use a boat for inshore fishing during the night. In the early morning the entire family will be on the beach to help pull the boats and assist with the catch. You can help too!

Many Canarians are involved with sea fishing, the main catches being tuna, swordfish, mackerel and sardine, all of which are used for export and canning. The seas around are full of fish, great shoals are found in the waters that lie between Lanzarote, Fuerteventura and

North Africa; but unfortunately the fishing fleets are poorly equipped.

Sport fishing is popular in these waters and many world record catches have been made, especially from Puerto Rico, Gran Canaria.

National holidays

Shops and offices are closed on the following national feast or fiesta days. Bars, restaurants, theatres and cinemas are open, however, and public transport operates though sometimes the services are limited (as on Sundays).

January	01	– New Year's Day
January	06	– Epiphany
March	19	– San José
(variable)		– Good Friday – Easter Monday
May	01	– Labour Day
(variable)		– Corpus Christi
(variable)		– Ascension
June	29	– San Pedro and San Pablo
July	18	– National Day
July	25	– Santiago Apostal
August	15	– The Assumption
October	12	– Dia de la Hispanidad
November	01	– All Saints
December	08	– Immaculate Conception
December	25	– Christmas Day

In addition each city, town and village, holds religious festivals and *fiestas* for its own patron saints. Christmas (*Navidad*) is celebrated with shops being decorated and there are scenes of the Nativity and the Three Wise Kings, for it is mainly a religious festival.

December 31st (*Noche Vieja*) is much enjoyed with parties, bonfires and fireworks. At midnight the New Year is heralded with the eating of twelve grapes, one at each strike of the clock, amidst great merriment and hooting of car horns and ships' sirens.

January 6th is the day for religious services, then the giving of presents – the most exciting day of the year for all children. Families dress in their best clothes and parade the streets and plazas, with the children showing off their new toys.

Fiestas and festivals

These are taken very seriously in the Canary Islands; religious services and processions are full of fervour. Visitors are always allowed to join in the processions and are made welcome if due respect is observed.

Once the religious part of the day is accomplished the fun and games start. Sport is part of the Canary way of life at all ages, and singing and dancing come naturally – even wee toddlers are encouraged to join in, whatever the hour. Folklore too is part of every fiesta and some interesting customs are still observed. For instance at the festival of **Bajada del Cristo** in Telde, Gran Canaria, an unusual statue of Christ is paraded through the streets of the town. Brought back by returning conquistadores, it was made by the Mexican Indians from maize, mixed with water into a kind of papier mache, and is still much revered.

Fiestas are full of fun with beauty queens, decorated floats, many bands, drum majorettes and clowns. The larger fiestas in Las Palmas (Gran Canaria), Santa Cruz de Tenerife and La Palma are more like the carnivals of South America with elaborate costumes and masks, and fireworks and dancing continuing all night. The streets can be very crowded in the larger towns where care should be taken against pickpockets. The highlight of the Carnival in Santa Cruz de Tenerife is before Lent, when a cavalcade of many colourful groups and personalities parade along the Avenida de Anaga, followed by decorated floats and much music. Be there by mid-day to get a seat (300 pesetas). The celebrations go on until midnight.

The floral carpets created to celebrate **Corpus Christi** (May/June), are a tremendous feat of endeavour, true works of art. These are said to have started in La Orotava, when an aristocratic lady laid some flowers on the cobbled street outside her house before a religious procession. People copied her, so evolved the carpets of flowers. Now intricate religious scenes and colourful floral patterns are created, using chalk patterns or metal frames which are later removed. Coloured volcanic sands, pebbles, salt and grains of cereal are used in some villages, while others only use leaves and flowers. After the religious procession has trodden over the carpets a battle of flowers creates much gaiety. You can see floral carpets at La Laguna in Tenerife.

At Tacaronte in the north of Tenerife, the **Fiestas del Cristo** last for two weeks from 7–12 September. The principal events are held on the two Saturdays and Sundays with solemn Masses and street processions. There are also livestock shows, cycle races, sporting

Carnival – Las Fiestas del Invierno

More of a way of life than a fiesta, the 'winter festival' is really a celebration of the end of the winter and the coming of spring. The Spanish word *carnaval* is said to have been derived from *carne valle*, the Latin for 'good bye meat', meat being taboo during Lent. The traditional time for Carnival is just before the beginning of Lent, February and early March.

All the Canary Islands celebrate at least one week of Carnival. In Santa Cruz de Tenerife it goes on for two weeks. There is no doubt that this event is looked upon by all Canarians as the happiest time of the year. For a few days they put aside their worries and problems to dress up in something bright and cheerful. Then in this disguise they go out into the streets to sing and dance the nights away. Often fireworks (*fuego artificales*), help the party along as do the *coche engalandos* ('private cars in fancy dress').

The election of the Carnival Queen and Junior Queen is taken seriously. Local bands rehearse their pieces and dance groups practise for months. In homes all over the islands shiny bright fabrics, often star spangled or glittering gold and silver, are stitched into elaborate costumes; thousands of sequins, pearls, feathers and lace go to make the Carnival costume, with wigs and masks to add to the fun. On the day of the grand Carnival procession (Cosa) an air of excitement starts at dawn with road sweepers singing their way along the streets. Shops are closed, bars and restaurants prepare for a busy time. (Incidentally the Canarian fiestas are not a time for drunken rowdyism.)

All day people come from towns and villages to forgather in chattering family groups. Never on time, the start of the parade is accompanied by many noisy bands cheerfully blasting away, then the groups follow, each being cheered and clapped with enthusiasm.

The arrival of the Queen brings gasps of pleasure, as with her attendant maids she sits atop a large float on a golden throne, her ornate high head dress of feathers waving in the breeze as she acknowledges the cheers of the crowd. Clowns, Micky Mouse, King Kong, lions, tigers, witches and tramps, all and many more pass in a kaleidoscope of colour. *Comparas*, the heart of the Carnival, are spectacularly dressed groups that rumba, samba and salsa their way, Rio-style, down the streets.

And when it is all over, groups (often one family from grandmother to the baby in a pushchair) all dressed alike will wander to the funfair to enjoy deep fried doughnuts (*churros*), toffee apples (*manzana garrapunda*), steak filled rolls (*pepitos*), and best of all spicy pork kebabs (*pinchitos*) and drink rum and cola (*una cubata*).

Tourists join in the singing and dancing, but it is the Canarians who make Carnival the best time to be in the Canaries.

events, a car rally and Canarian wrestling (*lucha*). Dances and balls take place most evenings with folklore and classical concerts. As well, it is a time for lots of drinking for this is the time of the grape harvest, and Tacoronte is in the heart of Tenerife's best red wine producing country. Tourists are welcome to join in all the celebrations.

It is worth noting that overnight accommodation is particularly hard to find at fiesta time, so do book in advance.

Canary music and dancing

The Canarians are a musical people, who love to sing and dance on every occasion. From a very early age toddlers are encouraged to make music; visitors to the islands are charmed to see tiny children who clap their hands and sing to a natural rhythm while at play.

Carnival is holiday time for all Canarian families, who love to dress in colourful costumes and parade, singing and dancing, in the streets.

Each island has its own folk dances and songs, but the general influence is Spanish and South American. The flute and tambourine are popular but the islands' most typical instrument is the *timple*. Much like a smaller guitar or ukelele, the *timple* was first made at Teguise in Lanzarote where there are still craftsmen making this delightful instrument.

Canary folk song and dances have a typical swaying movement, with languid drawn out melodies; gestures and brightly coloured costumes combine to make a unique and exotic impression. The *folia* is slow, the man demonstrating his feelings for the woman with dignity and restraint. *Folia* songs have been compared with Portuguese *fado*. The *isa* is a light and jolly dance similar to an English country dance.

The costumes worn by men and women are highly decorative. The women wear brightly coloured, often striped, skirts over long white petticoats; sometimes the overskirts are delicately embroidered and looped up. Dainty lace-trimmed aprons and embroidered waistcoats fit neatly over white blouses with large puff sleeves. Black ankle boots, scarves and hat complete the picture. It is the type of hat which helps to identify the islander: in the eastern islands, the scarf covers the face more and the hat is wider brimmed. In Tenerife and La Palma the hat is tilted towards the back of the head.

The men's costumes include white shirts, black knee length trousers over white underbreeches, long red waistcoats and colourful cummerbunds or sashes. Woollen knee-length socks and white spats over black shoes are worn and a soft black felt hat. Sometimes a thick cape completes the costume.

Students from various Spanish universities can frequently be seen in carnival costume, singing and playing in bars, restaurants and plazas to collect money for charity.

At fiesta time glittering masks are sold, and everyone delights in dressing up. Young girls paint their faces and nails, flashing smiles in all directions, and young men wear flowing capes and carry guitars.

Exhibitions and galas of Canarian music and folk dancing are held regularly on all the islands, throughout the year. Some are planned for the tourist, but most are for the delight of the happy Canarians, whose greatest pleasure is to make music and dance. For those interested in island and regional costumes, a visit to the Casade Carta Ethnological Museum is well worthwhile. There are more ways than one to wear a hat! Open all week, small admission charge.

Folklore

Canary folklore thrives with the different islands keeping to their own traditions. This is very noticeable in the varying styles of dress, singing and dancing. Religious fiestas often begin with a *Romeria* (pilgrimage), a long procession of people with gaily decorated horses and carts.

Special programmes for each town are preserved and presented each year. Acrobats, clowns and dwarfs perform in the street, great battles are re-enacted with much vigour. In Santa Cruz de la Palma the Fiesta of the Descent of the Virgin has taken place uninterruptedly for three hundred years.

Handicrafts

All the islands retain many craftsmen and women, in some instances their skills are unique. Craftsmanship has played an important part in architecture as can be seen in the old Canary houses and churches. Implements like yokes and ploughs, kitchen utensils, beautiful looms for weaving, furniture, cedar chests and pipes for smoking, all have over the years been carefully carved from the many different types of wood growing locally. Musical instruments, too, like the Canarian guitar (*timple*) and castanets (*chacaras*) are still being made by traditional methods. The typical Canary **basketwork** had its origin in its use for agriculture.

Vara (twig) basketwork is very sturdy; it is made from strips of young wood like chestnut. In La Palma it reaches an outstanding quality, whilst in Tenerife it is executed with darker, wider and thicker strips of wood.

Cana (cane) basketwork can be pure cane for making delicate baskets, or a mixture of cane and twig for strength. *Palanqueta*, where strips are obtained from the stalks of bunches of dates, gives a highly decorative effect. Very sturdy baskets are made on the island of El Hierro, especially at Sabinosa.

Other basketwork produces hats, mats and handbags made from the palm leaf. The central stem of the palm, the *pirgano* can be used for fans and brooms. In La Gomera there is a strong cottage industry using the dried leaves of the banana plant. Some delightful ornaments are created including attractive flower bouquets in baskets, lively dolls and amusing snakes. They make unique souvenirs. Straw can be used on its own or tied with bramble, to make hampers and containers for dried fruit. Each island keeps to its own traditional work.

There is renewed interest amongst the young in the ancient arts, especially amongst potters who work alongside the old crafts people. The main characteristic of typical Canary **pottery** is its simplicity and non use of the wheel, the craftsman's hands being the only means of lifting and rotating the clay. A small amount of sand is put under the clay to stop it adhering to the ground or bench. In the village of Chipude tucked away in the craggy mountains of La Gomera the shapes of the pots remain the same as in Guanche times. In La Palma, the Benahorita people (the ancient inhabitants) bequeathed a unique type of pottery which has a wonderful glaze, and is marked with prehistoric spirals and geometrical designs. It can be purchased at Mazo and in Santa Cruz de la Palma.

Weaving is still worked on handlooms. Traditional *traperas* rugs, made from rags, are sometimes now woven with wool. Always in bright colours, they make lovely souvenir presents. Among the places where you can see this work done is the *artesania* (craftshop) near Hermigua in La Gomera. At El Paso in La Palma you can find a unique example of silk weaving.

It is also in La Palma that wonderful silk shawls are delicately **hand embroidered**. The *bordados* tablecloths of La Palma are of such a high standard of craft that they are considered amongst the finest work of the islands. Although expensive to purchase they make magnificent heirlooms.

The handicraft that tourists can most easily observe and purchase is **open threadwork** (*calcados*). The work is done mainly in Tenerife, Gran Canaria and Fuerteventura, but it is a cottage industry pursued when conditions do not allow work in the fields. *Calcados* is executed by stretching the cloth on a frame, and drawing the threads together to form an intricate pattern. Usually each piece is worked by more than one person. Each island has its own designs and it is interesting to compare these. The same patterns appear on the blouses and skirts worn by the folk dancers.

Various schools of needlework throughout the islands are now open to visitors and the articles sold there are usually a little less expensive than in the shops. Seeing pretty young twelve-year-olds patiently working their needle must surely make you reach for your purse to keep alive the art of hand embroidery.

It is impossible to write about the preservation of handicrafts and traditions in the Canaries without mentioning the work of César Manrique. Born in Lanzarote, he is an artist and sculptor of international renown. Lanzarote has become an ecological focal point for the way he has protected the environment and harmonised new developments with the landscape. No more high rise apartments, bill posters, advertisement boardings or rubbish in Lanzarote: it has to be seen to be believed. It was he who designed the superb Lago Martinez of which the people of Tenerife are justly proud.

The list of handicrafts of the islands is long, and one must mention a few more: delicate lace-work done by the convent sisters, rag dolls dressed in typical costume, woollen shawls, native clay figures, polished volcanic stones. (The *peridot* is a green semi-precious stone which is made into attractive jewellery.)

Thanks to the patience of the islanders and the support of many tourists, the folklore and crafts are being preserved.

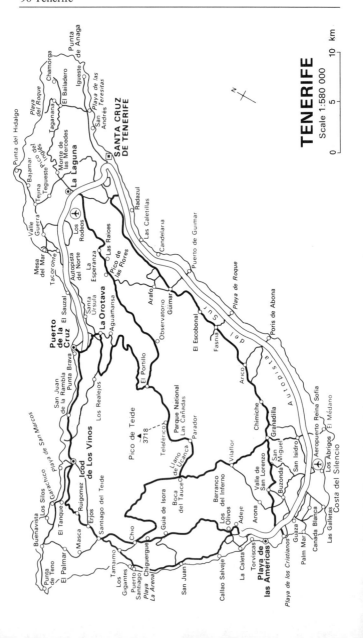

TENERIFE

Scale 1:580 000

EIGHT

Introducing Tenerife

Island of Eternal Spring

Tenerife, 112 km from the coast of Africa and 1120 km from the Spanish peninsula, is usually the first island that comes to mind when people think about the Canary Islands. It is the capital of the western province, which includes the islands of La Palma, La Gomera and El Hierro, and it is the largest of all the islands, at 2354 sq km and a population of 650,000.

A mild climate and the undeniable beauty of the island prove to be a constant attraction. Diverse scenery, the abundance of excellent accommodation and entertainment, plus the ease of modern travel, have made Tenerife one of the most popular holiday resorts in the world and a long-standing favourite with the British tourist.

The dominant feature of this roughly triangular-shaped island is the massive Mount Teide (3718m), a gigantic volcanic cone, the highest summit in all Spain. Teide is nearly always snow-capped and can be seen from most parts of the island. It is impressive to be lying in the sun or swimming, then to look up and notice the sun also shining on the great snow peak in the distance. Even when the snow has melted, the peak still has white pumice sand covering the top, giving the impression that it is covered in snow. Mists can come over Teide quite suddenly then quickly clear giving brilliant sunshine again.

A central mountain ridge runs almost the entire length of Tenerife. The natural volcanic crater of Mount Teide, which has been declared a National Park, is of great interest and importance to the island. Fragrant pine woods now grow on all but the highest lava rocks. Vegetation and flora flourish in the fertile valleys lush with banana plantations. Citrus groves and vines are cultivated almost down to the sea's edge. The Valley of Orotava, on the northern coast, above Puerto de la Cruz, is noted for the fertile richness of its soil. It is intensely cultivated with banana, vines, fruit and vegetable crops, and reputed to be one of the finest landscapes in all the Canaries.

The coastline of Tenerife offers much variation in scenery, from steep cliffs to sandy beaches. In places the sands are black from lava rock, elsewhere golden and gentle, and everywhere the views are spectacular and varied.

Because of the large mountain range in the centre of the island, temperatures can vary slightly from place to place. Generally speaking, the south-west of Tenerife is drier with a less moist atmosphere than the north-east. Low clouds in winter can sometimes obscure views, but these usually clear in a few hours and agreeable springlike weather is maintained most days of the year. Average temperatures lie between the minimum 17°C in winter and the maximum 23°C in summer, so do not expect a tropical climate.

The resorts range from Playa Cristianos and Playa de las Americas in the sunny south – lively places with high-rise hotels, apartments and good swimming – to quieter places like Puerto de Santiago, with black sand and old houses grouped around the small port. At nearby Los Gigantes (The Giants), huge black cliffs rise majestically from the deep blue sea and modern apartment blocks allow visitors to view the wonderful scenery.

The fine old city of Santa Cruz de Tenerife, capital of the island, is a busy place offering much that is of interest for sightseers and shoppers. The harbour is the second largest in the Canaries, ocean going liners seem to sail right into the heart of the city, and there is always hustle and bustle.

However, Puerto de la Cruz in the north retains its position as the principal international tourist centre of the Canaries. World famous hotels and lesser establishments provide an all-the-year-round welcome for holidaymakers. Modern high-rise buildings cluster along the sea's edge and the long promenade, lined with tourist souvenir shops, cafés and bars, is bright and busy. Here you will find César Manrique's renowned Lago Martianez, a brilliantly landscaped leisure complex of lakes, swimming pools, sun terraces and flower gardens, providing entertainment by day and night.

Tenerife is easily accessible by air and by sea from all parts of the world. Formerly there was only one airport, Los Rodeos in the north of the island; but now there is a new, larger, more sophisticated international airport, Reina Sofia, in the south and this is where most holidaymakers land. Los Rodeos is still used for inter-island flights and smaller aircraft. Santa Cruz is the port of arrival for visitors coming by sea.

History

The early history of Tenerife is shrouded in legends of the primitive Guanche people. The great Teide mountain and surrounding peaks were used as places of worship but no cave inscriptions have been found in Tenerife. Tacaronte in the north of the island was the ancient Guanche kingdom.

Tenerife was finally conquered in 1496 by Alonso Fernandez de Lugo, ninety-four years after the first Spanish expedition led by Jean de Bethancourt. The island was not relinquished easily, the Guanches were unsubmissive and put up great resistance but after three years de Lugo finally triumphed, having killed Bencomo, chief of the Guanches. The capital was established at La Laguna where de Lugo built the Iglesia de los Remedios (Church of Remedies) now the Cathedral. The lake from which the city took its name has since disappeared but La Laguna remains a busy and imposing town, and is now the home of the archipelago's only university.

However as the port of Santa Cruz developed into a centre of commerce it gained in importance and in 1823 became the capital of the island, being created a free port in 1852.

The island's history after the conquest of colonisation centred around the planting of sugar cane and vines. Helped also by the banana plantations of the late eighteenth century, the economy of Tenerife grew. Englishmen settled, particularly in Puerto de la Cruz, and a strong trade with the Canaries developed.

English people of means began to discover the agreeable climate and were sent to Tenerife to convalesce, with the result that some decided to remain permanently. In 1886 the Grand Hotel was opened in Puerto de la Cruz by Bernard Walsh, who changed his name to Valois. During the first season over 500 guests arrived, the first of the tourist trade. In 1887 Mr Ernest Har wrote in the *British Medical Journal*, 'The cooing of the birds, the splash of the fountains, the many hued flower beds, the far spreading expanse of the blue sea and the towering hills behind us, the blue sky and an all-pervading sun overhead, the delicious warmth but exquisite freshness of the air tell us that we have reached safety and happily the haven of our rest and are safely lodged for this promising winter in one of the choicest of the gardens of the earth, Puerto Orotava, the very pearl of the Fortunate Islands.' This very long sentence, written so many years ago, is still relevant today, when so many people have the opportunity to enjoy these blessed Canary Islands.

Today it is in Tenerife that British interest is most strongly represented, both by residents and tourists.

Fiestas and festivals

January 5	Cabalgata de los Reyes Magos (Santa Cruz)
January 6	Festival of the Three Kings (Garachio)
January 22	Fiesta de San Sebastián (Garachio and Los Realejos)
January 22	Fiesta de San Antonio Abad (Icod)
February 2	Fiesta de Sans Blas (Candelaria)
February (date varies)	Fiesta del Invierno or Carnival (Santa Cruz and Puerto de la Cruz)
March 2	Fiesta del Patriarch San José (La Guancha and El Tanque)
March/April	Holy Week celebrated all over island.
April/May	Festivals of Spain, bullfights, theatre, ballet, etc.
May 1 to 5	Fiesta de la Cruz (Santa Cruz) to celebrate foundation of the city.
May/June	Corpus Christi, celebrated everywhere (especially La Orotava and La Laguna), floral carpets.
June 24	Fiesta de San Juán (Icod)
July (1st Sunday)	Fiesta de San Benito Abad (La Laguna)
July 16	Fiesta del Gran Poder de Dios and Fiesta de la Virgen del Carmen (Santa Cruz and Puerto de la Cruz), fireworks, sailing and regattas.
July 25	Fiesta de Santiago Apostol (Santa Cruz) celebrating victory over Lord Nelson's attack.
July 27	Fiesta de San Cristóbal (La Laguna)
August 15	Feast of Our Lady of Candelaria (Candelaria)
August (3rd Sunday)	Fiesta de Cristo del Gran Poder (Bajamar)
September 7 to 21	Festivals of Santisimo Cristo (La Laguna and Tacoronte)
October 3	Fiesta de Nuestra Señora del Rosario (Fasnia)
October 5	Fiesta del Cristo de la Miscordia (Garachico)
October 7	Fiesta de Nuestra Señora del Rosario (El Rosario)

October 12	Fiesta de Nuestra Señora del Pilar (Granadilla)
October 21	Fiesta de Santa Ursula (Santa Ursula)
October 24 and 25	Fiesta Nuestra Señora de los Remedios (Buenavista de Norte), concerts, Canary wrestling and dancing.
November 16	Fiesta de Volcan (Guia de Isora)
November 25	Fiesta de la Catalina (Taganana)
Nov/Dec	Opera (Santa Cruz)
December 22	Fiesta de la Navidad (Santa Cruz)

The Burial of the Sardine

This important event always takes place on Shrove Tuesday, just before the beginning of Lent.

A huge silvery mock sardine (a symbol of the island), about six metres long, is carried on a platform on the shoulders of eight youths, through the streets at night. Accompanying it is a children's band and a procession of 'wailing mourners', all dressed in widows' weeds: male and female with black hats, veils and high heeled shoes sob and shriek their way along, cheered on by clapping and laughing crowds. Every now and then the Sardine is tossed in the air, having a final fling before being taken on to the beach!

There is a mock funeral service conducted amid much moaning and groaning from the mourners. Finally the Sardine is set alight in a huge bonfire, which is followed by a wonderful firework display.

So ends this night of fun and frivolity – it is a great and important Canary spectacle.

Climate

The climate in Tenerife is always mild, even in winter, when there can be snow on the mountains, yet the sunshine so warm that visitors can sunbathe at a height of 3,000m.

Because of the prevailing north east wind that part of the island is prone to more cloud than the south west. So if you prefer moist and greener surroundings then choose the northern parts. The southern region is mostly dry and dusty and on a few occasions can suffer a *sirocco* or *calima*, which is dust carried by hot winds from North Africa. Temperatures rise to their highest in July and August but rarely above 25°C or below 18°C in winter. The island's spring-like climate creates a feeling of well being and it is particularly advantageous for people with arthritic ailments.

What to wear

Lightweight clothes are worn all the year by visitors but the Canarians tend to wear thicker clothes during December and January. As it rarely rains an umbrella is sufficient for any wet days. Comfortable footwear is important, feet tend to swell in a warm climate so sandals or flip flops are best. However, do pack a pair of stout walking shoes for exploring the countryside and visiting Mount Teide and you will need a warm pullover or windproof jacket in the mountains sometimes.

The major resorts have upmarket restaurants where smart evening wear is seen. A tie and jacket are required when visiting the Casinos. However, elsewhere dress is now very casual.

You will not be allowed in churches or museums if wearing shorts or swimwear. Some remote beaches are unofficially nudist. Most hotels allow topless sunbathing. Remember the sun's rays are very strong so the use of sunhats is recommended.

Where to stay: a selection of accommodation

Tenerife has three main tourist centres. In the north Puerto de la Cruz offers all types of accommodation from the big and cheerful types of hotels along the sea front to the quieter and more restful locations above the town. Santa Cruz has hotels and pensions much favoured by the Spanish and business clients. In the south Playa de las Americas is now the most popular resort in the Canary Islands, a place for fun-loving sunseekers. A little quieter is neighbouring Los Cristianos. Costa Silencio is densely packed with apartments and bungalows and on site entertainment.

For tranquil venues choose El Medano and Los Gigantes in the south, while in the north Bajamar, Punta Hidalgo and San Marcos are resorts where it would be advisable to rent a car.

(Opposite) Top: *Awaiting the Carnival parade, these pretty children stand under a tree away from the hot sunshine.*
(Opposite) Bottom: *The tiny bay of Playa de Teno, where a few tenacious fisherman keep their small boats.*

The average cost in Tenerife for four-star hotel package accommodation in a double room, with breakfast, per person for one week is between £299 and £449, depending on season. Apartments are from £254 and £406. Prices include flight.

Santa Cruz de Tenerife

Mencey ***** Hotel Avenida Dr Jose Naveiras 38. Tel: 27 67 00. Open all year. In a quiet residential area to the north of the city, just off the Rambla. This is a magnificent luxury hotel with a dignified atmosphere, built in the thirties and recently renovated. It has imposing marble columns and floors, glittering chandeliers, spacious lounges and many conference/banqueting rooms and secretarial services. 298 rooms are luxuriously decorated, airconditioned, colour TV, video, music channel, minibar and direct telephone. Spacious marble bathrooms. There are 26 junior suites and one presidential suite. Room service. The restaurant overlooks the tropical gardens. There are bars, hairdressing salon, shops, swimming pool, gymnasium, sauna and tennis courts. Early booking over the Christmas period and the Carnival in February advisable.

Plaza *** Hotel Apartments. Plaza de la Candelaria 9. Tel: 24 58 61. Open all year this business hotel is easily located in the city centre, amongst the shops on the western side of Plaza de la Candelaria. Furnished in Spanish style with leather covered furniture, it is clean and friendly. 64 rooms, single and double, have modern bathrooms, telephone and TV. On the top floor is a solarium, bar and lounge. There is a lift.

Tamaide ** Hotel Residencia. Rambla General Franco 118. Tel: 27 71 00. Open all year, a small hotel in the Rambla, the main street that runs through the residential heart of Santa Cruz. Suitable for business people who require a quiet location close to the five star Hotel Mencey. 65 rooms, breakfast only.

Anaga ** Hotel. Calle Imeldo Seris 19. Tel: 24 50 90. Open all year, with an unobtrusive facade, this hotel is situated behind the harbour and in the business centre of the city. Spanish style leather furniture,

(Opposite) *Once almost lost amongst the folds of the deep green valley, the tiny village of Masca is now being discovered by tourists.*

it is clean and friendly. 126 rooms are adequately furnished with modern bathrooms. The restaurant has an international cuisine. There is a lift to the top floor where a terrace, with bar, gives views over the city towards the sea.

Horizonte * Hotel. Santa Rosa de Lima 11. Tel: 27 53 59. A small commercial hotel with 55 rooms, close to offices, shops, banks and restaurants. It is a friendly Canarian hotel simply furnished and useful for a short business stay or to see the capital city, which has much old-fashioned charm.

Medano (south)

Medano *** Hotel. Playa del Medano. Tel: 70 41 50. This hotel near the harbour has the distinction of having its own sun terrace right out over the sea, supported by piers, so that at high tide it is possible to dive straight into the water. It is a quiet pleasant place with 65 rooms. It is advisable to book in advance in winter. The beach here is safe enough for the disabled to enjoy a swim.

Playa Sur Tenerife, *** Hotel. Playa del Medano. Tel: 70 40 00. Mainly used by windsurfing enthusiasts as the grounds are at the edge of sand dunes and the beach. There is a sports school here where windsurfing equipment can be hired and tuition given. 70 rooms are adequately furnished.

Los Cristianos (south)

Gran Hotel Arona **** Hotel. Tel: 75 06 78. Fax: 75 02 43. 403 rooms. A new large, modern hotel, built in luxurious style at the quieter end of Los Cristianos, right by the beach and promenade leading on to the harbour. All rooms have full bathroom and sea view, balconies, air conditioning, music, telephone, TV, mini bar and safe box. Three restaurants, three bars, three swimming pools, gymnasium, squash court, sauna, hairdresser, entertainments, night club, plenty of sun terraces and outside bar.

Paradise Park **** Hotel. Urbanizacion Oasis del Sur. Tel: 79 39 07. Located in an elevated position at the eastern end of Los Cristianos, 15 km from the airport. This modern hotel has 112 rooms with TV and luxury style decor and terraces that face the sea. A courtesy bus takes visitors to the shop, beach and port. Restaurants, bars and lounges are comfortable. Nightly entertainment includes folk dancers and flamenco. Day nursery, swimming pool, solarium, gymnasium, sauna and squash.

Princessa Dacil *** Hotel. Tel: 79 08 00. Situated in an elevated position overlooking the harbour. Catering mostly for package holiday visitors. Swimming pool, tennis, sauna, gymnasium, mini golf, disco and dance floor. A good clean family hotel, pleasantly furnished.

Tenerife Sur *** Hotel Apartments. Avenida en Proyecto. Tel: 79 14 74. At the eastern end of Los Cristianos this pleasant hotel has 137 rooms, all with terraces. The swimming pool has plenty of area for sunbathing, while the beach and town are an easy 10 minute walk. It has its own restaurant and small supermarket and car rent firm. Close by are other shops and restaurants.

Andrea's ** Hotel Residencia. Avenida Valle Menendez. Tel: 79 00 12. Well established and suitable for business and short stay holidays. It is located at the beginning of the old town, near shops and five minutes walk to the harbour. The old fashioned furnishings are clean and the staff pleasant. Breakfast only, but there are plenty of cafes and restaurants nearby. 42 rooms. Close to bus station, taxis and tourist office. Open all year.

Silvia * Hotel. Calle del Valle Menendez. Tel: 79 25 05. Small with 22 studios and bedrooms. There is no breakfast served but next door is the Tosca Restaurant, also cafés, bars and shops. It has a central position for taxis, buses and tourist office and a five minute walk to the beach and harbour. Open all year.

Playa de Las Americas (south)

Mediterranean Palace ***** Hotel. Avenida del Litoral. Tel: 79 44 00. A newly built luxury hotel in opulent and spectacular style. Its blue and white frontage makes it a notable edifice along the seafront of the residential part of Playa de las Americas, close to Los Cristianos. Its sophisticated ambience meets you in the form of the top hatted porter on arrival (no scruffy jeans here). Inside, huge lounges are cool with gardens of ferns and modern furniture. 494 rooms include 41 junior suites, 12 having private swimming pools. Airconditioned, colour TV, taped music, dial direct telephones and all marble bathrooms. This is the hotel with just about everything from conference rooms, swimming pools, terraced garden for nude sunbathing. Secretary and hostess service. Animation sports, games, sauna and gymnasium. Not the place for an inexpensive holiday.

Bitacora **** Hotel. Avenida Michan Doña Ramon. Tel: 79 15 40. Opened in 1985, this large high rise is situated at the southern end of town within easy distance of main shopping arcades. A typically well organised package holiday hotel and always busy. 314 rooms have two beds and a sofa that converts into two extra beds. Airconditioned, telephone, piped music, minibar and terrace. Complete bathroom.

Five rooms are suitable for disabled. Main restaurant, terrace buffet by two swimming pools, one heated. Area for children and waterchute. Plenty of lively entertainment with international shows. Hairdresser, shops, tennis courts, one squash court and gymnasium.

Bouganville Playa **** Hotel. Tel: 79 14 62. This was one of the first high rise hotels to be built here. All 481 rooms have a sea view and terrace. Adequately furnished with telephone, taped music and full bathroom. The floors in the main lounges and restaurant are tiled. Four bars, restaurant with buffet lunch. Three swimming pools, tennis and squash courts, pool table and pinball machines. Shopping centre, hairdresser and fitness centre. Close to a busy road and ten minutes walk to town centre.

Conquistador **** Hotel. Avenida Litoral. Tel: 79 23 99. Well established and large, used by package holiday operators. It stands at the south eastern, quieter end of the resort and near the sea. 485 rooms are furnished in a modern style with terrace, telephone, music, air conditioning and full bathroom. Restaurants, snack bar, two adult swimming pools (one heated), children's pool, volley ball, tennis, table tennis, billiards and games room.

Esmeralda Playa **** Hotel. Urbanizacion Torviscas. Tel: 79 03 78. Open all year and used by several British tour operators. Opened in 1986, large, it has a cheerful atmosphere. The decor is practical, this hotel is recommended for children. Cots can be hired. All rooms have terrace with seaview. Airconditioned in summer. The adult pool is heated in winter and there is a baby pool in the tropical garden. Tennis, squash, table tennis, gymnasium, sauna, sports centre and plenty of entertainment at night. The bus stop is 100m away.

Gran Tinerfe **** Hotel. Tel: 79 12 00. In the centre of town by the beach. This is a popular family hotel used by several tour operators of different nationalities. 360 rooms include 11 luxury penthouses, 3 suites, 20 doubles with sitting rooms and 45 chalets in the garden, all with full bathroom. This is a relaxed hotel with babysitting service, laundry and doctor on call. Refrigerators and TV for rent. Built on three levels, the lower having direct access to the beach. Swimming pools, tennis courts, sauna, convention rooms, entertainments and night club.

Las Dalias **** Hotel. Urbanizacion San Eugenio. Tel: 79 27 12. A typical holiday hotel with a modern decor. Suitable for families with children. All rooms airconditioned with terraces. Situated 150m from the sea and centre of town. Tennis, squash, solarium and playground. Plenty of entertainment, conference room, open all year.

La Pinta **** Hotel Apartments. Urbanizacion San Eugenio. Tel: 79 58 58. Newly built modern style building, 229 units have full bathroom and equipped kitchen, telephone and piped music. Overlooking the new Marina Puerto Colon and 25m from a manmade beach. Airconditioned. Restaurant, bars, barbecue, garden, solarium, pools. The hotel has a fresh appearance. Open all year.

La Siesta **** Hotel. Tel: 79 22 52. This recently constructed hotel of low design is 300m from the sea. 280 suites all have lounge, bedroom and full size bathroom, piped music, direct telephone, safe deposit, colour TV, video and spacious terrace. 80 suites have cooking facilities, refrigerator and room service. A large garden of tropical palms, bright flowers surround three swimming pools, one heated and another for children. Two tennis courts. Grill and barbecue. Entertainments, TV and video lounge.

Park Hotel Troya **** Hotel. Tel: 79 01 04. Opposite Troya beach. Well established package holiday hotel in busy centre. 288 rooms with bath, telephone and terrace. Suites, family rooms and apartments. Airconditioned lounge and restaurant. Outdoor swimming pool, tennis courts, sun terraces. Entertainments. Shops, supermarkets, bars and restaurants nearby.

Torviscas Playa **** Hotel. Urbanizacion San Eugenio. Tel: 79 02 00. One of the newest hotels with a position along the manmade beach at the western end of the resort. Large and with plenty of sun terraces with tropical plants by the three swimming pools. Conference room seats 700, night club, tennis, squash, fitness centre and shops. All rooms are airconditioned and have terrace, telephone, electronic safe and optional colour TV. Away from the centre of Americas and by the attractive promenade of Torviscas where there are plenty of small cafés and restaurants.

Vulcano **** Hotel. Tel: 79 20 35. Opened December 1986 it is 17 kms from the Airport and 300m from the sea. With luxury decor and 371 rooms on eight floors this hotel is spacious and dripping with trailing plants and spectacular chandeliers. All bedrooms are airconditioned with luxury bathrooms, balcony or terrace. There are 12 suites and 6 rooms for the disabled. Main restaurant and poolside buffet. Plenty of sports and entertainment programmes with international nightclub shows and disco.

Los Hibiscos **** Hotel. Urbanizacion San Eugenio. Tel: 79 14 62. Situated at western end, 150m from the sea and 14 km from the airport. This is one of the few hotels that is not a high rise. 138 studio rooms and 180 bedrooms are built around the swimming pools, gardens and tennis courts. All rooms pleasantly furnished with telephone, music, full bathroom and terrace. Restaurant with buffet meals, snack bar, two bars, games for children. Access to all public rooms and entertainments in other four star company hotels in the locality.

Compostela Beach *** Hotel Apartment. Avenida Litoral. As its name suggests this is right by the beach and 1,500m from the harbour of Los Cristianos. Apartments for 2,3,4, and 5 persons, with bathroom, terrace, kitchen, telephone and safe box. Restaurant, cocktail bar with terrace in tropical garden. Solarium, swimming pool, some entertainment for children. Suitable for young families.

Puerto de la Cruz (north)

Melia Botánico ***** Hotel. Richard Yeoward s/n 38400. Puerto de la Cruz. Tel: 38 14 00. A first class hotel in every way, set in an atmosphere of luxury it is located almost opposite the Botanical Gardens in a quiet area 2 km to the north east of the town. Open all year, 282 airconditioned spacious bedrooms have modern bathrooms, colour TV and telephone. Balcony. There are suites on the Ambassador Floor. Like most five star hotels there are conference rooms seating 250 and private dining rooms. With a cool plush decor of marble and glistening chandeliers. The service is quiet, efficient and attentive. Swimming pools, barbecue, tennis courts and evening entertainment including a swinging disco, all are set in a superb garden with views of the sea and mountains.

Melia San Felipe ***** Hotel. Avenida de Colón 13. Tel: 38 33 11. This large modern high rise has an excellent position for those requiring top quality. Right on the seafront at the eastern end of the town. Open all year, 260 airconditioned rooms are nicely furnished in a restful decor, pleasant bathrooms, telephone, minibar and terrace with panoramic view. Conference rooms, comfortable lounges and gracious restaurant and bars. The Olympic size swimming pool with diving board has sunterraces where meals are served. Tennis courts, sauna and evening entertainments.

Atalaya Gran **** Hotel. Tel. 38 46 00. In the peaceful Taoro Park this well established hotel has a quiet decor and Spanish atmosphere with polite service. Modern music is played in the reception area. Surrounded by a thick tropical garden the large heated swimming pool has a nearby bar. Sports include bowls, tennis, garden chess, table tennis, billiards and gymnastics. 183 rooms with complete bathrooms, terrace, telephone and mini bar. The hotel is fully airconditioned. Nightclub La Sabina. A hotel bus runs regularly down to Puerto which is 3 km. Open all year.

A tropical garden, swimming pool, mountain views, plenty of sunshine and a comfortable hotel. This one is situated in the quiet area above Puerto de la Cruz.

Gran Hotel Tenerife Playa **** Hotel. Avenida Colón. Tel: 38 32 11. Well established and large, open all year. Close by the promenade and Martianez Lake. It has 339 rooms (33 are suites), all have bathroom, telephone and terrace. Room service from 0800 to 2400 hrs. 24 hour laundry delivery service. Safe boxes, TV rental, baby sitting and medical service. Used by package tour operators, this hotel is always busy. Amongst the facilities are conference rooms, hairdressing salon, massage and sauna. Reading, games and TV rooms. Self service restaurants. The sixth and ninth floors are terraces and solarium. Outside are two swimming pools, one heated. Table tennis and children's playground in a tropical garden. Next door to the entrance is a disco.

La Chiripa Garden **** Hotel. Calle Suiza, Urbanizacion San Fernando. Tel: 38 20 50. In a high position in the residential north of town on the edge of Taoro Park development. This hotel is quiet and has a Spanish atmosphere. 267 rooms all with terraces, some apartments with sitting room and kitchen. Breakfast and dinner are buffet, lunch is grill pizzeria. In the well established garden there is a poolside bar, two tennis courts, volley ball and minigolf. Helpful is a day nursery, shopping gallery, hairdresser, sauna, massage and well equipped gymnasium. An entertainments committee provides amusements and evening programmes. A hotel bus runs regularly to the town centre. The surrounds are hilly with a steep road down to the sea.

Las Vegas Sol **** Hotel. Avenida Colon 2. Tel: 38 34 51. In the centre of the town this high rise overlooks the Lake Martianez. It consists of 223 single and twin rooms, all have bathrooms and most have a terrace. As in all Sol hotels the atmosphere is lively with plenty of entertainment for all age groups. Outdoor pools for adults and children are heated, mini golf and a tennis court. Solarium, sauna, massage parlour and hairdresser. In the restaurant it is buffet service for breakfast and lunch, for dinner it is buffet and traditional service. Cafeteria and bar by the pools. This is a useful hotel for those who wish to be right in town by sea and shops. Open all year.

Maritim **** Hotel. Los Realejos. Tel: 34 20 12. Situated 2 km west of Puerto on high ground overlooking the ocean and near to Loro Parque. There is a courtesy bus service to the town centre. This extremely tall concrete hotel has 461 rooms, all have a full bathroom, radio, telephone and balcony. Some junior suites and apartments are equipped with kitchenette, oven and refrigerator. This large complex is designed as a complete holiday world that includes colourful tropical gardens, swimming pools, tennis and volley ball with a full programme of sports and entertainments for all ages in a relaxed atmosphere. Convention halls, open all year.

Orotava Garden Sol **** Hotel. Calle Aguilar y Quesada. Tel: 38 52 11. A high rise Sol hotel, open all year and used by package tour operators. A short walk from the sea front and the Martianez Lake with plenty of shops nearby. 211 rooms (4 suites) have bathrooms, telephone, terrace and background music and comfortable decor. There are conference rooms. The restaurant is airconditioned with buffet and à la carte service. Two swimming pools and outdoor bar. This is a good family hotel with relaxed atmosphere where children are welcome, playground, miniclub and plenty of entertainment. Hairdressing and sauna.

Parque San Antonio Sol **** Hotel. Ctra de las Arenas. Tel: 38 38 51. Open all year. In picturesque and quiet situation on an elevated position north of the town, close to public transport. Attractively set around a central tropical garden and swimming pools. From the terraces there is a magnificent view of Mount Teide. 211 rooms have bathroom, balcony, and telephone. Comfortably appointed with air conditioned dining room, sauna. Like all Sol hotels plenty of entertainment. The centre of Puerto de la Cruz is fifteen minutes drive down hill.

Tigaiga **** Hotel. Parque Taoro 16. Tel: 38 35 00. This well established, Swiss run, popular hotel has a lovely elevated position towards the back of Puerto, in the Parque Taoro. The tropical gardens are a special attraction for botanists. On the first floor is a secluded terrace for topless sunbathers. 4 suites, 65 twin and single rooms have en suite bath rooms with hairdryer. Comfortably furnished with private safe, colour TV and refrigerator can be hired. Terrace with a view of Mount Teide or Taoro Parque. Two lifts and one accommodating wheelchairs. Each Sunday canary folk dancing and local wrestling (*lucha Canaria*) are staged in the gardens. Organised walks are arranged. Dancing, fashion shows and entertainment in the evening.

Condesa *** Hotel Residencia. Calle Quintana 13. Tel: 38 10 50. Like the Marquesa two doors away this residential hotel is an old style Canarian building which still retains its charm, despite the modernisation and being in the busy centre of the old town. A delightful indoor patio has attractive wooden balconies and comfortable furniture. Many ferns and plants making a gracious lounge. The 45 rooms have bath, radio, telephone and balcony. A place for the quieter holiday visitor.

Los Principes *** Hotel. Plaza Dr Victor Perez, Tel: 38 33 53. This hotel was first opened in 1967 and renovated in modern style in 1986. It is situated in the heart of the shopping area and within easy walking of the promenade and old town. 59 rooms have bath, telephone and most have balcony or terrace. Two sun terraces and small pool are on the roof top. A tidy hotel.

Marquesa *** Hotel. Calle Quintana 11. Tel: 38 31 51. Built in 1712 and renovated in 1984. This is a real gem of a place for those who like an old building with character, lots of dark wood work and potted plants. The decor of the 88 rooms is simple but adequate. An excellent restaurant is usually busy with hotel guests and the public and extends to an outside terrace which faces the walkway and plaza. It is an experience to dine there on a warm evening by candlelight and live music.

Monopol *** Hotel. Quintana 15. Tel: 38 46 11. Owned by the family Gleixner for over 60 years this truly Canarian style hotel has an old world charm. With a cool patio where carved wooden balconies, tropical plants and rubber trees climb up three storeys. The cane furniture is covered with the same colour material as the folk dancers' skirts. 100 rooms have bath, shower and some have balconies. Heated swimming pool and three sun terraces. Sitting rooms, card tables, table tennis, billiards, restaurant and two bars. Lifts. Open all year. This hotel will appeal to the tourist who requires a restful venue yet wishes to be close to shops and sea in the older part of Puerto.

San Telmo *** Hotel. Paseo San Telmo 18. Tel: 38 58 53. Opposite the San Telmo beach, which is black shingle, rock and sand. This small family run hotel is convenient for the fishing harbour, old town and shopping centre. The decor is Castillian style with plenty of woodwork. 91 rooms have bathrooms, telephone, music and terrace. Restaurant, two lounges, TV and card room. The swimming pool and bar are on the top floor which has a panoramic view and is a real suntrap.

Maga * Hotel. Calle Iriarte 9. Tel: 38 38 53. Open all year this simple establishment is in the old part of town, five minutes walk from the harbour. Clean and friendly, the 24 sparsely furnished rooms have bathroom but no terrace. There is a lift from the first floor. Breakfast is served in the ground floor bar. Attached is a pleasant restaurant serving international food. Parking is in the street, from which some noise can be expected.

Punta Hidalgo (**north near Bajamar**)

Neptuno *** Hotel. Calle Punta Hidalgo. Tel: 46 04 61. 75 rooms with terrace, and mountains/seaview. 32 apartments with two bedrooms, living/dining room, kitchen and bathroom. 27 bungalows in gardens, most with bath, telephone, sitting room and terrace. Two sea water pools, solarium, bowling, tennis and table tennis. International restaurant. This hotel is situated at the north eastern corner of Tenerife and some way from other resorts. There is a bus service but car rent is recommended.

Mount Teide

Parador Nacional Canadas del Teide ** Hotel. Tel: 33 23 04. 23 rooms, TV, views, swimming pool, tennis courts, garage and gardens. Superb situation close to summit of Mount Teide, excellent for walking. Can be cold at night. Price for double room per night 7000 pesetas, with balcony 7,500 pesetas.

Camping

Nauta Camping, a long awaited Class 1A camping park, opened in April 1984 in the sunny, dry south of the island. It is built on level ground three miles from the coast at Las Galletas and six miles from Los Cristianos. In the distance to the north is a splendid view of Mount Teide, which towers 12,000 feet from a ridge of volcanic mountains.

This architect-designed park has an overall plan which will eventually make it into a self-contained camping and sports complex with its own restaurant and social centre. Among future attractions will be tennis, squash, French *boules* and table tennis. Wooden chalet type one room *cabinas* can be rented for four persons, and include electricity and free swimming. A children's play park is located near the supermarket, with a children's swimming pool nearby. Close to these is a larger separate pool for adults which is to have an outdoor bar and sunbathing terrace. Campers can enjoy nearby riding, golf, sailing and waterski. There is excellent windsurfing and swimming at El Medano, eleven miles away.

Already available are numbered pitches with electricity hook-ups, marked out with flowering plants and shrubs. Tents are situated separately. There are three modern toilet blocks in the caravan area and one in the tent park. Fitted with good quality basins, shower units, mirrors and power points, these have free hot water, as does the outside washing-up area. There's a laundry room equipped with washing machines and dryers, a chemical toilet disposal point, and dustbins are emptied several times a day. The reception is open from 1000 to 2000 hrs. There is a well stocked shop. Refills for Camping Gaz 907 bottles are available from some petrol stations and ironmongers (*ferreteria*). Tel: 78 59 71 or 78 51. Fax (922) 78 50 27. Open all the year. Charges per night in pesetas: adults 300, tent 300, car 300, caravan 400, motorhome 400, motorcycle 210, electricity 200, 4-person chalet 2,000.

At **Punta del Hidalgo**, in the north east of Tenerife, a new campsite is being built which is due to open in 1993. It is situated close to banana plantations and the beach of black lava rock pools, where the locals much enjoy fishing.

This is a popular place for walking, especially around the headland to Playa de los Troches and up into the Anaga Mountains. Near the camping ground a marina and lighthouse are under construction as this area is designated for tourist development.

In the north-west of the island, a small camping place has recently been opened called **Buenavista del Norte**, which at present takes some thirty five units. You take the right fork at the entrance to Buenavista, following signs to Las Animas. The road becomes a dirt track after about 1.5km and goes past banana plantations for a further 3km. The site is some 300m from the beach which is rocky and has a difficult access at present. Washrooms, showers and toilets are under construction. The camp is being marketed for older, quieter people. Large families, loud music and noise are not allowed. Owner, Ernest Rudi Freyberg. Tel: 84 06 86. Fax: 84 13 06.

NINE

Leisure activities

Shopping

In Tenerife the only problem is what not to buy! The saying that 'if you have the money it is there' is very true. Being an island with a free trade port (in terms of tonnage Santa Cruz is Spain's busiest port) the choice of goods is limitless. It's a shoppers paradise, if you have the strength to go in and out of the great mass of shops, which all seem to stock a little of everything. Best buys must include cigarettes, cigars and liquor, cameras, watches, clocks, radios and electrical goods. Sometimes real bargains can be had after much bartering, but only in the large towns. Smaller places have fixed prices.

Tenerife embroidery, hand-sewn tablecloths and mats, attractive local costume dolls make pleasing souvenirs. Ceramics from Spain, especially the porcelain Lladro, may be found at advantageous prices. Special to the islands is *cobana*, a liqueur made from bananas. Strelitzias (bird of paradise flowers) travel well and can last for at least three weeks in water. Cactus plants, if bought at a shop that has treated them for export purposes, are popular souvenirs. Plants can also be bought at the airport.

Museums and art galleries

La Laguna
Museo de la Casa Osuna (Casa Osuna Museum) Calle Soly Ortega (near the Cathedral), La Laguna. Interesting collection representing the history and art of Tenerife.

La Orotava
Casa Tafuriaste (Ceramics Museum) La Luz, La Orotava. Open

daily from 1000 to 1800 hrs. On the road between Las Candias and La Luz. A faithfully restored Canary mansion housing one of the most comprehensive collections of regional ceramics in all Spain. See a master potter at work, visit the pottery shop and watch a video film.

Los Realejos

El Castillo Parque Museum (The Castle Museum Park) On the C820 Puerto de la Cruz–Icod Road (at Los Realejos). History, flora, agriculture, volcanoes, farming, ceramics, handicrafts. Children's adventure playpark, camel rides. Open daily 0900 to 1800 hrs. Free bus every 30 minutes from Café Columbus, Puerto de la Cruz.

Santa Cruz

Museo Arqueologico (Archaeological Museum) Palacio Insular, Avenida Bravo Murillo, Santa Cruz. Exhibits include Guanche mummies, skulls, pottery, jewellery, life size models of early inhabitants. Open 0900 to 1300 Monday to Saturday.

Museo Municipal de Bellas Artes (Fine Arts Museum) Calle José Murphy 4, Santa Cruz. Small interesting collection of pictures includes local artists. Open 1400 to 1900 hrs Monday to Friday.

Museo Militar (Military Museum) Calle de San Isidro, Santa Cruz. Includes 'El Tigre', the cannon that shot off Nelson's arm at the Battle of Santa Cruz 1797. Open 1000 to 1400 hrs, closed Mondays.

Palacio Insular Plaza de España, Santa Cruz. The Cabildo (the Island Government), also an Archaeological museum and Tourist Information office.

Santiago del Teide

Ceñtro Alfarero de Arguayo (off C80 between Chio and Santiago del Teide) Ceramics museum with the old kiln, working pottery and small shop. Locally known as the Museum of Cha Domitila. Open Monday to Saturday 1000 to 1300 and 1600 to 1900 hrs.

Valle Guerra

Casa de Carta (Ethnographic Museum) On the road from Tacoronte and Tejina. A fine example of Canary Island architecture, early eighteenth century, set in tropical gardens. Colourful traditional costumes, handicrafts and old weaving. Open 1000 to 1300 and 1600 to 1900hrs summer, 1500 to 1800hrs winter. Closed Friday.

Sports and pastimes

Because of the mild climate and the proximity of the sea it is possible to participate in a wide selection of sports. Good facilities are provided on the major islands.

The Canarians enjoy all forms of leisure activity and keep themselves very fit.

Land sports

• **Archery** can be enjoyed in the grounds of a number of hotels.

• **Billiards** is played in many hotels and bars on the island; tourists are welcome.

• **Bowling alleys** will be found in all the tourist areas and cities, often with 12 fully automatic tracks, and smaller ones in some hotels. Very popular with the Canarian youth. There is floodlit bowling at parque Loros, Playa de las Americas (behind City Centre).

• **Canary wrestling** (*lucha Canaria*) is the oldest and most typical of Canary sports, with traditions rooted in early history long before the Spanish conquest. It is a carefully preserved sport which young Canarians participate in with great keenness. *Lucha Canaria* is played by two teams of twelve wrestlers (*luchadores*). A special ring of 9m diameter is used with a thick layer of sand to prevent injuries. The wrestlers go barefoot, dressed in shirt and shorts, the purpose of the fight is to floor one's adversary. Canary wrestling is incredibly popular, and boys start to learn at the age of three and carry on until about thirty five. Every town and village has a team and there is much rivalry. There are many grips and kicks to be learnt, all very technical. It is advised that visitors do not participate in this particular sport. Tourists can see the wrestling at fiesta time.

• **Cock fighting** is permitted in all the islands. The tourist office has details but it is an event for the locals.

• **Flying** Sports airfields are found in Tenerife. Visitors can have the opportunity to see the islands by air. Advance booking is necessary. Aircraft like the Cherokee 180, which takes three passengers, are used. Information from Tourist Office or travel agent.

• **Football** This game comes top of the popularity polls. In every small village a space has been cleared for a football pitch. Local teams compete in an inter-island league. The big stadiums are in Las Palmas and Santa Cruz, both in the Spanish League.

• **Go-karting** is a very new sport to the islands. **Karting Las Americas** is open from 0900 hrs until late at night. It is situated ten minutes away from Playa de las Americas. As well as karting there is

Canary wrestling requires strength, technique and skill. The sport is shown regularly on Canary television.

a bar, restaurant and barbecue. A free bus runs from Playa de las Americas and Los Cristianos.

• **Golf** In Tenerife there are three golf courses. One is in the north east close to Los Rodeos Airport. El Penon Golf Course is 18 holes and open to visitors. A snack bar and restaurant are in the grounds. Green fees and details may be obtained from the Club de Golf de Tenerife. Apartado 125, La Laguna, Tenerife. Tel: 25 02 40. In the south, the Amarilla Golf and Country Club has been created out of parched desert scrubland. Off the main road some 5 kms west of the Reina Sophia Airport, towards the sea, an 18 hole course in the midst of a modern villa development is proving very successful with international golf professionals attending tournaments. Green fee 3500 pesetas, club hire 1000 pesetas half set. Bookings can be made three days in advance but a handicap certificate is required. Smart casual dress, not brief athletic shorts or bare feet. Further details from Apartado 8, San Miguel de Abona, 38620, Tenerife. Tel: 78 57 77.

Property owners and visitors staying at Golf Del Sur are able to play on this 27-hole course. It is also open to non-residents who have official handicaps (men 28, ladies 36). Players are expected to be properly dressed. Course is open from 0800 to 1900hrs. Green fee for visitors 4600 pesetas. Tel: 70 45 55.

• **Keep fit** classes and programmes for physical training, jogging, judo and karate are organised in some of the larger hotels, especially those run by Germans and Scandinavians who are particularly keen on physical fitness and run large sports programmes for holidaymakers. Some addresses are:

Gimnasio San Eugeneio, Centro Comercial San Eugeneio; Monday, Wednesday and Friday 1700 to 2030hrs (popular martial arts, adults and children). Gymnasium Inter Gym, Apts Tenegua, Avda Melchor Luz, Puerto de La Cruz, Tel: 38 09 24 (aerobics, bodybuilding, keep fit, sauna, solarium, karate). Bouganville Gym, Hotel Bouganville Playa, Playa de las Americas; Ken Miller, Tel: 79 29 56 (judo, karate and sport fitness programmes).

• **Mountain and hill climbing** are enjoyed in Tenerife and the Tourist Office will give information and literature describing walks on Mount Teide. The owner of the Hotel Tigaiga in Puerto de la Cruz sometimes leads parties of walkers high into the Cañadas, Mount Teide. The Refugio de Altavista is a modern cabin which is an ideal overnight stop to enable climbers to see the dawn on Mount Teide.

• **Mountain biking** Bikes for sale and rent at Motorsun El Camison, Playa de las Americas. 450 pesetas for four hours, 800 per day. Different speeds available.

• **Para gliding** The National Para Gliding School is at Callao Salvaje (between Playa de las Americas and San Juan). Initiation and advanced courses. Tel: 78 13 57.

• **Riding** is popular and horses may be hired and riding lessons taken at El Club Hipico, La Atalaya, near Los Rodeos Airport. Tel: 25 14 10. Riding is available to non-members at the Amarilla Golf Club and Country Club, Costa del Silencio. Tel: 78 57 77.

• **Squash** courts are to be found in some of the larger hotels. At the 28° Squash Club in Los Cristianos players of all standards are welcome. Sessions every Wednesday at Hotel Palmeras, Playa de la Americas. English-speaking coach. Players and spectators welcome. Floodlit courts. Tel: 79 09 91.

• **Tennis** is a much practised sport amongst the Canarians and tourists. Public tennis courts are part of most of the modern tourist complexes; with the warm nights many are open until late at night, being floodlit. Most large hotels have tennis courts and coaching is available. In Tenerife, the Club Ingles, San Antonio, Santa Cruz is open to visitors.

• **Walking** The Canary Islands offer a splendid variety of scenery and terrain for walking. Miles of golden sands enable barefoot exercise. Inland treks require stout shoes for much of the land is stony and very hard. Remember to take a map if you venture off well-known routes, as distances can be very deceptive, especially if one intends to climb along the gorges (*barrancos*) or over the mountains. Another warning: there is very little evening and dusk falls quickly between 1800 and 1900 hrs in winter. Best to check with a local person before you set off on any long walk and let someone know which route you intend to choose. Take some rations, a compass and a hat – it's great fun walking in the islands, if done with caution.

In recent years several footpaths and trails have been way marked so that visitors can get into the countryside to see the unique natural flora and fauna in panoramic scenery. Icona Instituto Nacional para la Conservacion de la Natutraleza La Laguna (Tel: 25 99 03 and 25 64 40) have a series of tourist walking maps and instructions for excursions. Of special interest to walkers is the Information Centre in Teide National Park with details of walks both guided and alone, audio visual, leaflets, maps (and toilets). To participate in a guided tour you must contact the Servico de Interpretacion in advance or the Centro de Coordinacion, La Laguna. Tel: 25 99 03. An English speaking service is provided.

Water sports

Nautical activities abound around the island, for the warm sea temperatures greatly encourage beginners and experienced water sports people to indulge to the full.

• **Fishing** comes naturally to Canarians who spend many hours of their spare time with a rod. Often they are contributing to the family diet. Most tourist places have jetties, harbour walls, rocks and beaches suitable for fishing. Rods, tackle and bait are for sale. Boats with rods may be hired from a number of fishing ports and villages.

• **Deep sea fishing** The waters around the islands are noted for big game fish and every year fishermen from all over the world return for international competitions. Many record catches have been made in these waters.

Sport fishing is expensive but the demand is high. The cost to charter a boat and crew is about 20,000 pesetas per day; sometimes the owners will do a split charter for less. Boats are of a high standard and powerful. Great excitement is felt when around 1600 hrs each

Many types of volcanic lava can be seen in the Teide National park, where now a little vegetation struggles to grow.

afternoon, these fast little boats return to harbour, their tough captains chewing a fat cigar with great nonchalance, while admiring tourists gasp with wonder at the huge fish. Marlin, tunny, shark, swordfish and barracuda are the big ones, with mackerel and sardines being used as bait. Fishing trips for shark, stingray, conger and other Atlantic fish, from Los Gigantes harbour towards La Gomera. From 1000 to 1700 hrs. Includes tackle, food and drink. 5000 pesetas .

- **Diving** The seas around the archipelago have interesting underwater volcanic rock formations. Coral barriers and marine life make sub-aqua diving and swimming a fascinating pastime. Beginners courses in sheltered harbours, and boat excursions to interesting sites, are arranged. Cost of diving excursions starts at 1,200 pesetas.

• **Jet ski** Can be hired from Yamaha (opposite Palm Beach Club), Playa de las Americas and Puerto Colon. Half hour costs 2,500 pesetas.

• **Sailing** Every island, except El Hierro, has a yacht club. Many Canarians own either a sailing or motor yacht. The sport is very much on the increase and new yacht marinas are being developed. Water sport schools are big business in the tourist resorts, frequent outings are arranged for all classes of sailors and beginners. In Tenerife the Real Club Náutico, Carretera de San Andrés, Santa Cruz, welcomes visitors. A number of tourists take boats by trailer to the islands, especially in the winter season. Details of sailing schools and events are advertised in hotels and the local paper. All types of boats are for hire.

• **Swimming** The Canarian beaches (*playas*) offer interesting swimming all the year round with the sea temperature never really cold. El Hierro, La Gomera and La Palma are rather short of good beaches but Tenerife has a wide choice; golden sands, black sands, fine pebbles and rocky pools, always with lovely clear water. Seas are mostly calm, but remember this is the Atlantic, and big rollers can soon blow in, turning a tranquil sea into a fury of white foam and pounding breakers. Undercurrents around rocky areas can sometimes be dangerous. In tourist resorts a red flag is flown when bathing is considered unsafe by the lifeguards. One of the best beaches includes Teresitas.

Public swimming pools are found in Santa Cruz de Tenerife and elsewhere. All the big hotels, apartment blocks and villas have outdoor pools including smaller ones for children.

• **Water ski** schools are mostly found in the southern parts of the islands where the waters have a lower swell. Courses for beginners and more experienced water ski enthusiasts are well advertised in shops and hotels.

• **Windsurfing** This fascinating sport is rapidly gaining immense popularity around the coasts. Many visitors arrive with their own boards on top of vehicles. Windsurfing can be a bit more tricky than it looks and professional advice is given on many beaches. Learning in sheltered waters helps to give confidence. El Medano in the south has a windsurfing school, boards and sails can be hired and instruction given. For example half day costs 4,000 pesetas. Tel: 17 62 88. In Playa de las Americas (opposite the Palm Beach Club) boards can be hired 700 pesetas for one hour. If it is all too difficult do not despair, you can always hire a *pedallo* (pedal boat) for 400 pesetas per hour – for two!

Places to visit for entertainments

The north

Aquamansa Trout Farm (between La Orotava and Las Cañadas) Only trout farm in the Canary Islands, managed by ICONA Institute for Conservation. Mostly open all year. Fresh trout costs 450 pesetas a kilo. Open 1000 to 1400hrs. Monday to Friday. Tel: 33 07 01. Picnic area and aviary.

Bananera El Guanche (between Puerto de la Cruz and La Orotava) Tropical plants, trees and cacti. Video show on cultivation of bananas.

Botanical Gardens (La Paz, above Puerto de la Cruz) Open 0900 to 1800hrs. Renowned for collection of tropical trees and plants.

Camellos El Tanque (on road Santiago del Teide to Icod de los Vinos) Open daily for camel rides. Refreshments.

Casa de los Balcones (La Orotava) Open Monday to Saturday 0815 to 1830 hrs. Tel: 33 33 96. Canary balconies and patios. Handicrafts and embroidery.

Garcia Sanabria Municipal Park (Rambla General Franco) Santa Cruz. Large park with shady trees. Sculptures, floral clock, play park.

Ladi Leather Factory (Santa Ursula) Leather goods, belts, jackets and shoes. Free bus from Café Columbus, Puerto de la Cruz.

La Rosaleda (La Paz, Puerto de la Cruz) Garden with many roses, wildlife, tropical lagoons. Open daily 0900 to 1700hrs. Free bus from Café Columbus.

Loro Parque Punta Brava, Puerto de la Cruz. Large park with performing parrots and dolphins. Popular show place, many species, including tigers.

Tigaiga Hotel (Parque Taoro, Puerto de la Cruz) Tel: 38 35 00. Sunday 1100hrs. *Lucha Canaria* (Canary wrestling), Canary folk dancing. Admission 200 pesetas.

Risco Bello (Aquatic Gardens) Parque Taoro, Puerto de la Cruz (above town). Tropical gardens, lakes, grottos, waterfall, pottery. Open daily 1000 to 1830 winter, to 2030 hrs summer.

Zoolandia (El Ramal, La Orotava) Zoo set in tropical gardens. Open daily 0900 to 1800hrs. Free bus from Café Columbus.

The south

Aquapark Octopus (San Eugenio Alto, Playa de las Americas) Family Water Park. Open daily from 1000hr until dusk. Free buses from resorts.

Camel Safari Guaza (on road from Guaza to Las Galletas) Camels are bred here, rides, restaurant. Tel: 31 03 00. Free buses from resorts. Open 1000 to 1700hrs. Suitable for young children.

Bananera Jardines del Atlantico (between Valle San Lorenzo and Las Galletas) Exhibition, tropical trees, zoo, model of Tenerife's water system, museum. Open daily from 1000 to 1800hrs. Free bus from Los Cristianos and Playa de las Americas.

Centro de Orquideas Orchids (La Galga, Valle San Lorenzo) Many orchids and plants. A treat for botanists. Open 0800 to 1400 and 1800 to 2000hrs.

Damon Park (Ten Bel, Costa del Silencio) Adventure park for children. Train, minigolf, boats. Open 1000hrs till dusk.

Desierto Feliz Cactus Park (off motorway near Los Cristianos) Numerous cacti and desert species. Open daily from 1000 to 1800hrs. Free bus from Playa de las Americas and Los Cristianos. Tel: 78 01 92.

Donkey Safari Donkey trekking. Ten minutes from Los Cristianos, Finca El Bailadero, Cardon Alto Buzanada. Tel: 76 60 11. Half or full day treks, all age groups, small children welcome. Setting out from fruit farm. Adults 3,750 pesetas, children 2,000. Free buses from southern resorts.

Tenerife Zoo (off motorway near Los Cristianos). Many animals and plants. Open daily, free bus from resorts. Tel: 75 13 86.

Coach excursions

All hotels have leaflets listing and describing coach drives and the cost. Your tour operator will be delighted if you book through them. Popular excursions are:

Around the Island Full day, includes a visit to Mount Teide.

Puerto de la Cruz and Loro Park Full day through the green Orotava Valley, shopping in Puerto de la Cruz and a visit to Loro Park to see the dolphins and parrots perform.

La Gomera Full day by coach and ferry to tour this island, which has a wonderful ancient forest and deep green valleys.

Octopus Aquapark Full day to enjoy the Water Park, sunbathing and fun for all the family in the water.

Camel Safari Half day to see the camels and ride a short way amongst the cactus and desert, followed by a barbecued meal.

Santa Cruz Half day in the capital city, sightseeing and shopping.

Casino Night Evening visit to a casino with adjoining restaurant.

Sea excursions

The south of Tenerife, with its calm seas, has a number of excursions for holidaymakers who like to be on the water. Coaches from all the resorts bring visitors to join in the fun.

From Los Cristianos, several types of boats make full day excursions to see the whales, dolphins and swim off the boat before an informal lunch. It is interesting to see the island and Mount Teide from the sea. Also from the same harbour fishing trips are popular. Big game fishing boats leave from Porto Colon (Playa de las Americas) to hunt for shark, tuna and whale.

San Juan has a fine sailing ship, built in 1919, the *Nostramo*, which sails along the coast, past Los Gigantes and Masca, with lunch on board. Sunset cruises can also be arranged. The *Marino Riquer*, a 100 year old sailing ship, departs from Santa Cruz harbour for cruises along the coast.

Something different is a sea excursion in a yellow submarine. The Golden Trout Subtrek is docked at Los Galletas and from there it dives every day to observe the colourful marine life.

Batros Los Cristianos Harbour. Sightseeing trip from 1100 to 1530hrs. A cheerful family sea voyage to three miles offshore to see dolphins and pilot whales. Swimming from boat when moored in sheltered bay. Lunch and free drink included 2,900 pesetas. Tickets on board, at hotels and travel agents. Tel: 79 44 66.

Isabel II Boat Trips Los Gigantes Marina. Ship sails by famous Acantilados Gigantes steep cliffs and searches for dolphins. Free drinks and swim in Masca Bay.

Golden Trout Subtrek Las Galletas. Tel: 73 00 13. Free bus from Playa de las Americas and Los Cristianos.

TEN

Touring Tenerife

Getting about

Travel around the Island of Tenerife is comparatively easy. There is a good system of regular bus services to all the main towns. Outlying villages have a less frequent but adequate service. The Tourist Office in Santa Cruz will provide free timetables and routes. Bus station (*estacion de autobus*) locations and numbers are:

Santa Cruz Avenida Tres Mayo. Tel: 21 93 99.

Puerto de la Cruz Hermanos Fernandez Perdigon. Tel: 38 18 07.

Playa de las Americas Bus stops (*parada*) are along the sea front.

Los Cristianos Along main road leading out of town.

Car hire firms are plentiful with a vast range of vehicles from limousine, estate car, minibus, saloon to jeep. Bicycles, scooters and motorcycles are available for hire by the hour, daily and weekly.

It is advisable to have a good road map of the island, such as Firestone E-50 or V-1 where main routes are shown. Very few roads are impassable but some minor roads have poor surface without tarmac. Frequently in country places there are no edges to the roads and travel is slow.

Taxis are everywhere; a green light on the top of the vehicle means that it is available for hire. Fares are usually displayed at taxi ranks. Some taxis have meters, the minimum charge being 225 pesetas. It is sensible to confirm the fare before commencing the journey. If a long distance or day trip is to be made it is sometimes possible to make an agreement with the driver for a reduced fare. Some typical taxi fares (at the time of writing) are:

Los Cristianos to

Reina Sofia Airport	1,700 pesetas
Playa de las Americas	400 pesetas
Puerto de la Cruz	9,000 pesetas
Santa Cruz	6,150 pesetas

Playa de las Americas to

Reina Sofia Airport	1,700 pesetas
Los Cristianos	400 pesetas
Puerto de la Cruz	9,100 pesetas
Santa Cruz	6,150 pesetas

Puerto de la Cruz to

Reina Sofia Airport	8,000 pesetas
Los Cristianos	9,000 pesetas
Playa de las Americas	9,100 pesetas
Santa Cruz	2,900 pesetas

Santa Cruz to Reina Sofia Airport   6,000 pesetas

Taxi rank telephone numbers are: Los Cristianos 79 03 52; Playa de las Americas 79 14 07; Puerto de la Cruz 38 49 10.

Many open-air cafés and restaurants are to be found in Los Cristianos. The shady palm trees and level tiled pavements along the seafront make it very suitable for disabled holidaymakers.

Coach trips are numerous, the many travel agencies (*viajes*) have offices in all tourist centres and towns. Tours round the island and to places of entertainment are well advertised. Most of the hotels display details of events and journeys, and prices vary little between operators. Couriers are generally multilingual, friendly and informative. Money spent on sightseeing coach trips is good value and they are worthwhile, especially if time is limited.

Public footpaths enable walkers to visit beauty spots and Tenerife has maps available marked with scenic walks. These are obtainable from bookshops.

Some places of special interest

The places briefly mentioned here are described in more detail in the chapters about touring the island. Distances are given from Santa Cruz de Tenerife (capital).

Adeje (81 km) Important southern town in quiet setting above Playa de las Americas.

Barranco de Infierno (73 km) Near Adeje, this spectacular valley has become one of the island's most popular walks, to see the hidden waterfalls.

Candelaria (23 km) Centre of pilgrimage. Fine church by the sea. Red stone statues of Guanche Kings.

Costa del Silencio (56 km) In the south, arid and sunny with many apartments. Golden sandy beaches.

Garachico (65 km) Old port, interesting streets and monuments. Scene of volcanic eruption, 1705, which engulfed both town and harbour.

Icod de Los Vinos (61 km) At the foot of Mount Teide. Manorial houses. Famous for Dragon Tree. Wine growing area.

La Laguna (10 km) Important city, university, historic buildings, gardens, quiet.

La Orotava (35 km) Centre of beautiful valley, elegant town, fine buildings, Canarian balconies. Handicrafts, shopping, needlework school.

Los Abrigos (67 km) On the Costa del Silencio, unique small fishing village which consists almost entirely of fish restaurants.

Los Cristianos (75 km) South west tip of island, port for ferry to Gomera. Watersports, swimming, sandy beach, apartments, hotels, cafés, restaurants, promenade, marina. Popular holiday resort.

Los Gigantes (84 km) Puerto Santiago, fishing port, small tourist resort, impressive basalt cliffs called Los Gigantes nearby.

Masca (96 km) Once a hidden village only approachable on foot or donkey, now a newly made road allows visitors into the lush valley where its few old houses are gradually being turned into tourist restaurants. You need to have a good head for heights.

Mirador Pico del Ingles (20 km) Panoramic view point in the north, Monte de las Mercedes, thick forest.

Playa de las Americas (64 km) Modern tourist resort, good entertainment and nightlife. Some rock and sand swimming. Water sports, hotels, apartments, cafés, restaurants. Family fun.

Playa del Medano (60 km) On the coast 12 km south of Granadilla. Popular small seaside resort with hotels and apartments along 2 km of fine sands. Excellent swimming in bay, splendid windsurfing when windy.

Puerto de la Cruz (38 km) Major holiday town, bright entertainments, hotels, apartments, villas. Man-made swimming pools, some rocky sea swimming, night life, shopping, Botanical Gardens.

Punta del Hidalgo (30 km) A sleepy resort lying below the Anaga Mountains with rocky seashore. New marina and campsite being developed.

Punta de Teno (75 km) Extreme north-west point with two lighthouses, one still working. Wild barren landscape, good seaviews. Small bay with tiny fishing harbour. Good for picnics but no shade.

San Marcos (64 km) Sheltered horseshoe-shaped fishing harbour. Now small quiet tourist resort. Black sands, good for swimming. Near banana plantations.

Santa Cruz North-east coast capital. Modern cosmopolitan city, busy port, good shopping, open and covered markets. Hotels, apartments. Art galleries, museums, churches.

Tacoronte (20 km) Old village in north of island. Guanche capital, sixteenth-century church. Vine growing area, famous for Malvasia wines.

Taganana (31 km) Remote small village in northern tip of the island. Attractive rural setting. A few tourist shops and bars.

Teide National Park (Las Cañadas) (53 km) Extinct volcanic crater, plateau, funicular to Spain's highest mountain, peak of Teide 3718 m, snow capped most of the year. Fantastic rock formations. Parador.

Teresitas Playa (7 km) Man-made mile long beach, golden sand, water clean and safe for swimming, sun bathing, beach café. No accommodation.

Vilaflor (89 km) South of Mount Teide on the C821, highest village, 1400m. Agricultural area, crops grown in terraced volcanic lava, white houses with pretty gardens. Fine views of coast.

Beaches

Tenerife has few long stretches of sand but there are numerous small sandy bays that can be explored on foot. Your tour operator or local tourist office can help you find them. Here we list the better known and more accessible beaches.

El Médano By the seafront of the town is a yellow sand beach with shallow waters, safe for young children and disabled visitors, with cafés and bars nearby. Towards the south-west are undeveloped sand dunes and seas used by windsurfing enthusiasts when the wind blows, which is often. Can be dangerous for swimming. Further swimming can be had by walking round the headland of Montana Roja to Playa de la Tejita where there is some nudism.

Las Teresitas Man made golden sands with palm trees and shallow water, protected by a ridge of rocks. Safe for children but not much shade. Carpark and buses from Santa Cruz.

Los Cristianos Near port and plaza, man-made yellow sands, clean, with sunbeds, pedalos and windsurfing. Towards the east some swimming off rocks. Bus stop fifteen minutes walk. To the west grey man-made beaches stretch as far as Playa de las Americas.

Playa de la Arena Situated close to Los Gigantes, this black sand beach has a modern promenade with bars, cafés and shops, leading to Puerto de Santiago.

Playa de las Americas Beaches along this popular resort are all of black sand and consist of man-made sheltered bays. These sands become very hot, so take beach shoes, sunhats and layout mats or use sunbeds. Further pleasant beaches at Torviscas and Playa Fanabe are man-made.

Puerto de la Cruz A newly constructed beach at the western end of the resort called Punta Brava is black sand and, except when the sea is rough, provides pleasant swimming. Along the main seafront is the Lago de Martianez consisting of swimming pools, sunbathing terraces. Entrance fee.

San Marcos Tiny black beach in sheltered harbour safe for children, nearby restaurants. Interesting to watch small fishing boats returning in the morning.

Tours around the island

The majority of visitors to Tenerife stay either in the north, mostly at Puerto de la Cruz, or in the southern region at Playa de las Americas and Los Cristianos. A minority choose places like San Marcos in the north or Costa del Silencio and Los Gigantes in the south.

The tours described in the following chapters of this section begin for the most part in one of the main cities, and travel roughly in a clockwise direction around the island, so it is easy to break into them wherever you may be staying. Visits to Mount Teide and surrounding points of interest are also described.

Tenerife sunsets can be spectacular but you need to remember that there is little twilight. Try to avoid returning in the dark along unlit mountain routes; most are tortuous. You should enjoy your travels in this varied and beautiful island.

Many of the old Canarian houses have red tiled roofs, white walls and attractive carved Canary pinewood balconies. The lower windows have wrought iron bars.

ELEVEN

Santa Cruz de Tenerife

Santa Cruz de Tenerife, with a population of some 200,000, is the capital of the island and of the whole province. It has in residence the Civil and Military Governors and all the Government Offices, as well as the Provincial Tourist Office covering Tenerife, La Gomera, La Palma and El Hierro. The capital has been developing as a port and centre of commerce since the nineteenth century. Rich merchants and businessmen have built imposing houses along its wide avenues, gracious and cool with tall trees. Large squares and gardens are to be found amongst the activity and noise of the city.

Arriving by sea one sees the city silhouetted against its background of mountains. Dominating the scene is the Plaza de España which lies close to the quay where ocean going liners and ferries dock. The tall Monumento a los Caidos, in the centre of the Plaza, commemorates those who fell in the Spanish Civil War. It is seen at its most impressive at night when the centre of the memorial is lit to form a cross. This plaza is an excellent starting place for a walking tour (or for finding a taxi).

If you are driving in Santa Cruz it is advisable not to try and park in the streets of the city centre. A large carpark with an attendant (*vigalante*) is located along the seafront, Avenida de José Antonio Primo de Rivera. There is no height barrier. A new underground car park with entrance from the Plaza España has a height restriction. The cost is 125 pesetas for one hour.

City tour 1

Plaza de España – Avenida de Anaga – Museo Paso Alto: 2 km, walking time about 1 hour

Facing the Monumento is the **Palacio Insular**, a huge building housing the Cabildo, the islands' government offices. On the ground floor, at the entrance, is an interesting scale model of the island. In the same building is the Spanish **Tourist Office** where bus timetables, island maps and information on accommodation are freely given. Around the corner in the Avenida José Antonio Primo de Rivera, is the Tenerife Tourist Office and information bureau. The Tourist Offices will provide you with a free street map of Santa Cruz. We recommend that it is used, since the city is large with many streets looking alike, so one can get confused. If you have the Firestone Map E-50 of the island, the 'B' side has good street plans both of Santa Cruz and Puerto de la Cruz. However, do not be afraid to ask passers-by for assistance; quite often they will act as your guide, with obvious pleasure. The Customs House and Oceanographic Museum are also situated in Avenida José Antonio Primo de Rivera.

On the corner of Avenida Bravo Murillo and facing the Plaza España is the tall stately building that houses the Santa Cruz main **Post Office** (*correos*). The letter box is outside along the Avenida Bravo Murillo. Note that for posting abroad you should use the box marked *extranjero* (foreign).

The **Archeological Museum** in the Avenida Bravo Murillo has a fine collection of Guanche relics including primitive cooking utensils, tools and mummified corpses, complete with teeth and hair! The museum is open from Monday to Saturday, 0900 to 1300 and 1600 to 1800 hrs.

After exploring the Plaza de España and its environs, you may like to sit at one of the pavement cafés or better still walk up the steps of the Olympo restaurant/cafeteria, where you can sit on a terrace, enjoying a coffee or meal watching the scene below. As you take in the panorama of gaiety and movement, with the warm sunshine and blue skies above you, the ships in the harbour, the high mountains adding to the backcloth, you know you are really in the Canary Islands.

From here too, you can gaze along the broad highway of Avenida de Anaga, bright with hibiscus and flowering shrubs, but it is also a pleasant place for a stroll with seats conveniently placed for the weary. It runs along the docks where cruise and cargo ships are constantly moving in and out of the busy harbour. Santa Cruz has one of the deepest harbours in the world; the Queen Elizabeth II calls regularly during her cruises to the Caribbean.

It is along the Avenida de Anaga that you catch the bus to take you to Teresitas Playa, the white, sandy, man-made beach just north of Santa Cruz. On Sunday morning all along the Avenida de Anaga an open air market (*Rastillo*) throngs with Canarians and tourists, out to find a bargain. It is a cheerful occasion and worth a visit but make sure your money is in a safe place. Right at the end of this avenue at the junction with the Rambla del General Franco, is a sculptured monument, set in a small garden, erected to commemorate General Franco and the civil war.

The coast road continues, becoming the Carretera de San Andrés, the main road to the fishing port of San Andrés and the beach resort of Teresitas Playa. Just before the Cepsa petrol station and opposite the Muelle Norte (dock gates), on a road leading north there is a large store, 'Sovhispan', which sells a mixture of Soviet, Spanish and foreign products. Here you can find colourful wooden dolls from Russia and real Russian vodka; naturally, it is a popular place with Russian sailors as well as the general public.

The **Muelle Norte** is the port where the Trasmediterranea Jetfoil departs for Las Palmas (Gran Canaria). A smart new building has a booking office, cafeteria, bar, toilets and waiting area. Useful is a small bus that runs from the Trasmediterranea office on the docks, Muelle Ribera by the Plaza de España, to connect with the departure of the Jetfoil.

It is at the Muelle Ribera that the Trasmediterranea ferries from Cadiz and the other islands arrive and depart. You may care to use the small shop, bar and toilets by the ticket office. It is mostly frequented by port workers and taxi drivers. Another small *tapas* bar is located southwards towards the container port.

Just past the dock gates, on the sea side, is the Real Club Nautico, the yacht club. Close by is the **Museo Paso Alto**, a seventeenth-century fortification now housing a naval museum where historic relics are preserved. The gardens have an array of cannons of which the most famous was El Tigre (The Tiger) now removed for safety to the Museo Militar Regional de Canarias, Calle San Isidro (quite nearby). Open 1000 to 1400 hrs, Tuesday to Saturday. This is the cannon which caused Lord Nelson to lose the battle of Santa Cruz (24th July 1797) in which he lost an arm. There are many tales of this epic fight and the gentlemanly behaviour of the opposing sides (they

(Opposite) *The sheltered harbour at San Marcos has a nice little beach of black sands and several good fish restaurants.*

exchanged casks of wine), when the Spanish acknowledged the bravery of the British fleet even to assisting with the treatment of wounded. Indeed a prominent street in the city is called Horacio Nelson, near the Plaza de Torres (bull ring).

If you feel that you have walked far enough, there is a regular bus service that will return you to the Plaza de España, but remember to wait at the bus stop on the right side of the road!

City tour 2

Plaza de España – Parque Municipal Garcia Sanabrit – Plaza 25 de Julio – Plaza Weyler – Plaza de España: walking time 2-3 hours

If you want to shop it is a good idea to start at the Plaza de España; all roads go in an arc from the square. There are small shops, all appearing to sell the same goods, and to obtain the best bargain it is necessary to try several different shops. Prices vary, especially amongst the Indian traders who are past-masters at selling goods to tourists. If you do not like to barter it is better to shop at a Canarian owned store: usually they have fixed prices and the whole transaction is more relaxed, even slow. Do not be afraid to ask advice from a Canarian, most of them are pleased to assist and go out of their way to help you.

Walk north from the Plaza de España and the Plaza de Candelaria, which is pedestrians only. On the left you will find a McDonald's Restaurant; not far away is a Body Shop. They look strangely modern amongst the small Canarian shops. Continue up Calle Castillo until you reach Calle de Valentin. Here you can turn left and walk straight along until you reach the **Mercado de Nuestra Señora de Africa**, the main city market. But we suggest you turn right to reach Plaza Alferez Provisional. Nearby you will find what is reputed to be the smallest Marks and Spencer's in the world. By crossing the Plaza northwards you can go up Calle del Pilar and make for the Parque Municipal Garcia. on your way you see shops with high quality

(Opposite) *The Pride of Tenerife (tajinaste or viper's bugloss) seen here outside the Parador and in sight of Spain's highest mountain, Mount Teide.*

goods such as **Galerias Preciodas** (on eight floors), where items are price tagged. This shop is useful for toiletries, handbags and items of clothing.

Arriving at the **Parque Municipal Garcia Sanabrit** you will find just inside the entrance, a floral clock, much photographed by tourists. It is an accurate time piece as well! This large park is clean and cool with many walks and stone seats. An outstanding floral display, water gardens, aviaries, a small zoo, fountains and statues all blend to create a resting place for the city dweller or weary tourist. Children will enjoy the playground and the crazy golf. In the centre of the park tall fountains splash, and the statue of a voluptuous lady makes a notable contrast in style to the modern bust of Garcia Sanabrit, the gentleman for whom the park is named. Here young children love to feed the pigeons and office workers eat their lunch in the shade of the tall trees.

Across the park it is but a short walk along the Avenida 25 de Julio to the Plaza 25 de Julio. This is a singular little square: all the seats around it are tiled in Art Deco style, highly coloured and glazed, depicting 1920s advertisements for Martini, New Zealand butter, matches, and so on. A circular fountain in the centre has yellow, blue and green tiles in similar style. Tall trees surround the plaza, where children come to feed the birds.

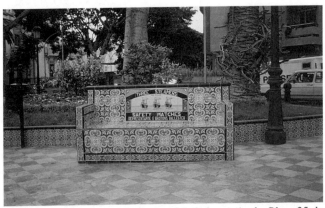

An example of the interesting colourful tiled seats in the Plaza 25 de Julio, Santa Cruz de Tenerife. They are surprisingly comfortable too, providing a cool seat on a hot day.

Going south down the Avenida 25 de Julio you will see the Anglican Church of Saint George and some fine old mansions. Further down is the Plaza de Weyler and the impressive Capitania General (headquarters of the Captain-General) where General Franco planned his uprising at the start of the Civil War. From Plaza de Weyler it is an easy downhill walk along Calle del Castillo towards the sea and, once again, the Plaza de España.

One shop that must have a special mention is the Caribbean Center, No. 7 Y Clavijo, a charcuterie and delicatessen with a splendid array of mouth-watering things to eat: huge hams hanging from the ceiling, cheeses, patés, salami, cold meats, pies, tins of speciality foods, sauces, sweet-meats and candies. The excellent bar offers a tempting selection of *tapas* (Spanish appetisers that are almost a small meal). Try the filleted sardines in a spicy sauce or *tortilla* (savoury omelette). Best of all, try some *papas arrugadas*, little wrinkled potatoes cooked in salt water and eaten with *mojo picon* sauce (see Chapter Five).

City tour 3

Plaza de la Candelaria – Museo Municipal – Old City – Plaza de la Iglesia – Market – Avenida Bravo Murillo – Plaza de España: walking time about 2 hours

Close to the Plaza de España is the Plaza de la Candelaria, with a notable eighteenth-century marble monument, honouring the Virgin of Candelaria. Around the base are represented Guanche kings worshipping the island's patroness. Also in this plaza is the **Palacio de Carta**, a monument of National Artistic interest. This is a seventeenth-century mansion with an open air central patio and wooden balconies, and some beautiful gardens. Perhaps you will not see it at first, as the Banco Español de Credito have restored the building to use it as their main bank in Santa Cruz.

At the top of the Plaza de la Candelaria, on the right-hand side, you will find **Artespana**, one of the big chain of shops created by the Spanish Government to offer the visitor typical Spanish goods. Objects from different regions are on sale: Canary Island laces, embroidery, ceramics, jewellery and souvenir ornaments, all reasonably priced.

You will notice signposts for the **Museo Municipal** (municipal museum) which is in nearby Calle José Murphy. It contains mainly

Spanish paintings and sculptures with a section dedicated to Canarian painters. It is open afternoons only, Monday to Friday. If you are interested in looking round the museum you will really have to make a separate visit. That will also give you the opportunity of visiting the eighteenth-century **Church of San Francisco** tucked away in a tiny plaza behind the museum. It has a Baroque portico; inside a beamed ceiling rises loftily, pictures dark with age line the walls and a blaze of candles is reflected in the beaten silver. Like most Spanish churches it is a haven of peace and coolness.

Leaving the Plaza de la Candelaria, and walking south along Calle Candelaria, one enters the old part of the city. In the Plaza de la Iglesia you will find the mother church, **Iglesia de Nuestra Señora de la Concepción**. Built originally in the sixteenth century it was reconstructed after a fire in 1652. Set in a rather faded square of old balconied houses, it is the tall eighteenth-century Moorish-looking tower that one notices. The interior of the church is baroque. There are many items of historical interest there. The much revered image of Our Lady of the Conception over the high altar was brought to the island by Alonso de Lugo. In the five naves are kept the most valuable historic mementos of the Canary Islands: the Cross of Conquest, used by Alonso de Lugo in 1496, together with the banners captured from Admiral Horatio Nelson at the battle of Santa Cruz in 1797.

A short walk across the Barranco de Santos leads you to the Calle José Manuel Guimera and the **Mercado de Nuestra Señora de Africa**, the central market, which is open from Monday to Saturday. Being the main market for the whole island it is large – several different covered areas and courtyards hold fresh and frozen fish and meats – and always busy. Fruit and vegetables are piled high, the scent of flowers and spices pervades the air. This is one of the finest markets in the whole of the Canary Islands, and it is well worth a visit just to see the spectacle even if you do not require any produce – though it will be hard to resist buying a little bunch of pink carnations from a cheerful flower seller in a big straw hat, or a delicious cheese, or some enticing fresh strawberries.

Across the road from the covered market, in a wide cool street, you will find two rows of stalls which sell just about everything – shoes, clothes, baskets, pottery, china, tools, bags – a real flea market. On Sundays this market is devoted to selling stamps, for philately is a popular hobby with the Spanish.

Not far from the market in a rather run down part of the town, is a red-light district, where 'madam' can be seen at the window touting for business. At night the street corners are busy with taxis arriving with clients.

It is a pleasant walk from the market down Calle San Sebastián. Then turn left into Avenida Bravo Murillo, and in a few minutes you will find yourself in the familiar Plaza de España.

Other places of interest

Restaurants, cafeterias and bars are numerous in Santa Cruz, offering a wide range of menus, from typically Canarian to Creole and Chinese at various prices. At most establishments, including hotel restaurants, the menus and prices are displayed outside. If you wish to reduce the cost of your meal it is cheaper to eat at the bar; meals eaten at tables or out on the pavement are usually more costly.

Do not be afraid to try a typically Canary eating-house catering for the locals. Plastic covers on the tables and lots of conversation can be expected and sometimes long waits between courses, as most items are freshly cooked to order. The menu is usually chalked on a blackboard. It is quite in order for you to walk into the kitchen and look in the fridge or the cooking pots before you decide what you would like to eat.

Fresh fish, chicken and pork chops are always delicious, so are the Canarian *sopas*, almost a meal in themselves. Puddings are usually caramel flan or gateau and lots of fresh fruit is served. Coffee is an extra charge.

A theatre and cinema provide entertainment, a few of the hotels have a band for dancing and some restaurants and bars have live music. Several discos provide fun for the young.

A much brighter selection of night life is found in Puerto de la Cruz and south of the island at Playa de las Americas, where the choice is plentiful.

Restaurants in Santa Cruz

Cabarra Taberna Just off the Duque de Santa Elana, eastwards along the seafront from the Plaza de España. Look for the Banco Atlantico and turn the corner. This restaurant is next to Bar Marina. Good class food with local and international menu.

Cafeteria Castillo Calle Castelo, up from the Plaza de la Candelaria. A simple bar café with tables outside serving *tapas*, coffee and good fresh doughnuts. Notice the old pictures on the walls inside the bar. Nice to rest here and watch the passers-by.

Caseta de Madeira In the Barrio de Cabo. Tel: 21 00 23. Maybe difficult to locate without a map or taxi, it is well known. A genuine *typico* small restaurant set amid lobster pots and old shanties, on a rough road west of the port, not far from the main bus station. You may be the only tourist here. Fresh fish and Canarian cooking. Open 1300 to 1500 hrs and 2000 to 2300 hrs. Closed Saturday evening and Sunday.

La Fragua Calle General Antequera 19. Tel: 27 74 69. 200m from the Hotel Mencey, this little restaurant serves first class fresh fish and meats with a varied cuisine. Among the specialities are sirloin steak with cheese, avocado and mushroom sauce. Fried rice and prawns and salmon salad.

Meson la Mancha Calle Heliodoro Rodriguez Lopez. Near Supermarket Orsueco and Plaza de R Dominicana. Tel: 23 15 16. Typical cuisine and fine wines from La Mancha. Try the garlic soup *(sopa de ajo)*, roast lamb *(menestra de cordera)*. You will find few tourists here.

Meson Los Manjes (The Monks) Walk from the Plaza de España east, along Duque de Santa Elana, to Banco Exterior on corner. This restaurant is up the street to the left and easily located. Opposite are several cafeterias and snack bars.

Oh La La Duque de Santa Elana. Along seafront east from the Plaza de España. Clean fast pizzeria, croissanterie, cakes, pastries and savoury snacks.

Olympo Plaza de España. Located at the northwest corner of Plaza de España on the first floor, this café restaurant is a very popular place for all to meet and have refreshment. Can be busy at lunch time but service is fast and efficient. International menu at reasonable price. Good view of the harbour.

TWELVE

The north-east corner

Island tour 1

Santa Cruz – Las Teresitas – Igueste – Taganana – Monte de las Mercedes – La Laguna – Santa Cruz: about 64 km

To the north and east of Santa Cruz de Tenerife the area is mountainous and the population sparse except in the old city of La Laguna. Leaving Santa Cruz, continue along the coast road, Carretera de San Andrés, past the Yacht Club, and the Balnearo (public swimming pool) – close to a busy warehouse and docks area – and you will arrive at **San Andrés**. This is a small fishing village, completely Canarian, without any tourist attractions, but with several small, clean bars and fish restaurants along the main road by the sea.

Leaving San Andrés turn immediately off the main road, seawards, to reach **Las Teresitas**, the mile long artificial beach of which the locals are so proud. Tons and tons of sand were imported from the Sahara Desert during 1960. It is fine and white, being swept and cleaned regularly. Protected from the ocean by a long low breakwater, the seas are usually calm and safe, and with Tenerife's ideal winter climate it is the perfect place for all-the-year-round bathing. Sun umbrellas of palm fronds give the beach a holiday appearance; large car parks and restaurants cater for holidaymakers. The windsurfing school is popular.

New hotel complexes are planned for this area, with opposition from some Tenerifos, who wish it to remain undeveloped.

The coastal road out of San Andrés climbs quickly up to a headland and mirador, from where one can look down on the extensive Teresitas beach below and in the distance shipping and the busy Santa Cruz port. Continuing on this road which winds close to the cliff edge you will see a sign for **Playa de las Gaviotas**. A quite steep road descends quickly to a small and quiet beach. There are no facilities here.

Six kilometres from Teresitas one reaches the end of the tarmac road at the pretty village of **Igueste**, set in lush vegetation either side of the valley (*barranco*). Well built houses cling to the sides of the steep mountains of Anaga. A short walk from the carpark leads to a peaceful plaza and the village church.

Returning by the same route to the junction for Teresitas beach, take the inland road signed **Taganana**. This is winding and has some blind hairpin bends as it climbs steeply, giving fine scenic views of the coast and mountains. Eventually you reach a junction with directions west to La Laguna and east to Chamorga. For Taganana and the view point at **El Bailadero** you go through a tunnel northwards.

For those who do not mind a bumpy road a detour can be made via Las Bodegas to **Chamorga**, a beautiful unspoilt hamlet in the mountains of the Anaga peninsula. Drivers of vehicles need to keep their eyes glued to the tortuous roads so holidaymakers who want to enjoy the scenery should take the local bus which runs regularly from San Andrés to Taganana, or a taxi. Should you be feeling more adventurous, then proceed on from Taganana to **Playa del Roque**. The road is narrow and winding but the scenery is magnificently wild with great craggy mountains above and black lava rocks at sea level. Often great Atlantic rollers dash onto the pebble beach sending swirls of foam over the road. There is a notice warning that bathing can be dangerous here. Watch out for the end of the road. Do not attempt to drive up to Benijo, it is very difficult to turn. There are two simple and good fish restaurants here at Playa del Roque.

The Anaga peninsula is a splendid place for experienced walkers, but take care of low clouds descending and mist in the valleys.

It is necessary to return by the same road from Playa del Roque to sleepy Taganana. Several *typico* restaurants in the village cater for excursion coaches as this remote place becomes more well known. Stop once more at the El Bailadero viewpoint to admire the green terraced escarpment with its spectacular mountain peaks, red-roofed houses and waving palm trees, while out at sea lie the tiny volcanic islands of Roque de Dento (de Tierra on some maps) and Roque de Fuera, haunts of seabirds.

We now reach the road junction and a sign for La Laguna and **Monte de las Mercedes**. The road is still narrow as it winds through the village of Casa de la Cumbria. Botanists will delight at the amount of flora in the Anaga region. If you drive slowly you may find, amongst the steep terrain, the delicate bell-shaped orange *Canarina Canariense*, a scrambling plant with tuberous roots.

Elsewhere in damp shady places the rock roses (*Aeonium Urbicum*) have noticeable pale green to blue glaucous rosettes that grow to a width of eight inches. Many endemic plants of the island are to be found in this north-east corner of Tenerife, clinging to the dark brown volcanic rocks and cliffs.

The Anaga ridge, 1024m high, is magnificent and the road affords tremendous vistas into the valleys and across the top of the pine forests. You are sure to stop at the mirador (viewpoint) called the Englishman's Peak (Pico del Inglès), named after a gentleman who walked from La Laguna to this outlook in one day. In good weather there is the fine sight of Mount Teide rising into the blue sky.

Descending slowly into the depths of the forests another mirador, Cruz del Carmen (920m), is an ideal place for taking photographs, having vistas of both sides of the island and the seas beyond. Now your route drops fast through the Monte de las Mercedes.

In the village of Mercedes there is a road junction giving directions to Tegueste, Trejiona and Bajama. A quiet country route runs amongst high agricultural land towards these north-eastern towns. But this tour continues south for another three kilometres towards La Laguna.

When you have reached the village of Las Mercedes you are on the edge of a fertile plain that surrounds the university town of La Laguna. Here animals graze and crops are grown, a restful scene after your awe-inspiring drive from Teresitas and Taganana.

The former capital and now the second largest town in Tenerife, with a population of 80,000, **La Laguna** is still a place of importance for here are the cathedral and the university. The town was founded in 1497 and the original quadrilateral plan is still in evidence, though the lake which gave it its name has disappeared. A one-way traffic system flows in its narrow streets, lined with tall houses, many with wrought-iron balconies. Picturesque promenades have mansions and monuments. An air of grace and dignity gives La Laguna a sense of bygone magnificence. An ancient dragon tree in the garden of the Seminary is of interest to the visitor, likewise the monastery garden is quiet and restful.

The cathedral Santa Iglesia was built on the site of a sixteenth-century church, Los Remedios, its neo-classical façade dating from 1819; but the nave and four aisles were built in neo-gothic style in 1905. Another important church is La Concepción, now a national monument. It is an early example of the sanctuaries that were built at the time of the conquest. In Calle San Augustin the Palacio Episcopal (Bishop's Palace) has a beautiful stone façade and a delightful patio and courtyard.

At Corpus Christi (during May and June) the streets of La Laguna are carpeted with flowers. On the 14th September, the crucifix from the San Francisco Monastery is venerated in a massive procession and there are general festivities enjoyed by day and night. Canary wrestling, a sport that goes back to Guanche times, is much applauded. Visitors are advised not to join in the contests!

From La Laguna you have a choice of taking the autopista either to Puerto de la Cruz or straight back to Santa Cruz. Note the modern statue at the busy autopista junction on the western side; it is of Friar Anchieta. Born in La Laguna, he went to South America to accept work amongst the natives and convert them to Christianity.

An alternative route from La Laguna to Santa Cruz (avoiding the busy autopista) is to take the road signed **La Cuesta**. Follow this through Valle Jimenez and climb up to **Los Campitos** to then descend near the huge reservoir Embalse de Los Campitos, seeing below you the sprawling capital of Santa Cruz and its great harbour where ships from all over the world anchor.

THIRTEEN

Southward on the east coast roads

Island tour 2

Santa Cruz – Candelaria – Poris de Abona – San Isidro – El Médano – Los Abrigos – Aeropuerto Reina Sofia – Costa del Silencio – Las Galletas – Cañada Blanca – El Palm-Mar Guaza – Los Cristianos: 105 km

Driving south from Santa Cruz de Tenerife the road follows the coast along by the docks. Fast moving traffic speeds out of town at all hours of the day, sometimes in a six lane sweep. Traffic lights, at times from above, control the intersections. Signs are well placed but do make sure you are in the correct lane: this is a fast modern motorway that has the TF5 Norte and TF1 Sur (north and south) routes, the former leading to Puerto de la Cruz.

The Autopista del Sur (TF1) runs parallel with the coast line. Leaving the city of Santa Cruz, with its factories and harbour installations, one is soon in an area that is dry and almost barren. The central range of mountains is some distance away to the right, the sea a few kilometres to the left of the road which stretches on through rather featureless countryside. Only small cactus, prickly pears and tall cardons are able to survive the sparse dry soil.

The autopista skirts a number of small fishing villages which lie along rough little roads on the seaward side. These have only tiny beaches and are purely Canarian. A new *urbanización* at Radazul has a deepwater yacht marina. After the resort of **Las Caletillas** the autopista reaches the first place of notable interest for the tourist.

Candelaria, 23 kms from Santa Cruz, could easily be passed on the autopista (junction 9) for it lies at sea level and almost out of sight. The old town is dominated by an imposing church set unusually close to the sea. The Basilica de Nuestra Señora de la

Candelária was built on the foundations of an ancient church and is now an important place of pilgrimage for all Canarians.

Inside the church is the statue of Our Lady of Candelaria, much venerated. There are several versions of her story in the folk history of the island. It is related that before the island of Tenerife was taken over by the Spanish, some Guanche shepherds saw an image of the Virgin and Child washed ashore near Candelaria. Not knowing what it was, they reported it to the king who instructed that it be carried to a cave in the village. There the statue was installed and homage was paid to it and according to legend the statue performed many wonders.

Autopista TF1 Sud – Junction Numbers

1	Ramblas – Avenida Maritima
2	Autopista del Norte TF5
3	Hoya Fria
4	Santa Maria del Mar
5	Radazul
6	Tabaiba
7	Barranco Hondo
8	Las Caletillas – Igueste Candelaria
9	Candelaria
10	Arafo
11	Puerto de Güimar – Güimar
12	Punta Prieta
13	El Tablado – El Escobanel
14	Fasnia – Los Roques
15	Cambio de sentido
16	Las Eras
17	Arico – Poris de Abona
18	Abades
19	El Rio – Tajao
20	Chimiche
21	Parque Eolico
22	Granadilla – San Isidro – El Médano
23	Aeropuerto
24	Los Abrigos – San Miguel – Las Galletas – Amarilla Golf – Golf del Sur
25	Parque de la Reina
26	San Lorenzo – Guaza – Las Galletas
27	Arona – Los Cristianos
28	Playa de las Americas
29	San Eugenio – Parque Acuatico
30	Torviscas – Playa Fanabe

When the Spaniards took over Tenerife they built a sanctuary for the statue which was looked after by Dominican monks. Because the victory over the Guanches was partly ascribed to her, the statue became the patroness of the island. The story is not quite complete, for in 1826 a freak storm created a tidal wave which swept into the sanctuary and carried the statue out to sea, never to be recovered.

A new statue was sculptured and a church was rebuilt on the site of the original one. In 1958 the present Basilica was completed and the tiny Virgin and Child, dressed in sumptuous robes, was placed high above the altar, with candles and gold and silver adornments to create a blaze of light in the vast church. Every year on the 14th and 15th August pilgrims come from all the islands to light candles, place flowers and worship at the shrine.

Our Lady of Candelaria

In 1464, Sancho de Herrara, a young nobleman from Fuerteventura, went to Candelaria to see the statue; he asked the Guanche King if he could take it back to Fuerteventura to Christian territory but his request was refused. So one night he stole it and took it back to Fuerteventura where it was installed in a church. The next morning when a priest entered the church he found that the image was facing the wall, so he turned it back again, a procedure that was repeated for several days. Then an epidemic broke out which was thought to be a punishment and Herrara was forced to return the image to Candelaria.

The church is open weekdays 0730 to 1300 and 1500 to 1930hrs. On Saturday, Sunday and fiestas it will close for church services.

Outside the church in the large square, along the sea wall, are ten stone statues which represent Guanche chiefs. These roughly hewn figures all have handsome but different features and stand impressively with their backs to the sea, representing the legendary bravery of the native inhabitants of long ago.

There are several pleasant bars and restaurants for refreshment in Candelaria, also parking on the seafront towards Santa Cruz.

Continuing along the Autopista del Sur one reaches the busy road leading to **Puerto de Guimar** which handles the produce being exported from the fertile agricultural areas around Guimar, situated inland on the old main road, the C822. Passing through the industrial area you reach the town square where there are restaurants, bars and fast food café. The beach is rather nondescript but there is parking along the promenade. Entry to the yacht club is by permit only.

Continuing along the autopista the road passes through a tunnel. Small *playas* with few facilities line this part of the coast.

Away from the main tourist route **Poris** (at junction 17) remains sleepy but is developing slowly. Some restaurants provide typical Canarian meals and close to the beach is Casa Julian, a well established fish restaurant. Along the sea shore you can walk (except in rough weather) out to the headland and the lighthouse at Punta de Abona, an important landmark for shipping.

Returning to the autopista, travelling south again, there are a series of undeveloped *playas* located amongst the dry and dusty desertlike landscape. The deep *barrancos* and craggy rocks are weather worn and, apart from the green cardon cactus with its poisonous milky latex and Tenerife's most abundant plant the euphorbia, the scene appears desolate unless one looks inland to the mountains and the splended cone of Mount Teide. The euphorbia *Regis Jubae* was named after King Juba of Mauretania whose ships reached the Canary Islands about 30BC and found these plants growing everywhere.

Junction 22 of the autopista is the exit north for **San Isidro**, a lively and useful town close to the southern resorts. A good place to have car repairs done, buy household goods and materials. It has chemists, banks, supermarkets and restaurants. If you wish to shop where the locals do, this is the place.

By turning south at this junction you will quickly find yourself heading for El Médano. While on the coast by El Médano you have the opportunity to drive a short distance out of town eastwards. From the harbour, along the coast road past the modern Windsurf Hotel at El Cabezo. The road ends just before you reach a tiny sheltered bay. At present it is a scramble down to the sandy shore for a picnic, swim and nudist sun bathing.

El Médano has a small fishing harbour and a charming plaza. Several fish bars and restaurants are to be found. The beach is flat and safe, the water clean and it is popular with the Scandinavian paraplegics having a remedial stay at nearby Los Cristianos. Asthma sufferers, too, recommend El Médano as ideal for a winter holiday. Although El Médano is only eight kilometres from the airport, it is not in the aircraft flight path, so any noise is not unduly disturbing.

Close to the plaza is a tourist information office, small carpark and bus stop. On the promenade there are public telephones. Médano has a few tourist shops and a supermarket.

Cueva del Hermano Pedro

Whilst in the vicinity of El Médano, an interesting excursion can be made to the Cave of Hermano Pedro. To reach this from the autopista you turn off for El Médano and drive towards the sea. Just before reaching the town you take a right turn signed Los Abrigos (there is an old fishing boat marking the junction). The road winds along towards the coast, going past an entrance to the beach by the Hotel Playa Sur Tenerife. Continue on for less than a kilometre then turn right taking the road marked Hermano Pedro. This leads almost to the end of the airport runway. Before a dip in the road park your vehicle and go on foot into the bottom of this dusty *barranco*, called Los Valos. In front of you up a few steps you will find the cave.

The legend is that young Pedro, born in 1616, was the son of a poor family living at Vilaflor on the way to Mount Teide. He spent his early days tending goats. Often he made his way to these caves so that he could shelter from the hot midday sun. In the silence of nature he felt a religious calling and often prayed in the cool cavern. On the 18th September 1642 the young Pedro embarked on his great mission to America. For a while he lived in a priest house in Habana. Later he travelled to Guatemala and Santiago de los Caballeros (15th February 1651). After an earthquake he founded the Bethlemitas religious order which became of great importance to the Guatemalan Christians. Over the years because of his miraculous works he was considered to be a saint, and the people of Tenerife came as pilgrims to visit the cave where he spent his childhood. They would bring oil lamps, candles and votive offerings, while those with ailments felt the religious atmosphere was beneficial, even curative.

Today the cave is still a place of religious pilgrimage and many bizarre offerings and flowers can be seen near the tiny altar. The number of visitors to the cave has increased since Pedro's beatification by the Pope in the Vatican, especially at weekends and on the feast day of San Pedro y San Pablo, and also on Pedro's birthday.

A pleasant walk from the central plaza can be enjoyed by going along the promenade, or on the sands westwards. It is at this part of the *playa* that windsurfing enthusiasts forgather, also there is a thriving Windsurfing Centre. Most winters, important championships are held at Playa del Médano. It is very picturesque to see these agile sports people creating a colourful, fast moving scene of leaping sails on the turbulent blue and white waters.

Close by is the volcanic cone of **Montana Roja** (Red Mountain) – a name derived from the reddish volcanic sand (though it has been said that it is named after a bloody massacre of Guanches). If you continue to walk behind the Montana Roja across a disused airfield you reach Playa de la Tejita, and an almost deserted beach. It is a place for nudism; a small bar provides drinks but there is no shade. Continue on this minor road by the coast passing banana and tomato cultivations and you reach the fishing village of Los Abrigos. Once just a tiny harbour with a few fishermen's cottages. With the building of the nearby airport, staff and aircrew discovered the little fish restaurants here, and gradually the place has developed so that now every house has become a restaurant and the narrow harbour road is a solid mass of cars at meal times. Nevertheless it is one of the nicest places for fresh fish dishes.

A poorly surfaced minor road from Los Abrigos winds its way northwards to join, eventually, the autopista at junction 24. Before reaching the autopista a left turn will take you to the entrance of the Amarilla Golf and Country Club. A welcome splash of green in the sandy desertlike landscape. A further few kilometres west brings you to another verdant area, Golf del Sur.

Aeropuerto Reina Sofia, Tenerife's busy international airport, is reached from the autopista at Junction 23. Because of the increase in the number of arrivals and departure flights this modern airport building has already become too small, consequently at times it is overcrowded and uncomfortable. It is believed that plans are in hand to enlarge the runway and airport buildings. Facilities at present include travel agents (*viajes*) where you can book hotel and apartment accommodation, car rent firms, tourist gift shops, money exchange bank, newsagent, bars and restaurant, luggage trolleys and Airport Information desk. Toilets include facilities for the disabled.

Buses from the airport go to Santa Cruz and Los Cristianos and there is a bus information desk in the airport building. There are generally plenty of taxis to meet incoming aircraft; fares are controlled with an increase after midnight.

The next part of the coast, south of the autopista is known as the **Costa del Silencio**, obviously named before the airport was built. Down by the sea a large tourist development called Ten Bel is an enormous holiday complex of some 45 hectares, with a multitude of facilities amongst the studios, apartments and villas. Nearby El Chaparral is another dense development of holiday residences. All these modern buildings have failed to obscure the quiet, old fashioned charm of **Las Galletas**, where a recently enlarged harbour has fishing boats and yachts, as well as the modern attraction of a yellow submarine called the Golden Trout. There are daily excursions to explore the underwater marine life. By this harbour is a useful Tourist Information Office.

North of Las Galletas, amongst the many banana and horticultural plantations at Cañada Blanca, is **Camping Nauta** (see Chapter Eight: Camping) from where there is a fine view of Mount Teide. To the west on the coast is **El Palm-Mar**, a small urbanisation that has yet to be failed to develop and has no facilities, though bathing can be had from a rocky beach. Montana de Guaza, 429m, close to the sea makes a challenging walk to the summit. The village of Guaza, by the autopista, has a Mobil petrol station, open twenty-four hours. Here you will also find *typico* Canarian restaurants. On the southern outskirts of Guaza the **Camel Safari Park** is a good place for a family outing. The camels are surprisingly tame and the safari ride will provide a good photographic souvenir.

A ten-minute drive west on the autopista brings you to the intersection for Arona (inland) and **Los Cristianos**, which lies down hill towards the sea.

Island tour 3

Santa Cruz – Igueste – Arafo – Güimar – El Escobonal – Fasnia – Arico – Granadilla – San Miguel – Valle de San Lorenzo – Los Cristianos: about 120 km

An alternative route from Santa Cruz to Los Cristianos takes you along the original old road going south, Carretera del Sur, which runs mostly parallel with the autopista. This drive is a complete contrast to the fast monotonous motorway, being very slow and tortuous. it winds its way between *barrancos* (valleys) and along narrow roads, but it is delightfully peaceful and scenic with little traffic. Do not take this route if you are an impatient driver, or in a hurry.

From Santa Cruz we suggest that you start by going along the Autopista as far as juction 7, thus avoiding the industrial and commercial areas on the outskirts of the capital city. Turning inland towards Barranco Hondo and the C822 southwards, you will start to climb into the dry, dusty hillside away from the coast. This is real desert country full of caves and candelabria cactus. At first it may seem a little dreary until you see the gathering of houses of **Igueste**, its church steeple being the tallest building.

Now you will have to get used to endless sharp bends and curves as you make your way south.

All the time you will have a bird's eye view of agricultural land above Candelaria and the coastline, where on a clear day you may see the shadow of Gran Canaria on the horizon.

When you reach La Hidalga you may wish to make a short detour to visit the pretty village of **Arafo**. Driving up hill you soon reach an important crossroad, where on the right is a useful petrol station. By continuing up hill you are at the centre of the village with its large pink and white church. The district of Arafo is known for its wine and in August it is the scene of a colourful *romeria* (pilgrimage).

If you turn right at the aforementioned petrol station you will be on route to climb the high mountains on a good road to La Esperanza and Mount Teide. This is a lovely drive but more attractive is to do it in reverse, coming down from the mountains towards the coast. Should you wish for refreshment, three kilometres along this road from Arafo you can have a snack (*tapas*) or a meal at a restaurant, Las Cuevitas de Nemesio. But back again to the Arafo crossroads for this tour, we continue south-east signed to Güimar, 3km.

Güimar, once a Guanche capital, is now an important town and agricultural centre set on the side of a ridge of mountains. With narrow streets busy with traffic you may find it hard to locate a parking place. But if you are interested to absorb the atmosphere of a truly Canarian town then you will enjoy exploring, especially around the large eighteenth-century Iglesia de San Pedro Apostol church and by the old Dominican convent, now the town hall (*ayuntamiento*). A road south leads to junction 11 of the Autopista del Sur.

We continue west along the dusty road, shortly to have a stiff climb to reach the Mirador de Don Martin, 4km from Güimar, a high viewpoint that affords an extensive panorama over the agricultural Güimar valley, the ridge of mountains behind, the busy autopista, and south to the sea-washed coast. No doubt you will be intrigued by the large white building nearby. It is a derelict hotel, forlorn and neglected, its swimming pool empty. In the fields behind you are likely to see butterflies, the Blue Canary. Painted Lady and Red Admiral, amongst the profusion of wild flowers. It is a pleasant place for a picnic and the clear air is exhilarating.

Many small communities live along this high, winding C822; here the artisans and farmers go about their daily tasks hardly aware of the mass of tourists that crowd the southern beaches, their sign of progress being the number of TV aerials, video clubs and the many new Japanese Land Cruiser type vehicles parked by their dwellings.

Every house is bedecked with bright trailing plants; purple bougainvillea, orange begonia and pink geraniums mingle with cheerful window boxes of petunias and marigolds. Away from the main road unmade tracks wind up steeply to rustic homesteads (*fincas*) and green fields. Watch out for the local buses that sweep round corners as if on a switchback, also the odd cow, goat or donkey that may have strayed in search of greener pastures.

Past **El Escobonal** you will come to the Barranco de Herque, where the road has been cut through a deep cave in the mountain; if it has been raining waterfalls will flow down amongst the tropical greenery. Soon you will reach the terraced lands of Fasnia where tomatoes, potatoes, salad crops and vines are carefully tended, with tiny pumice stones used to help retain the precious moisture. (You can return to the coast and autopista from Fasnia, junction 14.)

All these mountain villages have bars and simple restaurants. They will welcome your visit but remember the pace of life here is slower, old folks sit on doorsteps watching their grandchildren skipping in the lane, small dogs bark as you approach, but wagging their tails too; all will respond to a *buenos dias* or hallo. The siesta is still observed here and shops and bars close during the afternoon.

So we continue on through the villages of Arico El Nuevo and Arico El Viejo, new and old, to **Arico**. Another road here leads down to the coast and Poris de Abona at junction 17. You may care to stop at Lomo de Arico where the village church of San Juan Batista is noted for its colourful interior panels.

If you are still enjoying this rural ride then continue on past the turning for Chimiche until you reach the very important town of **Granadilla**. It is there that the Central Property and Land Registry Offices are found. You are now leaving behind the unspoilt villages, as a modern way of life has now reached Granadilla. Here are banks, chemists, supermarkets and shops. There is also a huge emporium of furniture and household goods. Probably this will be your first glimpse of a policeman on this country route.

Many of the hotel and restaurant staff working in Playa de las Americas and Los Cristianos travel daily from this large market town, busy too with agricultural depots and maintenance yards. Many technicians and crafts people live here and in San Isidro which lies south close to the autopista at junction 22. Granadilla is some eleven kilometres from the coast at El Médano

Just a little further to go on this tour of the old southern road brings you to **San Miguel** amid terraces of fig and almond trees. It is quite a busy town with modern amenities, several restaurants and artisan shops as well as a large church in the central plaza.

Still on the Carretera del Sur we make for Valle de San Lorenzo, but do pause at the **Mirador de la Centinela** to admire the view of the shimmering coastline with the range of high mountains towards Vilaflor and Mount Teide as a splendid backcloth. Valle de San Lorenzo is a charming and quiet inland village, with several *tipico* restaurants. It is an easy drive from either Playa de las Americas or Los Cristianos to Buzanada and junction 26 or via Chayofa and the Los Cristianos/Arona junction 27.

So we have reached the end of this inland route and an intriguing glimpse into the rural life of many *Canarios*.

Restaurants in southern Tenerife

Adeje
La Concepcion Cruce Tijoco. Tel: 78 02 86. Off main road to Guia de Isora and Playa de las Americas. In tiny mountain village, attractive Canarian decor. Menu depends on what is in the pots that day. Open evenings but telephone to confirm. Speciality rabbit (*conejo*), goat (*cabra*) and roast pork (*lomo*). Fine views.
Los Arcos Edificio Los Arcos, Calle Tinerfe el Grande. Tel: 71 07 70. Set well away from the crowds, high up in the hills above Playa de las Americas, this restaurant is also a pizzeria with a varied menu. You will enjoy the attractive terrace.

Arafo
Las Cuevitas de Nemesio Tel: 51 34 02. Away from the tourist trail, this unique restaurant is in a genuine old cave, three kilometres north of Arafo. *Tipico* Canarian menu. Nearby bar serves *tapas* including goat stew.

Arona
El Patio Canario In a quiet location in this mountain town. A Belgian lady runs this pleasant restaurant, cooking Belgian and local foods.

Chayofa
Meson Chayofa Tel: 79 31 17. In pretty setting, high on a hillside overlooking Los Cristianos and Playa de las Americas. This distinguished restaurant is ideal for a party or special occasion. Cooking is on a stone grill without oil. Spanish, German and French cuisine. Different buffet each day. Bar 1200 to midnight. Restaurant 1200 to 1500 and 2000 to 2200 hrs. Closed Thursday.

Cruce Buzanada

Genero Ctra General. Clean family run bar and restaurant on the cross roads to Valle de San Lorenzo. Tipico Canarian menu and international dishes. Good value. Closed Monday.

El Médano

Pescador El Médano Edificio Chasna. Tel: 70 45 25. In centre of town. Clean tourist restaurant, menu of the day.
Sandria Tel: 70 44 03. A well established and small restaurant serving fresh fish, *paella* and quality meals. Quiet venue.

Guaza

Guaracarumbo Ctra Las Galletas. Tel: 78 58 19. Bar restaurant popular with locals, it has a large room upstairs for parties and dances. Varied menu including charcoal grill.

La Caleta

Cala Marim Large well established, high class restaurant by pebble beach. Very good *tapas* and fresh fish. Expensive.

Las Galletas

Las Rosas Calle General 9. On road to Ten-Bel from Las Galletas. Small, family restaurant. Simple style, mainly for locals. Well cooked food includes fish; inexpensive, menu of day.

Los Abrigos

Langostina Village by the sea, west of the airport and close to the Amarilla Golf Club (Golf del Sur). This is one of the many very good fish restaurants all close to each other. Fresh lobster, king size prawns, mussels and a large selection of other fish dishes. Pay by weight. Very busy at lunch time, tourists eat earlier than Canarians. Open evenings. Not expensive and good value. The whole village smells of fish!

Playa San Juan

Ali Baba Tel: 86 74 34. *Tipico* fresh fish and sea food; you pay by weight. Also menu of the day. Simple and clean.
Brisa del Mar At the beginning of village, eastwards. This is a large bar restaurant used by tourists and Canarians. The menu is on a black board and you are welcome in the kitchen to admire the cooking. Can be noisy when busy. Excellent food and friendly.

San Isidro
Bodega El Jable Calle Bentejui 9. Popular Canarian restaurant in busy mountain town. Open 1330 to 1600 and 1930 to 2330 hrs. Closed Sunday and Monday afternoon.

Valle de San Lorenzo
Hermano Pedro Ctra General 52. Tel: 76 61 54. Typical Canarian bar restaurant in mountain village, good simple service. Specialities Canarian menu, grilled goat and tasty local soups.

Villa Isobel
La Fragua Calle El Hierro 11. Tel: 78 62 55. Well worth seeking this cheerful restaurant where the kitchen is opposite the bar. Nicely cooked tasty Canarian food. The sucking pig and chateaubriand is delicious. The tourists eat early, later the locals arrive.

FOURTEEN

Los Cristianos and Playa de las Americas

Los Cristianos

Playa de Los Cristianos has in recent years changed from a small fishing village into one of the major resorts in Tenerife yet it still retains its friendly atmosphere. Newly planted tropical flowers and shrubs create a feeling of being a green oasis set down by a sandy beach and interesting port. Best of all it has an all year round warm climate.

Even the **harbour** has been enlarged; now it combines its responsibilities as a port with those of a successful yacht marina. In winter, especially during January and February, the bay in which is the harbour is busy with ocean going yachts, there to take advantage of the favourable Trade Winds to assist their long voyages to the West Indies. Here a ship repair and maintenance yard is used by both pleasure and fishing vessels. Boating, water ski-ing, skin diving, deep sea fishing – all are available.

The ferries for La Gomera leave regularly from the quay. Tickets for the one hour and twenty-minute voyage from Los Cristianos to San Sebastián, Gomera can be purchased on the quay or at any travel agent. The ferry *Benchijigua*, built in 1972, is fast and comfortable, being fitted with stabilisers; her hoot of farewell as she sails out of Los Cristianos harbour is a notable event and an efficient time check! There is also a regular Hydrofoil service between the harbour in Los Cristianos and San Sebastián, La Gomera, operated by Trasmediterranea. From here also, daily excursion boats take holidaymakers on cruises for fishing, diving and to see the dolphins and pilot whales.

To the west of the harbour new developments include an attractive walkway by the seashore which goes past a myriad of modern apartments, hotels, bars and restaurants. This now extends all the way into neighbouring Playa de las Americas. Indeed nowadays you will not find any demarcation between the two resorts.

Pedalos, beach beds, sunshades and windsurfing are available. Pedestrian ways with colourful cafés, tables, chairs and sun umbrellas create a relaxed tropical atmosphere. The modern white church, **Nuestra Señora del Carmen**, in the town centre has a large plaza which is a useful meeting place, but do not rely on the church clock for your time. A newly built **Centro Cultural** will house the Town Hall, concert hall, cinemas, botanical park and the Tourist Information Office; here the smiling Maria speaks English and patiently offers information and advice

Shopping in the town gives plenty of variety, smart boutiques, sports shops, expensive jewellery, perfumeries, tobacconists, radio and TV goods, with the latest models offered at competitive prices. The islands are no longer Duty Free, but it is worth shopping around and sometimes discounts can be obtained. Numerous small shops are full of tourist souvenirs, beachwear and children's toys. Plenty of supermarkets, some hypermarkets, open from 1000 to 2200 hrs, also on Sunday mornings. Cake shops (*pasteleria*) have mouth watering selections but they do not sell bread; bakers (*panaderia*) have a good variety of types for sale. Delicatessens like Tania at Parque Margarita (to the east of town) have the most tempting selection of high quality foods. Fresh and frozen meat from the butcher (*carnerceria*) and a small amount of fresh fish from stalls at the harbour provide meals for those who are self catering.

However, the vast choice of restaurants, cafés and bars that fill the streets and the sea front promenade means that the cook in the family can have a holiday too, and the bill at the end should be less than if in the UK. Look out for Chinese, Indian, Venezuelan, Mexican, Italian and Scandinavian menus. With so many British tourists, Sunday lunch menus of roast beef and Yorkshire pudding are popular, also fish and chips and British beers.

It is more difficult to find genuine Canarian dishes in Los Cristianos; you are more likely to get a proper *tipico* meal if you visit restaurants in the villages away from the coast.

In recent years Los Cristianos has seen a big increase in the building of property offered for 'time share' and, as with its neighbour Playa de las Americas, the street touts have become a nuisance. The authorities are aware of the problem and the adverse publicity and it is hoped that a solution will soon be found.

There are plenty of firms offering cars, bicycles and motor cycles for hire. Buses, taxis and coach excursions give alternatives from lazing on the sandy beach or by a pool. Two petrol stations are in the centre of town and a drive of just one and a half hours will bring you up to Mount Teide in the centre of the island. Walking in the country requires sturdy footwear and probably a sunhat. The twin peaks of Montana Chayofita, 116m, to the west of Los Cristianos and Montana de los Cuevitas, 394m, to the east lie behind the white holiday homes that cling to the steep slopes. Both offer challenging climbs.

This is a happy relaxing place for a holiday, with the spectacular Mount Teide in the back ground. A very favourable winter climate makes it an all-year-round resort: its peak period over the Christmas season often sees all accommodation booked. Although its mixture of high rise apartment blocks and hotels has spread inland in an untidy way, the sea promenade has been planned to give a long and attractive walk, going the full length of the bay. For this reason Los Cristianos is suitable for anyone who is disabled or in a wheel-chair. Tall palm trees and flowering shrubs give exotic colour; tiled pavements with tables, chairs and bright umbrellas, make it seem tropical. The beach has recently been enhanced by the addition of white sand from the Sahara, and is kept in good condition by regular sweeping and rolling.

Restaurants in Los Cristianos

Pleasant restaurants and cheerful bars jostle for custom; all display their menus and prices. Britain keeps its end up with 'The John Bull Bar', 'The British Bar', 'Churchill's Bar' and 'real English breakfasts' or 'fish and chips'.

Canton 2 Calle Barranquillo (near church). High class Cantonese restaurant with excellent service. The proprietor worked on the Queen Elizabeth II. Take away food. Air conditioning.

Casa del Mar Esplanada del Muelle. Tel: 79 32 75. Excellent fish restaurant, upstairs with harbour and mountain views. Good service and clean. International menu, good value and not expensive. Closed Monday.

Estrella Polar Turn off west from Calle General Franco by Mobil petrol station. This is a *tipico* simple bar restaurant run by Canarian fishing family. Good value.

Margarita Tel: 79 56 23. Past Hotel Tenerife Sur, eastern end of town, on corner of Calle Penetración. Small friendly Canarian bar restaurant with outdoor terrace. English breakfast, Sunday roast lunch. Inexpensive.

Los Cristianos in the south of Tenerife is one of the most popular places for British tourists, with hotels, apartments and cafés close to the seafront. The harbour provides good moorings, and is the base for many pleasure boats. The ferry sails from here to La Gomera.

Oli-Delga Avenida Suecia. Tel: 79 16 29. Spanish style bar restaurant with TV. Speciality fish and sea food. Good *tapas*, reasonable wine list. Closed Sunday.

Orinoco Edificio Simon (close to Supermarket Hermusa 4) Tel: 75 00 87. Bar and large well-run restaurant serving *tapas* and 'take away' as well as an excellent menu, friendly Venezuelan service. Try the steaks. Inexpensive.

Rincon Criollo Centro Apolo 38. Near Supermarket Yambo. Small family run bar restaurant, outdoor charcoal grill. Specialities Venezuelan *hallacas* and *arepas*. Inexpensive.

Rosie's Cantina Royal Palm, Oasis del Sur. Tel: 79 55 51. Mexican style restaurant, amongst the new hillside *urbanización* at eastern end of town. As well as Mexican chumichangas, fajitas, beef taco, enchiladas diablo, you can enjoy chicken, steak and fish dishes. Remember to start your meal with a Margarita, it will get you in a party mood.

Royal Below Royal Apartments at eastern entrance to town. Run by Canarian family from La Gomera. This small bar restaurant has a clean and friendly atmosphere. Meals are inexpensive and nicely served. Mainly Canarian menu.

Slow Boat Calle San Telmo. Good quality Chinese food in pleasant surroundings. Expensive but good value. Similar restaurants by Diamantes Apartments (to east of town) and Playa de las Americas.

Taj Tandoori Avenida Maritimo. Tel: 79 21 19. Genuine Indian cuisine in upstairs restaurant overlooking harbour. The daytime view is interesting, overlooking harbour, at night quite romantic. Open 1330 to 1530 and 1900 hrs to midnight.

Playa de las Americas

Playa de las Americas is a modern, carefully planned resort made entirely for the pleasure of tourists, which is now achieving international renown. Tall concrete hotels and apartments provide ample accommodation for sunseeking, pleasure-loving visitors. Delightful open air cafés, souvenir shops, bars, restaurants, night clubs and discos give a wide variety of music and entertainment. At every street corner large supermarkets lure in holidaymakers with tempting displays of cheap cigarettes and liquor. All the fun of the seaside is to be found at Playa de las Americas with its long promenade, trinket stalls, pavement artists, ice cream parlours and sun terraces.

Small dark sandy beaches have sun umbrellas, and even on the odd cloudy day the sea temperature will always make swimming enjoyable. The majority of hotels have swimming pools and lay- out chairs in colourful surroundings. It is quite in order for non-residents to visit any hotel and enjoy the entertainments and facilities. However inside the hotels you are expected to be adequately covered, whilst at night long trousers and a tie are worn by men. Evening dress is not necessary.

The choice of hotels and apartments in Playa de las Americas is wide. The tourist office in Santa Cruz de Tenerife has a complete list with full details, which they will send on request.

Playa de las Americas has a great variety of restaurants, cafés and bars. Flamenco and international dancers give a sparkling show at 'Maxim' in the Centro Commercial Salytien, where you can dine and dance. Other night clubs and discos provide music and dancing for all ages into the early hours of the morning. Playa de las Americas is not for anyone seeking a quiet holiday, but it is great fun for the young at heart. In recent years Playa de las Americas has enlarged in all directions, with a vast building programme of luxury hotels, apartments and shopping centres; Puerto Colon is the new port near man made beaches. One of the more attractive developments is called Torvicas and down by the shore a well sheltered beach of black sand gives safe bathing. A promenade of white pagodas and trellis work are ablaze with brilliant geraniums and trailing plants. On several levels are many bars and restaurants. Across the road in front of the stark white and green apartments are more bars and cafés, one is called Cheap and Chips!

Children as well as adults are well catered for at this cheery resort. Along the maritime promenade, near the Hotel Gran Tinerfe is the entrance to **Acuari Atlantic**, an aquarium of underwater life in the Canary Islands. Amongst the fishes to be seen are stingrays, sharks, sea turtles and many crustacean species. Open from 1000 to 1800 hrs, entrance costs 200 pesetas, children 100.

Another popular venue is the **Octopus Park**, a water park built on the side of a hill at Alto San Eugenio (part of Playa de las Americas), which is inland of the autopista. Free buses from the centre of town take you to the entrance. Open all year it offers fun for all the family.

Driving in Playa de las Americas can be quite a nightmare and parking during the day a real problem despite the one-way system; the situation is a little easier towards the eastern end of town which was built more recently. Here the roads and pavements are wider and avenues are lined with unusual tropical shrubs, and buildings not so tall.

Near every hotel and apartment block you will find a supermarket, often it will be of hypermarket size, with lengthy shelves of alcoholic drinks; your selection of booze for your Duty Free is wide. Prices do vary from shop to shop but only by a few pesetas. If you want a bargain ask one of the many elderly visitors who spend the winter months here. They have the time to wander round looking for special offers.

Playa de las Americas has the reputation for being noisy and brash, a crowded concrete hungle of neon lights, music and bawdy people. Certainly there is an element of this in the central older part of town and this is what a number of holidaymakers enjoy. However one has only to choose a hotel or apartment set back from the centre to find a quieter atmosphere.

Every year new developments are being opened both inland and to the west. The autopista is scheduled to continue on past junction 30, Torviscas and Playa Fanabe, along the coast as far as Los Gigantes.

For the energetic an easy and mostly level walk can be enjoyed from Playa Fanabe past Playa Torviscas, by the smart Puerto Colon with its luxury yachts, right along the seaside promenade all the way to Los Cristianos, a distance of seven kilometres. Plenty of bars, restaurants and shopping on this walk. The contrast of scenery is quite dramatic for the bare, high mountains come close to the coast, a stark background against the white, modern high rise hotels and apartments. All this close to the blue Atlantic which washes the blackish sands with a feathery white spume.

In places the jagged black lava rocks have been put to effective use, especially at Club Rocas where colourful and exotic gardens have been planted around the turquoise and white swimming pools and sun terraces. Here you have all one expects for a lazy sunbathing holiday. Across from the Club is the Hotel Jardin Tropical. One of the newer hotels and a veritable paradise of tropical gardens and balconies dripping with hanging plants. A spectacular vision of what can be created by man from an arid and desert landscape.

Continuing along the promenade eastwards, you are near one of the entrances to the **Casino** (from town it is below the Pueblo Canario); daily a low flying aircraft flies a banner telling everyone 'Casino open every night'. You must be over eighteen and have your passport to enjoy the gambling.

The new larger hotels provide real luxury in elegant settings, where you can relax by a pleasant pool to sunbathe or sit under a shady, tropical tree. Plenty of comfort with well staffed restaurants, sports facilities, saunas, hairdressers, boutiques and nightly entertainments means you can have a wonderful holiday without leaving your hotel!

But we hope you will take one of the numerous coach excursions, or rent-a-car, to see the beautiful mountain scenery, Mount Teide and the green villages of the north. Have an evening out at a night spot or restaurant. There is a vast selection of menus and varied ambiences, from the Gary Linekar's Bar, the friendly Fish and Chips café, the noisy karaoke, to the good value steak houses or the smart á la carte restaurants. Remember, too, the *tipico* Canarian mountain hideaways; taxi drivers have their special favourites, but book a return journey to your hotel!

There is much to be had from a holiday in the south of Tenerife, and Playa de las Americas is still the island's most popular destination.

Restaurants in Playa de las Americas

Banana Garden Palm Beach. (Next to Hotel Troya Park) Tel: 79 03 65. A popular restaurant and cocktail bar, situated in centre and down steps in a garden setting with cosy corners. International food at reasonable prices. Dancing to live music. Flamenco shows. Table reservations required. Open from 1900 hrs.

Beefsteak Charly Hotel Club Bonanza. Although in centre of town the atmosphere is pleasantly quiet. Menu of the Day and vegetarian dishes. Reasonable prices.

El Malaga In front of Mediterranean Palace Hotel. New Restaurant in Spanish style and cuisine. Tapas bar. Open from 1100 hrs until early morning. Flamenco show.

Fagans Calle Las Flores. Good English cooking with large selection of fresh soup and salads. Roast pork, lamb and turkey. Delicious desserts.

Gourmet Atlantic Between Hotel Las Palmeras and Parque Santiago 2. A clean and busy restaurant with interesting menu. Open evenings only 1800 to 2300 hrs.

Horizonte Club Atlantis. First class service. The set meal is very good value. Extensive à la carte menu. Recommended by local paper.

Mamma Rosa Apartamentos Colon 2. Tel: 79 48 19. A classy restaurant with smart modern decor and well dressed waiters. Outside patio. Table reservations. Italian fresh pasta, steaks, international menu and large selection of wine.

Maite Centro Comercial, Veronica 3. Tel: 79 01 59. Facing the sea this pleasant and busy restaurant gives fast, efficient and friendly service. Also used by Canarians, it is comfortable and clean, with white table cloths and napkins. The prices of the international menu are average, the food is nicely served with generous portions.

Papagay Beach Costa Torviscas. Opposite the Hotel Esmeralda this bar cafeteria serves English food and breakfasts. Roast beef on Sunday. Every Thursday roast lamb. Cocktails, sangria and ice cream.

Porky's Fun Pub Apartamentos Playa Azul. Traditional English food until 2000 hrs, including speciality English pork. 'Happy Hour' every night, cheap drinks 2200 to midnight.

The Cookery Nook Centro Comercial. Americas shopping, by Parque Santiago. Bar restaurant serving English breakfast, morning coffee, home made cakes and scones. Evening meals, special Sunday lunch. Children's portions. Open daily from 0930 hrs until late.

FIFTEEN

The west coast, heading north

Island tour 4

Playa de las Americas – Adeje – San Juan – Los Gigantes – Santiago del Teide – Masca – Erjos – Garachico – Icod de los Vinos – Los Realejos – Puerto de la Cruz: about 120 km

The tour to Puerto de la Cruz commences on the northward C822. The landscape remains dry and dusty with sparse vegetation, but distant mountain ridges soften the view giving various shades of rock indentations, particularly beautiful at evening light with the sun going down when a warm pink glow descends over the vista.

A turning off the main road seawards leads to **La Caleta**, a small sandy beach with a fish restaurant. The road runs between huge banana plantations, protected by high concrete walls. Often the entrance drives to the plantations are lined with red poinsettia bushes, a splendid sight. The banana leaves wave in the breeze and you can glimpse the peasants in their wide-brimmed hats busy at work or resting in the shade of the trees.

The next deviation from the C822 is **Adeje**, a small town built on the site of an old Guanche settlement. Buildings of note are the Casa Fuente, a ruined sixteenth-century fortification once the residence of the Counts of Gomera, the seventeenth-century Convent of San Francisco and the sixteenth-century Church of Saint Ursula. Within walking distance is the **Barranco del Infierno** or Hell Valley, a name conjuring up fearful stories – yet it is green and beautiful with old Guanche caves. To find this *barranco* follow the main street to the top of the hill, where there is a sign giving the direction. A small carpark on the left allows you to leave your car but if you go by bus you will have to walk up hill to the bar restaurant, which is perched at the start of the walk. (Cafeteria Otelo by the path to the Infierno has a large balcony; their speciality is garlic chicken.) It is about two hours of strenuous walking along the ravine, which is narrow, steep and quite rugged; stout footwear and a cardigan are required. The clear path takes you deeper into the undergrowth, past prickly pears and many wild plants, willows and ferns. So you zig zag your way to the bottom, a depth of 300m. In places there is no sunlight. At the bottom you find waterfalls and rock pools. Be careful, it is moist and slippery. It is said that the Guanches used the caves for burials and that Adeje was a prehistoric capital.

Just past **Los Olivos** the road divides, with an inland road providing an alternative mountain route on the C822 as far as Santiago del Teide (which is described on page 167). But here we take the road signposted Los Gigantes, which follows the coast quite close to the sea past more banana plantations that add a welcome touch of green to the landscape.

Hidden Coves

Along the south-east and south-western coast of Tenerife there are a number of quiet coves that can be ideal places for a picnic or secluded swim. Most of these bays have to be reached by taking a dirt track seawards from the main road; quite a number then require a rough hike, often past banana or tomato plantations, then a scramble down a footpath to reach the beach. For active and outdoor types, seeking out these remote spots can be good fun and the exercise invigorating.

Unfortunately the more people get to know these places the less ideal they become; for soon one finds a beach bar appearing, then an attendant with sunbeds. It develops and the peaceful atmosphere disappears. So do seek out your own quiet haven and enjoy it while it remains.

One such place that will eventually be developed is El Puertito, south of Callao Salvaje and Playa Paraiso. You can drive down a fairly level earth track for about three kilometres to reach this tiny sheltered bay, with its few houses, fishing boats and a small bar, which also serves fish meals and snacks.

The more adventurous will climb up through the village and walk along the top of the shallow cliffs east towards La Caleta. It is quite a hike on stony ground and at present involves crossing a very rickety bridge. Your reward is a 'hidden' sandy beach much favoured by naturists. How long will it be before the first developer arrives?

The modern high rise apartments at **Callao Salvaje** rather spoil the vista and the huge Marazul apartment hotel seems out of place amongst the green banana plantations.

San Juan, once a little known fishing village, is slowly developing. Its fish restaurant Brisa del Mar, overlooks the sea and the fishing boats. Being popular with the locals it is obviously a good place for a fish meal, so go early to get a table. San Juan port is now an important harbour for the local fishing fleet and it is interesting to watch a catch of glistening tuna being hoisted from the holds of the boats. Opposite the quay there is a tiny pebble rock beach suitable for swimming.

Another small port is in the village of **Alcala**, but it is not very good for swimming. The village has a large tree lined plaza and plenty of shops along the main street.

Two kilometres further west one reaches Playa de la Arena with a good wide black sandy beach and pleasant modern promenade. Recently built apartments and restaurants have turned this clean beach into a popular resort. Only in rough weather when the red flag flies is it advisable not to go into the sea. There is a Tourist Information Office on Avenida Maritima. Tel: 11 03 48.

Puerto de Santiago is an attractive fishing port with narrow streets that lead to the harbour – you may find it difficult to park your car near the port. Apartments and villas are now being built as the tourist trade takes over from fishing.

From Puerto de Santiago there are fine views of the renowned **Los Gigantes** (The Giants), as these enormous black cliffs are called. It has been developed into a holiday area with a hotel and apartments built against the cliffs. There is a yacht marina and sight-seeing boats take tourists to view the cliffs. El Club de los Gigantes, Calle Maritim, has possibly the most ambience on the island, and the food is usually excellent. There is fishing from the promenade. This not a good place for the disabled because of the steep roads.

Skuba diving and boat trips to see the dolphins and swim off Masca Bay are available from the harbour. Los Gigantes likes to keep its upmarket image. This is reflected in the quality and prices of its restaurants, boutiques and property.

Leaving Los Gigantes the road immediately starts a spectacular climb up to **Tamaimo** and Santiago del Teide at 975m. This amazing drive is full of twists and turns with fascinating views of the coast away below. As one leaves sea level the land becomes fertile and cultivated, with vines, tomatoes and potatoes yielding four crops a year. From June to October the children in this area are on holiday from school so that they can assist in the harvesting. The water for irrigation is brought down from the mountain in a series of navigation channels. Lettuce, beans and spinach are grown successfully on neat terraces.

At **El Retamar** the lava fields of the Chinyero volcano can be seen; the black soil together with the high humidity of the area helps the cultivation. Almond blossom in January gives the air a sweet perfume and adds to the delight of the place. **Santiago del Teide** is a busy centre for marketing the produce. It has a picturesque domed church and typical Canarian shops that are old fashioned village stores.

It is at Santiago del Teide that a minor road leads into the mountains to the village of Masca. In the past the village which lies 305m below rugged cliffs could only be reached by mule train. Now a narrow tarmac road with hairpin bends and a few passing places winds its way up and then down through the isolated pretty hamlet.

The village of Masca

Should you wish to drive to Masca make sure that none of your party suffer from vertigo and that you have good brakes! The Barranco de Masca (valley) lies hidden by high mountain ridges of rough basalt in a dramatic and peaceful landscape of palms, pines and verdant vegetation. At first the road rises steeply in a quick series of bends, then quite suddenly you are at a small high plateau, where a bar kiosk restaurant serves refreshments to anxious drivers. At this point you have magnificent views east and west. Here you have a bird's eye view of the hairpin bends and spiralling road below. Recently remade, this road is still very narrow with few passing places. On reaching the first cluster of small abodes park your car and take the pathway to the tiny village with its church and small school. If you are an experienced walker and suitably equipped, then consider taking the strenuous walk to the bed of the river as suggested in *Landscapes of Southern Tenerife* (see bibliography).

However you can still admire the scenery from one of the cafés or restaurants. We particularly like to climb up (no car for the last 250m) to La Pimentera da Salvadores, which is perched on the mountain side. Excellent paella and Canarian cooking or just a cup of coffee on the terrace is a real treat for anyone who likes the away from it all scene and the tinkle of the goat herds. Unfortunately this gem of tranquillity is getting far too well known. The Masca road continues more gently uphill towards El Palmar, or you can return to Santiago del Teide and continue on the C820.

From Santiago del Teide the C820 road reaches its highest point at **Erjos**, 1219m above sea level. On the north side of the pass, green grass grows on the high hills and cattle graze. In the early part of the year *escobon*, a white broom, and the yellow *codeso* (gorse-like shrubs) bloom freely. Tree heathers, with their pink and white blossom, give shelter to the small fields. Workers are busy pruning the vines. The white wine of the area is 14% strength and much sought after by locals and visitors alike. The road descends in a winding, pleasant way, the scene is green and prolific with vegetation, so different from the hot dusty south coast.

You will find on the left side of this pretty road **Camellos El Tanque** where you can enjoy a camel ride and have some refreshment. El Tanque has a wide main street with a church, banks, post office and shops. Soon after leaving, you will see a turning west, signed to Garachico TF142. This is a steep and winding route down to the coast. A less tortuous way is to continue on to Icod de los Vinos and then take a lower road to Garachico, which lies by the sea.

Garachico was founded shortly after the Spanish Conquest and two centuries ago its port rivalled that of Santa Cruz, but a volcanic eruption in 1706 almost wiped out the whole town. To get an idea of the devastation of the lava flow, visit the Mirador de Garachico on the C820 towards El Tanque; from there one looks down on the sweep of the lava stream all the way to the town, still an awesome sight; at the Mirador there is a tourist cafeteria and souvenir shop.

The town has now been rebuilt on the lava that slid into the sea. The only remains of the old town are around the Castillo de San Miguel, a sixteenth-century fort, the San Francisco Convent and a seventeenth-century Palacio de los Condes de Gomera – those

The town of Garachico, west of Icod, on the north coast of Tenerife, rebuilt on a site of an earlier settlement which was destroyed by volcanic lava in an eruption in 1706.

The Teno Peninsula

The most westerly point in Tenerife is the Punta de Teno, a rocky, almost deserted peninsula where two lighthouses mark the edge of the land. To reach this remote region you have the choice of including it in a drive from Masca via El Palmar to Buenavista or going the coastal route from Garachico, Los Silos and Buenavista. You can make the tour in reverse order. Both ways you will travel through some splendid scenery, also ideal for walking, passing from the high, craggy peaks of the Teno Mountains (Mount Baracan 1000m), through a pretty, green and winding valley of scattered farmhouses and cultivated crops, until you reach the coastal town of Buenavista, the most north westerly village in Tenerife.

Buenavista is important as an agricultural centre where coffee groves lie alongside banana plantations. The town has a sleepy atmosphere and a maze of narrow streets. The road west, TF1429, is signposted. On the outskirts the restaurant El Marino is a useful refreshment stop for there is no bar at Punta de Teno.

Once a rough track, the nine kilometres to the lighthouses is now tarmac. At one point it skirts a high cliff and goes through a dark and unlit tunnel. You will wish to stop at the Mirador de Don Pompeyo, where there are views of waving banana plantations and the coastline below. Soon you drop down to a grassy plain and a level road to Playa de Teno. This minute bay of sand has a slipway with a few small fishing boats. Nearby are the two lighthouses. Only one is in use and neither is open to the public. A remote place for a picnic or a night stop, if you have a motorhome. On a clear night you can see the lights of Los Gigantes along the coast to the south, and a wonderful starlit sky.

Return by the same road to Buenavista, then continue east through Los Silos, a charming place with an attractive white church and cobbled main street. Down by the sea Parque Sibora is a quiet development of villas. A tall apartment block has a restaurant nearby and an excellent swimming pool. From Los Silos it is an easy drive along the coast past the turning to La Caleta, a busy banana area, to reach Garachico.

Counts who seem to have had so many residences. It is said that when the developers were planning the new town they wanted to destroy a large rock out at sea, El Roque. Feeling that it was part of the old town, the inhabitants resisted and built a cross on the rock in commemoration of the disaster.

It is well worthwhile to plan a stop in Garachico, where there is parking by the harbour; several restaurants and bars are geared for the daily invasion of tourists. Down on the seafront a series of lava rock pools have steps down to the water making easy access for swimming, but the local lads like to show off their skill by diving off the rocks. When the wind is strong bathing is prohibited, for then the sea comes rushing in with great Atlantic rollers, creating a huge wall of white foam. You will find a nice restaurant by the sea where you can watch all the activities. One of the most peaceful places in this interesting town is the little garden set back from the harbour car park. It is reputed to have been the old harbour entrance before the volcanic eruption; now it is a sunken garden with tropical flora and little paths. An ancient wine press is a relic of the past, Of more modern times is a statue placed at a view point going west on the road to Los Silos. Erected in 1990, this lively bronze figure of a man walking with a suitcase, commemorates the many emigrants who went to seek a fortune in Venezuela.

Continuing eastwards, the coastal road heads towards Icod, and a turning off towards the sea leads to **San Marcos**, a small seaside resort in a bay sheltered by low black cliffs, with a beach of black sands. Its quiet and peaceful apartments and houses nestle closely together, while tourists enjoy swimming in the clear water. The arrival of the local bus is the big event of the day and cause for much talk and chatter. Often the womenfolk will put huge baskets on their heads to carry home the shopping.

Do not attempt to drive down to the harbour at San Marcos as parking there is very limited. Use the carpark and walk down the steps that lead to the seafront. Here are several cafés that have tables out of doors and the fish restaurants are recommended.

Returning by the same route through the banana plantations one reaches the main road and, turning eastwards, it is but 3.2 km to **Icod de los Vinos**.

The 'town of vines' is at the foot of Mount Teide and in the Icod valley, famous for its wines. Perhaps even more well known is the thousand year old Dragon Tree (*Drago Milenario*) claimed to be the oldest and finest specimen in the world and guarded by railings. Honoured by the Guanches, the blood red sap of El Drago was used for various medicinal purposes.

The church of San Marcos lies in an orange-tree shaded plaza, lined with elegant old manorial houses, having the traditional wooden balconies. There are splendid views out to sea towards Mount Teide. Try and get there early in the day as parking space is limited.

The C820 road follows the coastline through **San Juan de la Rambla** which has a pretty church in the square. Inland a higher road leads to **Los Realejos**, built in two parts, *alto* and *bajo*, upper and lower. It is in a setting of farmland and banana groves and is named after the final battle between the Conquistadores and the Guanches, when the Royal (*Real*) troops were victorious. The Church of Santiago in Realejos Alto is the oldest on the island. Visit El Castillo Parque Museo and see a pictorial and factual representation of the story of the Canary Islands. Entrance costs 700 pesetas. Free bus from Puerto de la Cruz, eastern end of seafront, opposite the Café Columbus.

On the rocky shoreline bananas grow in profusion. Las Aguas is a colourful hamlet just past San Juan de la Rambla, which is a distance of 12 km to the centre of Puerto de la Cruz. Los Realejos, which with La Vera is the garden city of Puerto de la Cruz, is 7 km from the centre.

Approaching Puerto de la Cruz from Icod de los Vinos, we suggest that you turn left and leave the main C820, just before KM36 at the Shell petrol station, signed Punta Brava. This is Carreterra del Norte, a busy road into Puerto; it leads downhill for $2^1/2$ km. A turning to the right takes you to Parque Taoro and the Casino. Further on a turn left marked Derhesa and Loro Parque is narrow, winding and not recommended. Better to take the next left turn also marked Loro Parque and Punta Brava. This is Avenida de Blas Perez Gonzalez, leading to the Castillo de San Felipe, where you should find space for parking. A level ten-minute walk (or taxi) will take you to the Plaza del Charco and the centre of Puerto de la Cruz.

Alternative inland route (Island tour 4)

Los Olivos – Guia de Isora – Chio – Tamaimo – Santiago del Teide: about 28 kms

The road junction past **Los Olivos** is clearly marked with the C822 going straight ahead towards Guia de Isora, while the coastal route is signed Los Gigantes.

The C822 takes you high up into the countryside away from the sea, but for the most part there are extensive views towards the coastal resorts and many large banana plantations that grow so well by the sea. As you gradually climb along the side of the mountain slopes you will pass turnings inland for the little villages of Taucho, La Concepcion, Tijoco de Abato and Vega de Herques. All are small hamlets which have recently been 'discovered' as good places to seek out typical bar restaurants, where you will receive a friendly welcome and a simple meal. Usually Canarian soup, grilled pork chops with small Canary potatoes, salad and locally grown oranges.

Continuing along the main road, which twists and turns as it crosses deep ravines, the vegetation becomes greener with a profusion of cacti and colourful wild flowers in the hedgerows and terraces. After passing through a couple of tunnels one reaches **Guia de Isora**, an important agricultural town with an attractive church set in a cool plaza. Shops, bars, restaurants and a petrol station are along the main road. A turning north of the town towards the sea leads down a steep slope to Playa San Juan.

We progress northwest passing a road to the right signed Las Cañadas and Mount Teide. The way becomes narrower as we reach **Chio**, where more petrol is to be found. Again the road divides, with the C822 dropping down very sharply in a series of bends to the agricultural valley below and eventually reaching **Tamaimo**.

The alternative higher road takes you through the valley of Arguaya where in February and March the almond blossom spreads a pink and white scented cloud. These are lovely rural rides with spectacular views, although the driver needs to keep an eye on the narrow way.

You may like to stop at the **Centro Alfarero de Arguayo**, a museum of ceramics where you can see pottery being made and where you can purchase unique handmade gifts. Open Monday to Saturday, 1000 to 1300 and 1600 to 1800 hrs. Tel: 86 31 27.

After being in the heady clear air of the mountains it comes as a contrast after passing through the scattered village of Las Manchas to reach the lower countryside and the open agricultural fields around **Santiago del Teide**.

SIXTEEN

Puerto de la Cruz

An international tourist resort

There are three roads that lead into Puerto de la Cruz. Coming along the autopista from Santa Cruz, you can leave at junction 18, signposted Puerto por Botanical y Maritima. Following the first option you will soon be in the area known as El Botanico, set on a hill overlooking the central part of town and the seafront; when you drive the Maritima route you will wind down to the Playa Martinez and Avenida Colon, which has become one way along the seafront. Driving in Puerto needs care, a good knowledge of the system helps and lots of patience; unfortunately there does not seem to be a map of the one-way system.

The third entrance to Puerto is at the western end of the main road from Santa Cruz, past the junction for San Nicholas; look for the TF132 to the right, it is just before the Shell petrol station, then follow Carretera General del Norte.

Puerto de la Cruz, set at the bottom of the beautiful Orotava Valley, with the snow-capped Mount Teide high above, must have one of the most perfect settings for a tourist resort. Once the port for La Orotava, it is referred to by the locals as Puerto. Now it is the principal northern tourist resort in Tenerife and one of the most important in Spain.

The large modern town, built at the edge of the rocky seashore, has a mushroom growth of huge hotels, apartments, restaurants, cafes and shopping streets. The old town is delightful, with open markets, and colonial houses and little streets leading to the old harbour. The promenade is attractive; many view-points are hung with flowers, arcades are crammed with souvenirs and bars beckon at every corner.

The natural beach at Puerto de la Cruz is small and rocky with dark sand and pebbles; nevertheless holiday-makers flock to lie under the blue skies in the warm sunshine.

For those who do not enjoy such conditions, there is the huge Lago de Martianez, built on land reclaimed from the sea, and Puerto de la Cruz's outstanding landmark. This renowned leisure complex is a masterpiece of modern design providing magnificent swimming pools, cafés, clubs and sunbathing terraces. César Manrique's ingenuity has been acclaimed worldwide. An amazing collection of sculptures and fountains add spectacle and interest to the colourful setting. Price of admission to the swimming pools and sunbathing area is 500 pesetas.

The Old City

In the old part of the town, at the western end past the Avenida de Colon, a tiny fisherman's chapel, Chapel San Telmo, stands by the water's edge. Close by, the town's mother church Iglesia de Nuestra Señora de la Pena de Francia, is set in a cool plaza planted with palm trees and tropical plants.

It is across the Plaza de la Iglesia that the Tourist Office is situated. Maps of the town and illustrated brochures are given freely, usually they include English translations. Bus time-tables are available.

Along one side of the Calle Santo Domingo the street is lined with flower-sellers, cheery Canarian women who give broad smiles to encourage you to purchase their colourful merchandise. Nearby is the town hall (*ayuntamiento*).

A little harbour, the original Puerto de la Cruz, is now only used for fishing boats. Brightly coloured, they lie on the black pebble beach where fishermen spend hours mending their nets. Plans are going ahead to build a new harbour and yacht marina.

Close to the harbour is the former **Royal Customs House**, the oldest house in the town, owned by a British family. In this area are several English type pubs with draught beer, long bars, beer mats and bar billiards. At night there is music to a piano and often singing until far into the night.

Another old house that has been converted into a centre for crafts is **Casa Iriate**, Calle San Juan 21. Built before 1790, it is one of the few houses that still has a courtyard you can enter freely, with galleries surrounding a lovely patio. There is a garden bar and a Naval Museum. Local people are at work making gold and silver filigree, carving ivory and wood, hand-tooling leather and embroidering the famous lace tablecloths. Artisans sell their produce at very competitive prices.

Back past the fishing harbour along Calle Mequinez and Calle Felipe is the football stadium Estadio Futbol el Penon. Along the same road is found the British Cemetery close to the **Castillo de San Felipe**. This castle was once used as a defence against pirates but it is now a pleasant restaurant.

Recently the seafront between the Castillo and Punta Brava has been modernised; once again the Lanzarote architect César Manrique's great skill has been used to create an attractive seaside leisure complex. His use of natural wood, stones and lava is much admired. Walking along the promenade you not only enjoy the sunshine and beach activities, but also have a fine view of the snowcapped and majestic Mount Teide, looking ethereal in the blue sky.

Clubs

Puerto de la Cruz has had a thriving British community for a great many years. The Anglican Church, the British Club and the British Yeoward School are all situated in the Parque Taoro area. The Wednesday Group, the Tennis Clubs and the Bridge Clubs are all organisations with numerous activities catering for the residents in Tenerife. A Citizens Advice Bureau gives assistance where required. The English Library, Taoro Park, has some 30,000 books including the latest World Atlas and Encyclopaedia Britannica. Temporary membership is available. Open Monday 1500 to 1730 hrs, and Wednesday 1000 to 1200 hrs. Friday 1600 to 1800. A reference room has British and American magazines. There is a small juvenile section.

Local transport

Buses run regularly from the bus station in Hermanos Fernandez Perdigon. Tel: 38 18 07. Fares are low and it is possible to cover the island more cheaply by bus than on coach excursions. The tourist office has up-to-date time-tables and fares. The main taxi rank is in Plaza Charco. Tel: 38 49 10.

Suzuki and Honda motorcycles are for hire from most car hire firms in Puerto. It pays to shop around as prices do vary. Make sure that you have the total charge correct and that it includes insurance.

Nightlife

The town abounds with entertainments of an international standard. The Casino Taora, set high above the resort, has a splendid bar with restaurant, open from 2100 hrs, and offering roulette, blackjack, baccarat and slot machines. Entrance costs 500 pesetas. For gentlemen a jacket and tie is requested. Your passport is essential.

In the evenings, below sea level in the Martianez complex, the international night club, Andromeda, gives sparkling live floor shows with top class artistes, including the Spanish ballet. In the same complex is disco dancing where the dance floor is open to the sky. With lights sparkling on the water, it is like being in a cave. Upstairs it is a restaurant, cafeteria and sun terrace by day.

In the larger hotels music for dancing is played every night, with special folklore evenings and guest artistes appearing. Visitors to the dancing do not have to be residents. No charge is made but the prices of drinks are increased, usually to about 400 pesetas.

There are several other night clubs. The Plaza de Toros la Rueda is open at 2100 hrs; there is dancing, a comedian, flamenco and mini bull fight in which guests may participate. In the Hotel Valle Mar, the night club Los Carrichos is lush and comfortable. Dancing and entertainment varies from guitar music and flamenco to pop groups. La Cueva at Los Realejos has wonderful views. The night club is set in a Guanche Cave and the entertainment is twice nightly. Discos and bars with music can be found in most streets near to the seafront. A taxi driver will take you to discos in other parts of the town.

Amongst the most popular discos are Regine, Felipe, El Penon, Victoria and Qata at Le Paz. A taxi driver will take you to discos in other parts of town, including the classy El Coto in the Hotel Botanico.

Loro Parque

Barranco de San Felipe marks the western edge of the town. A short distance on is **Loro Parque**, open 0830 to 1800 hrs daily, an amusement park that is a big attraction for tourists from all over the island. Loro Parque can be reached from the seafront in Puerto; outside the Cafe Columbus you will find a free bus, brightly painted with 'Loro Parque' written on each side. It runs every twenty minutes to the park gates. Inside in a tropical park are exotic plants and trees; everywhere are parrots (the Spanish word is *loro*), for this is said to be the largest collection of parrots in Europe. Some are flying freely, their bright plumage causing great splashes of colour in the trees. Flamingoes stand gracefully around a small lake quite undisturbed by the clicking of cameras.

Special attractions in the park are the Parrot Shows which are given in the cafeteria nine times during the day, at no extra charge. During this unusual performance, the parrots perform clever things like roller skating, riding a tricycle, jumping through hoops, counting and sorting out colours. It takes a few weeks for the parrots to learn their tricks but once learnt, they perform happily and expect applause.

Until recently the Parrot Show was the highlight, but now another attraction has been added without extra cost to the visitor. Walking past monkeys and crocodiles one sees a mosque-like structure, very oriental on the outside. Be prepared for a 'happening' when you reach the inside. Indeed there is a notice outside warning people that it might not be suitable for those of a nervous disposition or with heart complaints.

On entering the dome one sees a cinema screen which stretches from' floor to ceiling in a perfect 180° arc. There are no seats, everyone stands throughout the performance. The show starts without warning and one has the sensation of being on a roller coaster, body angling in a breathtaking way. Fire engines roar at speed and water ski-ing is simulated. This is not for the faint hearted, but a real thrill for the majority of holidaymakers, who come out dazed and ready to go to the bar!

The latest addition to the Parque is the Delfin Show (dolphins). The dolphinarium is an outdoor entertainment which delights everyone. Nearby an enclosure houses sealions; another is Tiger Island. A little further is the Gambia Market which sells authentic Gambian products. Plans are going ahead to greatly extend the area of the Park, so that it will include a Thai village, an underground aquarium, a gorilla exhibit and a theatre. Perhaps best of all is the fact that this commercial enterprise also does excellent work in helping to preserve endangered species.

Bananera El Guanche

A further free bus service is given by **Bananera El Guanche**. The five minute bus ride from Café Columbus towards La Orotava brings you to a family run plantation. This is a highly informative and easily understood excursion for the price of 500 pesetas entrance fee.

You will learn all about the cultivation of the banana, be given a free banana, plus a taste of banana liqueur and some local cheese and figs. The tour is very well arranged. An English-speaking guide will explain graphically on a blackboard how the banana grows. The cultivation is not easy, for the ground must be well prepared to allow the passage of water.

The banana plant is not a tree but a rhizome (like a large bulb). It is unusual as it is hermaphrodite, male and female flowers being on the same stalk, reproduction taking place without pollination. The bananas are the female part of the flower and at the tip of the flower is the male part, which is cut off after about two or three months growth.

The stem is cut green at six to seven months; a hand of bananas can weigh from fifteen to sixty kilograms. A further shoot then appears from the ground, the life of the plant is infinite. Because of the high price of bananas in the world market 96% of Canary bananas are sent to mainland Spain, which is a great pity, for the little Canary banana is of superior quality for flavour and sweetness.

At the Bananera you can see the bananas in all stages of growth plus a really colourful selection of exotic trees and flowers, including coffee, pineapple, mango, papaya, sugar cane and chewing gum trees. One large avocado tree produces 1,500 kilograms of fruit a year! The plantation is bright with bougainvillea, hibiscus, enormous red poinsettias and many other brilliant flowers and cacti, all clearly labelled.

At the bar/shop, local honey, cheese, figs, liqueurs and fruit can be purchased. Plants, fruit and flowers for export have been cleaned of soil and specially packed for entry into UK. There is free delivery to the hotel on the eve of your departure so that the boxes can go with your luggage on the aircraft. The owners of Bananera are at hand to answer any questions and will be pleased for you to take photographs. The view of the Orotava Valley is worth a picture too. Note that the bus service runs from 0930 to 1300 hrs and then from 1430 to 1830.

Every Sunday at 1100 hrs there is traditional dancing and Canary wrestling at the Tigaiga Hotel, Puerto de la Cruz. On Wednesday at 1100 hrs, there is a guided tour by an English botanist round the sub-tropical garden of the hotel where every plant is named. The owner of this hotel knows the island well and has prepared several walks of varying duration. Armed with a special leaflet and a packed lunch you can spend an entire day walking in the pines or lush coastal area.

High up in the Cañadas on the side of Mount Teide is the **Refugio de Altavista**, a modern cabin with dormitories, kitchen, lounge and bar. Staffed by local men, it is clean and useful for those who wish to spend a night on the mountain and see dawn break at the summit. Reservations must be made through the Patronato de Turismo in Santa Cruz de Tenerife.

Botanical Gardens

The Botanical Gardens, located on the eastern outskirts of Puerto in Carreterra del Botanico on the north side, were founded long ago in 1788 by orders of Charles II of Spain, as a place where tropical plants arriving from the New World could rest and become acclimatised to new surroundings before further shipment to Europe. Over the years the fame of the gardens has grown. Botanists and tourists delight in the size and colour of the exotic plants. A huge rubber tree, nearly 200 years old, and the orchid houses are among the splendid sights. Open daily from 0900 to 1800 hrs, admission 100 pesetas. A guide is available. We are advised that the gardens are to be enlarged.

Risco Bello, next to the Casino Taoro, is a peaceful garden open to the public daily from 1000 to 1800 hrs. Tel: 38 43 71. Entrance 500 pesetas. Belgian owned, the house has a cafeteria and restaurant. Walk near the Japanese bridge and lake, through grottos and by waterfalls. A useful meeting place in a gracious setting.

Rosaleda is another treat for garden lovers, located in the La Paz area of Puerto. You can take a free bus from the Café Columbus. See over 10,000 roses. Open 0900 to 1700 hrs.

Potteries

From the Café Columbus on the seafront of Puerto de la Cruz, a courtesy bus (free) runs to **El Barco Pottery**, six kilometres away towards Los Realejos. The pottery, park, bar and gardens are open daily from 0900 to 1800 hrs. Sundays 1000 to 1300 hrs. El Barco, where Tenerife pottery is made from Mount Teide clay, has local craftsmen at work making unique ceramic jewellery. Refreshments are available on the terrace. Hand-made pottery is also to be seen at **La Calera Pottery**, Las Arenas. There you can see the pots being thrown, baked and painted. From huge 'Ali Baba' vases to ash trays, they all make charming souvenirs.

Restaurants in Puerto de la Cruz

Restaurants, bars and cafés are open many hours of the day and night serving an enormous range of foods, a truly international cuisine in a bewildering variety of decors. Chinese, Indian, Bavarian, Italian, South American and Canarian, whatever your taste, you are likely to find it in Puerto. A good selection of budget meals can be found in **Calle San Felipe**, which has a vast selection of international restaurants. Approximate price for lunch, 900 pesetas. Dinner will cost about 1200 pesetas including litre of wine. Many places have speciality dishes with coloured photographs showing the meal and price displayed outside the entrance.

To help in your selection you may like to buy a copy of *Here and*

Now. Published in English, the paper costs 75 pesetas fortnightly. It carries lists of recommended eating establishments, plus interesting features on the islands, people and places to visit. You can obtain this tourist paper at local newspaper kiosks and bookshops in the main tourist areas.

In the Puerto de la Cruz area, of interest to visitors and locals alike are the so-called 'chicken-houses'. These are simple bar-restaurants, usually set up in an old garage which is part of the house. Here the entire Canarian family cook meals over wood burning stoves or charcoal grills. It is well worth seeing for local atmosphere; the food is cooked specially to order; chops, steaks and chicken, deliciously crisp and fresh. Prices are reasonable and usually written up on a blackboard.

Los Asadores La Calera. Recently renovated this 'chicken house' also serves tasty charcoal grilled pork dishes. Busy with 'take away' meals. Simple decor and friendly atmosphere. Good value.

Bellman Edif. Lunn, Plaza del Charco, 1st floor, Puerto de la Cruz. Tel: 38 11 10/38 05 70. Open 12.30-23.00 hrs. International cuisine.

Bello Horizonte San Juan de la Rambla. Tel: 36 01 12. French and typical Spanish cuisine. Grilled fresh fish.

Cafe Berlin Avda. Venezuela 11, Puerto de la Cruz. Tel: 38 00 38. Specialising in *Sangria*, Champagne, oysters, and pastries.

Bistro Avda. Generalisimo, Edif. Lavaggi, Puerto de la Cruz. Tel: 38 05 21. Open 5-11 pm. Closed Mon. Pizzeria, steaks.

Bistro Shish-Kebab Canary Centre, Carretera Botanica, Puerto de la Cruz. South European specialities.

Calypso Avda. de Colón (opposite the Lago), Puerto de la Cruz. Tel: 38 10 13. English breakfasts and international cuisine.

Capitan Metro Steak House Calle Cologan 6, Puerto de la Cruz. Tel: 38 04 44. International cuisine.

Castillo de San Felipe Set in genuine old fortress on seafront at western end of town. The first class restaurant has attentive service in an elegant atmosphere. Expensive.

China Avda. Venezuela, Puerto de la Cruz. Specialising in typical Chinese cuisine.

Casino Taoro Parque Taoro, Puerto de la Cruz. Tel: 38 05 50. Restaurant open from 9 pm. International cuisine.

Da Alda Avenida Venezuela 5. Tel: 38 41 70. Specialises in Italian cooking. Open 1200 to 1500 and 1830 to 2300 hrs.

Dorada Bavaria Plaza del Charco, Puerto de la Cruz. Tel: 38 02 52. Typical Bavarian restaurant.

El Caleton Plaza Manuel Ballesteros 14, Punta Brava. Tel: 38 60 55. It is worth the short walk from Loro Parque to reach this quiet restaurant, serving international and Canary dishes.

El Jardin Calle Mequinez 8. Traditional three course Sunday lunch. Chef has spent many years in London. Cheerful eating place with reasonable prices.

El Guanche Calle Dinamarca, Parque Taoro. Tel: 35 58 71. Opposite the Hotel Atalaya in quiet district above the town. This is a *tipico* Canarian restaurant that serves fresh fish and *paella*. often there is Canarian music.

El Pescado Avda. Venezuela 3b (behind Oasis), Puerto de la Cruz. Tel: 38 28 06. International cuisine.

El Pradino Calle de Lomo 17. Tel: 38 29 37. With a low ceiling and busy atmosphere, here you can enjoy authentic Italian cooking, such as picata Milanese, lasagne, tortellini, rigatoni and a selection of meat and fish. In the old town.

Ingrid's Bar Avda. del Generalisimo 20, Puerto de la Cruz. Open 10.30 am-2.30 pm, 6 pm-12 midnight. Closed Sunday. Gammon steak a speciality.

Inca Calle Felipe. This is where you can enjoy South American specialities. Look for it west of the Plaza General Franco.

La Parilla, Hotel Botanico Avda. Richard I. Yeoward, Puerto de la Cruz. Tel: 38 14 00. Five-star international grill.

La Parranda Cruz Verde 2, Puerto de la Cruz. Tel: 38 23 09. Speciality: fresh seafood. Closed Mondays.

La Taberna de Nacha Urb. Tucan, Guarico. Tel: 37 27 64. North of Carretera del Botanico, this bar restaurant serves splendid *tapas* and a traditional Spanish menu. Reasonable prices.

Los Quiquiriquis Las Arenas. Both tourists and locals enjoy this well known restaurant located to the south east of town, near the C820 and Shell petrol station. Huge T-bone steaks are cooked to perfection and are not expensive. Tel: 38 21 59.

Mago Paseo de Dan Juan 24. Tel: 38 38 53. In old part of town and behind Hotel Maga, this clean restaurant specialises in Canarian cooking as well as international. Try the paella but be prepared to wait while it is freshly cooked.

Maracaibo Calle Mequinez. In the old quarter, a friendly cheerful place to take all the family for a nice meal with a wide selection of dishes.

Magnolia Carretera del Botanico 5, near Hotel Molino. Blanco. Tel: 38 56 14. Open from 1300 hrs until midnight. A quiet high class restaurant with elegant atmosphere. Fresh fish and seafood, international and Catalan cuisine, noted for its shoulder of lamb. Owner Felipe has won many awards.

Meson Atlantico Guiz Verde 2. Tel: 38 65 61. Friendly small restaurant near Calle Mequinez, with good and varied menu. Credit cards.

Meson Valle Verde Calle El Penon 4. Tel: 37 06 27. Typical Canarian cooking, this small family restaurant gives good value.

Metro Burger Bar San Telmo 18, Puerto de la Cruz. Open 9.00-24.00 hrs. Specialising in T-Bone steaks, hamburgers, snacks, chicken and chips, English breakfast.

Mi Vaca y Yo Calle Cruz Verde. Tel: 38 52 47. In a rustic setting this well known establishment in the old town serves fresh lobster and fish as well as Canarian and international dishes.

Nino's (Snack Bar), Avda. Generalisimo 7, Edificio Iders, Puerto de la Cruz. Tel: 38 23 53. Specialities: bacon and eggs, steaks and chops.

Old Dutch Avenida Generalisimo (next to Guajara Hotel), Puerto de la Cruz. Tel: 38 19 56. Open daily 12-3 pm and 6-11 pm. Dutch specialities.

Restaurant Paco Carretera Botánico 26, Puerto de la Cruz (opposite Comercial Botánico). Specialising in *paellas* and meat dishes.

Palatino El Lomo 28. Tel: 38 23 74. In the heart of the old town, this *'palacio de la carne'*, good quality restaurant grill is recommended for T-bone steak, meat kebab, roast lamb, barbecue meals and grilled rabbit.

Pizzeria Ristorante da Ernesto Edificio Bahamas, Avenida Generalisimo. Tel: 38 67 02. Open from 1200 until midnight. Italian and international cuisine with a cheerful atmosphere.

Puerto Cruz Calle Perez Zamora. *Tipico* Canarian cooking and local wine. Good value and open every day.

Robin Hood Calle La Hoya, Puerto de la Cruz. Tel: 38 16 14. Dishes to suit all tastes.

Roda Gallega Calle San Felipe 34, Puerto de la Cruz. Tel: 38 03 99. National and International specialities. Open every day.

Rudi's Calle Inocencio Garcia 2 (next to Mercado Común), La Orotava. Tel: 33 32 57. Cafeteria.

Sancho Panza Calle Iriarte 36. Tel: 38 52 38. In a pretty part of the old town and near the shopping centre, this high class restaurant has a wide choice of menu, including fresh fish and lobster, prepared at the table with different sauces.

Tigaiga Hotel Coffee Shop Parque Taoro, Puerto de la Cruz. Tel: 38 52 51. Open daily from 10 am. Snacks and specialities.

Tiroler Alm Canary Centre, Carretera Botanico, Puerto de la Cruz. Tel: 38 24 70. Open 11 am to midnight. Closed Thursdays. Austrian cuisine.

Tosca José Antonio 1, Puerto de la Cruz, near fishing harbour. Self-service. Eat as much as you like for 600 pesetas.

VIP's Restaurant and Coffee Shop Hotel Las Vegas, Puerto de la Cruz. Tel: 38 34 51. Open all day. Light snacks and à la carte menu.

Wimpy Edificio Cariver, San Telmo, Puerto de la Cruz. Tel: 38 23 69. The home of the hamburger.

Other restaurants in north Tenerife

Los Realejos

La Finca La Longuera, 3 km west of Puerto and north of Los Realejos. A good fishing restaurant in country setting. Busy at weekends.

Miramar Urb. Valpariso, Los Realejos. Open daily for lunch and dinner. Hungarian specialities.

La Vera

La Historia West of La Vera. Tel: 38 41 74. Popular Tenerife cooking. Try the *potaje* (stew).

La Montaneta

El Tenderette Carretera El Jardin, south side of C820, Tel: 34 25 94. Excellent Canarian dishes, friendly service, normal prices.

Mesa del Mar

Club Parque Mesa del Mar Between Tacaronte and Mesa del Mar. Tel: 56 13 00. Open daily for lunch and dinner. International cuisine.

San Juan de la Rambla

Bella Horizonte Tel: 36 01 12. French and *tipico Canario* food. Fresh fish.

El Sauzal

La Ermita Los Angeles 66. Tel: 56 39 80. Modern restaurant on west side of road. Noted for fresh fish, sea foods and grilled meats. Open 1300 to 1630 and 1930 to 2300 hrs. Closed Wednesday.

SEVENTEEN

The extreme north coast

Island tour 5

Puerto de la Cruz – Santa Ursula – El Sauzal – Tacoronte – Valle de Guerra – Tejina – Bajamar – Punta del Hidalgo – Tegueste – Santa Cruz: 70 km

There is still more of the coast to explore between Puerto and Santa Cruz. From Puerto de la Cruz take the fast autopista 5, or for a more leisurely drive the C820, which we will now explore. Three miles east is the **Mirador Humboldt**, named after the famous German naturalist, who once described this area as one of the most lovely he had seen in his extensive travels. From there the view looks over the green vegetation of the Orotava Valley and snowcapped Mount Teide, the blue of the Atlantic adding to the scene.

Nearby **Santa Ursula** has a leather goods factory and some tourist souvenir shops which are off the beaten track. Very few tourists visit Santa Ursula so it remains tranquil. The central plaza with its church has pretty gardens, with seats under the tall trees. Old palm trees line the path ways.

Now you are near two places with famous historical names, La Victoria (the Victory) and La Matanza (the Massacre): both are connected with the conquest of the Guanches by the Spanish Conquistadores. Nowadays all is tranquil and rural in La Matanza, there is a small museum which has displays about the history and handiworks of the town.

The C820 now crosses the autopista then winds down to the town of **El Sauzal**. On the way you will pass some good fish restaurants; the locally caught fresh fish is on display awaiting your selection. Many smart villas are built on the hillside, this being a favoured area of business men from Puerto. A fine municipal auditorium at El Sauzal holds classical concerts of high repute.

The hills around **Tacoronte**, the next place of any size, were once a Guanche stronghold. Recently several artefacts and remains have been discovered in the area. The town has two interesting churches, Iglesia de Santa Catalina dating from the sixteenth century and Iglesia del Cristo de Los Dolores, part of a seventeenth-century convent. The slopes of the valleys near to Tacoronte are covered with vines – its Malvasia wines, like a light sherry, are famous and usually about 17% in strength.

Close to Tacoronte is the El Penon Golf Course, an 18-hole course open to visitors. A snack bar and restaurant are in the grounds. Nearby is Los Rodeos Airport.

The route C820 now reaches green fertile countryside, where terraced vineyards cover the slopes. The road twists and turns giving fine sea views. It is a little visited area: just the place for a peaceful drive. On this Tacoronte-Valle de Guerra road look out for the notice that marks the entrance to the **Casa de Carta Ethnographic Museum** (closed Fridays). If you are travelling downhill you may have traffic behind you, so be prepared to cut across the oncoming traffic on this narrow road, or continue past and then turn to be on the correct side for the entrance. If by chance you still miss the entrance, park by the simple bar and walk back down. It really is worth all this effort to see the colourful collection of Canarian costumes and fascinating ancient memorabilia, all nicely displayed in a genuine eighteenth-century mansion.

At the end of the village of **Valle de Guerra** you have a choice of continuing steeply down to the coast, westwards, to El Pris and Mesa del Mar. The latter is a resort popular with people from Puerto. Only a few tourists seek out this quiet northern retreat. Just two kilometres away is El Pris where you may care to walk along the beach or take a dip in the sea water pool. It is necessary to return on the same road to Valle de Guerra.

By driving towards the east, still passing through green agricultural land around **Tejina**, you will then wend downhill by banana plantations until reaching a seaside resort that is gradually becoming better known.

Bajamar, once a fishing village, is being promoted as a tourist centre, with a few hotels and several large apartment buildings. An assortment of shops, a promenade and municipal swimming pools (*piscine municipales*) make up this rather remote resort, which seems to be favoured by German visitors.

Practically joined to it by the Arenal beach is **Punta del Hidalgo**, at the extreme edge of the northern coastline. The town is slightly inland with most of the shops each side of the main street. Other buildings reach up the steep Macizo mountain side. In the middle of town is an unusual large red stone church. If you continue on the main road you will climb to a headland where there is a fine Mirador, with a little plaza that has an impressive statue; it was put up in 1990 to commemorate the writer of Canarian folklore, Sebastián Ramos. Not a lot of parking space, but it is worth stopping for the extensive panorama of very craggy mountains which stop abruptly just before the shore line. Down below, green banana plantations make a striking contrast with the black volcanic rocks, and in places the sea sweeps in creating foaming white pools. From the Mirador a track goes down to a cemetery by the sea at Playa de Los Troches.

Casa de Carta

It comes as a surprise when driving between Tacoronte and Valle Guerra near El Boqueron cross roads to see the sign Ethnographic Museum of Tenerife, a place one would expect to locate in or near a city. Yet it is a clever idea to use this splendidly restored eighteenth-centuy mansion to house a magnificent collection of artefacts relating to the past Canarian way of life.

Set in a spacious garden full of tropical plants and overlooking the agricultural landscape and town of Valle Guerra, the museum atmosphere is tranquil and full of interest.

Well laid out rooms show collections of ancient pottery, weaving and displays of needlework, together with reconstructed bedrooms and a kitchen depicting a past era. Perhaps best of all is the colourful collection of traditional Canarian costumes. At first the black dummy figures seem a little odd, then one realises they are just right to allow one's attention to be held by the wonderful hand woven materials and embroideries of the costumes. The exhibits show men and women in various garbs worn for work and fiestas.

It isa fascinating collection, so do allow plenty of time to have this glimpse into a bygone age of Canarian history.

Back in the centre of Punta del Hidalgo, look for a turning on the sea side with a notice Piscinas Municipales (public swimming pools). Many new villas and apartments line this road which ends in a T-junction by the sea. In front of you is a good fish restaurant that has a sun terrace, although the vista is marred by huge, high rise apartments. This being one of the most northerly points of Tenerife it can be very windy here. At such times the sea is whipped up and huge Atlantic breakers pound the shore sending angry waters surging into the lava rock crevices.

If you wish you can turn right and drive on the track along by the sea, past banana plantations for about two kilometres. It is a nice place for a picnic. On a calm day you can go down some concrete steps and look in the shallow pools for shrimps and tiny crabs, or the family can go fishing. This is a favoured spot for walkers who are able to go round the promontory to Playa de Los Troches. Canarians like to come here, especially at weekends, looking for octopus (*pulpo*) at low tide. Recently work has begun on building a marina and tourist complex here; already a new camping ground is nearly complete.

Hidalgo Point is an old district where many Tinerferos used to divide their life between the oar and the hoe. Like nearly all of the coastline it is hemmed in by mountains. The twin peaks called the Two Brothers are part of a legend about 'forbidden love'.

It is necessary to retrace the route back to Tejina, where you can vary your return by going via **Tegueste**; this is a lovely, quiet country road amongst fertile land. At Las Canteras the road divides, one going north to Las Mercedes, the other takes you into La Laguna. From there it is easy to return to either Puerto de la Cruz or Santa Cruz on the autopista.

EIGHTEEN

Las Cañadas and Mount Teide

It is impossible to go to the island of Tenerife and not be aware of Mount Teide. It is likely that, whether you arrive by sea or by air, you will see the famous snow peak before all else on the island. The volcanic cone, which reaches a height of 3718 m, is the highest peak in all Spain and nearly three times as high as Ben Nevis in Scotland. It is also incredibly beautiful, especially when seen from afar. Often in clear weather the pointed cone rises in great majesty way above a sea of clouds, an ethereal picture of nature in all her glory.

Situated almost centrally in Tenerife, Teide is part of a gigantic age-old crater. During successive volcanic eruptions which took place in this area, ravines and gorges began to form and make the base for this tapering snow-capped mountain. These gorges have been given the name of **Cañadas del Teide** and this area, 19 km in diameter, has now been declared a National Park.

This chapter described four routes leading from the coast to the peak. These roads all give varied landscapes and views on the climb up and down. When they reach the National Park all are dominated by the natural wonder of the Cañadas del Teide. Often snow-covered in winter, sometimes right down to the foot of the slopes, the area is dry and dusty in summer.

The National Park is covered in vegetation despite the inhospitable land. Twisted Canary cedars and pines manage to survive but the most common plant is the Teide broom, *Retama del Pico* which in spring has rosy white flowers that attract bees. The red *Tajinaste*, 'Pride of Tenerife' is a viper's bugloss with a stem of up to seven feet high, remarkable for its size and amazing colour. Other species in the park include the Teide violet and daisy, endemic to Tenerife. These hardy little plants are found at altitudes of 1677m to 2591m, and come into bloom about March.

Visiting strangers can only wonder at the wealth of plant life in this volcanic region. In the winter they will be impressed with the numerous pulvinate plants that are hidden under last year's stiff dry blossom shoots. Fauna in the park are relatively scarce, the *tizon* lizard being the only abundant species, with mountain rabbits numerous. The royal kite, the kestrel and the sparrow hawk are the predators. One of the most beautiful birds is the chaffinch which has a splendid bluish plumage.

Route 1

Santa Cruz (La Laguna) – La Esperanza – Pico de las Flores Mirador – El Portillo – Las Cañadas – Visitors Centre – Mount Teide: 56 kms.

Access to Mount Teide by way of Santa Cruz de Tenerife or La Laguna is by the C824. Clearly signposted out of the towns, it goes along the dorsal ridge of the mountains towards the peak. Views of both the north and south side of the island can be seen. Almost at once you are in the forest of **La Esperanza**. Dense Canary pinewoods lean southwards away from the prevailing winds from the north. On this route you will see many good restaurants, with easy parking especially popular with Tenerifos at weekends. At **Las Raices**, a memorial to commemorate the alliance with General Franco at the beginning of the Spanish Civil War in 1936 is set in a clearing of the woods.

It is a quiet road which twists and turns as one climbs higher, the air becoming fresh. At weekends Canarians enjoy a cool drive here. **Pico de Las Flores Mirador** is a good vantage point to view the contrast of the green cultivated north of the island with the arid dryness of the south. Shortly after passing the view point El Diabillo, you will see the T4133 going left and south to Arafo. This is a scenic route that twists through the *barrancos*. In spring it is ablaze with wild flowers

Continuing our route on the C824, in 14km another turning left leads to the Observatorio de Izaña. From this road there can be fine views of Mount Teide. The public need permission to visit this Observatory. It was here in 1910 that Jean Mascart observed and took the first photograph of Halley's Comet.

El Portillo, at 2000 m, is the meeting place of the Puerto de la Cruz and Esperanza roads. It is also the edge of the National Park and **Las Cañadas**, the volcanic crater. Several large restaurants and car parks serve the needs of the many tourists and coach parties.

This magnificent obelisk in a clearing in the woods near Las Raices, commemorates where General Franco had a meeting place in 1936, at the beginning of the Spanish Civil War.

Just past these restaurants and on the right of the C821 leading to Mount Teide is the entrance to the National Park Visitors Centre. Open to the public from 0900 to 1630 hrs. Closed Sunday and Monday. This is a permanent exhibition describing the Park, together with details of the geology, history, ecology and culture of the Canary Islands. Publications in English are on sale, audio visual shows are given throughout the day, and there are toilet facilities. A network of paths exists in the Park where visitors, including the disabled, can walk. Free interpreter guides take parties from the Visitors Centre, commencing at 0930, 1130 and 1330 hrs. Leaflets giving details can be obtained from Tourist Offices, or telephone 259903 or 256440, Centro de Coordinacion, La Laguna. It is well to remember that altitudes in the park exceed 2,000m and people with heart conditions should consider this before climbing. On the mountain the sun can be extremely hot and sunglasses and a hat should be worn. In winter the weather conditions change quickly and warm clothing is required. Always take drinking water and wear stout footwear.

Do not be put off by these comments for when in Tenerife it is a splendid experience to walk amongst the lava rocks and see the variety of strata left after the past devastations. The flora changes from season to season. To see the plants in bloom, make a visit from the end of March to July; in places the colour is breathtaking and at all times of the year the whole of the Parque Nacional del Teide is superbly panoramic.

Route 2

Puerto de la Cruz – La Orotava – Aguamansa – Las Cañadas – Mount Teide: 104 km return; one day tour by car, taxi or coach

Every day a bus leaves from the bus station in Puerto at 8.30 am for Mount Teide, returning at 16.00.

The road from Puerto de la Cruz and La Orotava, the C821, climbs steadily from sea level, giving striking contrasts of scenery. As buildings give way to cultivation the banana takes over. Acres of these huge leaved plants cover the land, the plantations nearly always surrounded by high concrete walls. Every now and then a plantation is open to the main road, but a deep ditch prevents you from taking the fruit or picking the precious red flower heads, so impressive on first sight.

As the road travels higher, vines take over from bananas, interspersed with small fields of vegetables and cereals. Much of the cultivation is done by hand. The small houses of the country dwellers are bright with pots of red geraniums, poinsettias and bougainvillea. Women work in the fields carrying heavy loads, often balanced on top of their heads.

It will cost about 1,000 pesetas by taxi to reach **La Orotava** (335m) in the heart of the beautiful Orotava Valley south east from Puerto. The town was once a centre for rich merchants who owned sugar cane plantations – now replaced by banana plantations – and it still retains a lot of charm. Many fine seventeenth and eighteenth-century Canarian mansions line the narrow streets, often with huge armorial bearings above the doorways and ornately carved pinewood balconies. The streets in La Orotava have a sense of antiquity.

The central square allows views of those splendid old red-roofed houses, as the ground slopes away towards the sea. In the Plaza Casanas, the principal church is the **Iglesia de la Concepción** originally built in 1503; most of the present structure was completed in 1768. The graceful baroque façade is flanked by high towers. A fabulous collection of trees, shrubs and flowers is to be seen in the Botanical Garden, a small replica of the one in Puerto de la Cruz.

It is in La Orotava at the feast of Corpus Christi that the squares are transformed, not with flowers but wonderful pictures created with coloured sands and pebbles. Religious scenes are clearly depicted in these loving works of art..

Many attractive shops, sometimes in graceful arcades, make shopping a pleasure. Along the Calle San Francisco is the **Casa Los Balcones**, built in 1632, still wonderfully preserved. The huge heavy doors open into a cool paved courtyard, banked with ferns and hanging plants. Now open to the public, it is a School of Embroidery, where young girls can be seen engaged in very intricate work. They smile self-consciously as curious tourists peer over their shoulders.

On display are many island crafts for it is also an *artesania*. Basket work, local costume dolls, shawls, lace tablecloths and also goods from mainland Spain are for sale. Prices are reasonable. Upstairs one is able to walk along the wooden balcony into huge high rooms, sparsely furnished with antiques and paintings. The ancient floors creak at one's tread and there is an aura of past history.

Leaving La Orotava still on the C821 the views are breathtaking as one looks down over the green valley and Puerto de la Cruz by the blue sea.

At **Aguamansa**, altitude 1,000m, there is a trout farm, carpark, arboretum, picnic tables and toilets. A kilometre beyond the carpark is a side road that branches off to the left, from there one can walk round the Caldera crater to see the columns of lava rocks shaped like organ pipes, Los Organos.

Further up, the pine trees grow quite dense and the air smells sweetly of wood and resin. It is in this area that forest walks have been marked and many botanical rarities can be found among the prolific Canary flora. In the course of five marked walks (which no visitor should miss) interested observers will become acquainted with a multitude of plants in their natural habitat. Several very good books have been written on the subject. *The Five Most Worthwhile Walks* and *The Flora of the Canary Islands*, the latter written by Hubert Moeller, will prove very informative.

At **El Portillo** the C821 road converges with the C824 from Santa Cruz and continues to climb until it reaches the **National Park of Mount Teide** and **Las Cañadas**. Las Cañadas means the ravines or gorges that were created by geological erruptions in remote times. All the gorges are different in size and have individual names.

Route 3

Playa de las Americas – Guia de Isora – Chio – Mount Teide: 60 km.

The third route goes from Playa de las Americas on the C822 to Guia de Isora and on to Chio, where the way is signposted to Las Cañadas. However, if you like narrow roads and wish to get off the beaten track, then make a short cut by going through Aripe and Chirche (or Chiguergue). Both roads are steep and afford good views of the busy coast; here all is rural with cactus and farmsteads (*fincas*) growing wheat, oranges, almonds and figs. In spring time wild flowers bloom and the bird song is sweet

This is a quiet route with little traffic and you will get a glimpse of Mount Teide as you climb higher. If the sky is clear you probably also have a distant view of La Palma and La Gomera to the west above a carpet of clouds. Soon Montana Chinyero (1510m) comes into sight. This is where in the year 1909 the last volcanic eruption in Tenerife happened. Further on, if you wish for a break from driving, there is a recreational zone on the right. Near **Montana de Cuevacitas** (1800m) another parking place allows you to walk and maybe visit some caves. Some aforestation on this route seems successful and the pines help to improve the stark volcanic landscape, they also make the air fragrant. Finally, when you sight Pico Viejo's dark crater (3120m) which erupted in 1798 you will come to a T-junction and join the road from Vilaflor at Boca de Tauce (see Route 4).

Route 4

Los Cristianos – Vilaflor – Boca del Tauce – Las Cañadas – Mount Teide: 62 km; half or one day tour by car or taxi

The tour from Los Cristianos starts on the TF511 signed to Arona. You immediately start climbing on a good road and soon reach the pretty village of Chayofa, which is becoming an upmarket development for residents who wish for a quiet, elevated position with good views of the coast. **Arona** is an important town with jurisdiction over Los Cristianos. The town hall is at the top of the town where you find a bank, shops, bars and restaurants. On the outskirts of Arona turn left on to the T5112 for Vilaflor and Las Cañadas. There is a petrol station on the right side. Climbing all the time, this scenic route gives panoramic views of the mountains.

Much of the agricultural land now lies to waste with farmhouses deserted, doubtless their inhabitants prefer to work in the tourist areas. In a few homesteads vines, figs, almonds and some cereals are still grown.

About 1km from Vilaflor you will reach the attractive Centro Artesania 'Chasna', worth a stop for refreshments and to see the well laid out display of Canarian handicrafts. It is interesting to note that the building was originally a factory for making cutlery set up by an Austrian who lived here for health reasons. If you visit in May and June you will see the *tajinaste* or viper's bugloss, the amazing Pride of Tenerife flower, whose reddish spike blossom comes before the leaves. The plant can grow to three metres.

You reach **Vilaflor**, at 1450 m the highest town in Tenerife. By then the air has lost its salty tang and is cool and fresh. Terraces of potatoes are cultivated in volcanic dust, tomatoes cling to bamboo canes and in the fields straw-hatted workers gather the crops into straw panniers, for transport to market. A few kilometres outside Vilaflor you reach the Pino Gordo viewpoint and a little higher up the road the picnic place of Las Lajas, where there are toilets, water and barbecue facilities. At **Montana Colorado** there are great red faced cliffs, some covered with cactus. Later the road encircles a huge laurel and pine forest.

As you drive higher you are likely to encounter what is sometimes called a 'cloud sea'. This is caused by the cold moist air, brought in from the north by the trade winds, making contact with the warm mountain slopes. Because of a further upper layer of warmer, drier air the cloud is prevented from rising and can be a thickness of 300 to 500m. It is a strange sensation to go from the sunshine by the coast, then into thick white cloud and thankfully the bright sunshine again as one gets nearer to Mount Teide. It is fun to bet on who sees Mount Teide first!

At **Boca del Tauce**, 2055 m, the road merges with the C823, and continues into the Cañadas del Teide and the National Park. The abrupt change in the scenery is very startling and spectacular, going from pine forest to volcanic rock scenery. It is from the Boca del Tauce area that the coloured rocks are collected and crushed to make the sand carpet at La Orotava at Corpus Christi.

Las Cañadas is the name of the ancient crater area from whose centre, at 2000m, surged the most recent Teide volcano, which erupted in 1909. The central cone is **Mount Teide**, 3718 m. All around this splendid mountain is a high plateau some 80 kilometres in circumference, the remains of molten lava which has poured from the bowels of the earth in great waves of destruction.

This surprisingly level place is a wilderness, with lava rocks and black cinder-like clinkers of enormous size; it looks like the remains of a huge coke fire. The road cuts across this strange land, so quiet and awesome. Some extraordinary coloured rocks are called Los Azulejos, after the ceramic tiles made in mainland Spain. They glint with the blue-green lustre of copper oxide. Elsewhere are areas of sand and pumice stone, the whole place seems strange and unbelievable.

Having passed Los Azulejos, on the right is a dirt track which goes for half a kilometre into the lava bed. A barrier across the road and some rest huts stop further progress. But do leave your car and walk on. For nature lovers and botanists this is a fascinating experience, almost too awesome to believe, for all around is the wonder of this great National Park. The track will eventually reach the Teide Visitors Centre.

At the centre of the volcanic plain stand unique lava boulders, uncovered by erosion, strange shapes against the blue sky. Known as **Los Roques de Garcia**, they are featured on many posters and postcards of Tenerife. Their weird configuration attracts all who visit Mount Teide.

A large parking place and viewpoint has been made to enable hordes of visitors to scramble happily amongst the boulders and crags – an international convention of tourists all bent on being photographed at this, the most spectacular sight in Tenerife. A large picnic area allows people to linger. People chatter happily in the rarified air, the hardy will even sunbathe if the day is particularly warm.

Close by the picnic place, the National Parador stands alone, surely one of the most remote of these establishments. It is a unique experience to stay in this 23 room *parador*, which is situated at 2,200 m, in splendid isolation amidst volcanic craters and just below the mighty peak of Mount Teide, which is often snow-capped. It is especially memorable in the evening light and early dawn when there are few guests about. Furnishing is not spectacular but the huge log fire is cosy and we found the Canarian cooking very tasty, particularly the rabbit stew. Take warm clothes.

The main road continues to the foot of the final slope of Mount Teide. A *teleferico* (cable car) takes 33 passengers up to within walking distance (about three quarters of an hour) of the summit, weather permitting. It is a breathtaking experience (literally, for the altitude is not for people with respiratory or heart complaints) walking over loose volcanic scree and sulphur smoke holes, some 24m deep and 48m wide, to the cone edge which is 914m from the crater floor. Remember to take warm clothes and stout shoes, for even on a brilliantly sunny day, the air will be sharply cold.

At the summit the views are stupendous, looking out over Tenerife, Gran Canaria, El Hierro and La Palma. In the foreground is the Pico Viejo crater, geologically unrelated, for its last eruption was in 1798. The mighty Atlantic spreads its blue cloak around these blessed islands.

Many brochures refer to Tenerife as "The Island of Eternal Spring' or "A basket of flowers floating in the sea'. Both these statements seem strangely true. At all times the weather is mild and spring-like, and the wide variety of flora is a delight to botanists and amateur gardeners alike. Areas of great colour and beauty abound. Even in the island's hot and dry places, the hard toil of the country dwellers has turned the valleys into green fertile areas, the fishing ports and hillside villages add character to this island of variety. Peaceful plazas with imposing churches, cool avenues of age-old trees where children play and chatter like starlings, deep dark forests, sweetly fragrant, offer pleasant contrasts to the tourist domains. Tenerife is indeed an island for everyone.

(Opposite) Top: *The Municipal Market, open daily, in Santa Cruz de La Palma. Note the stallholders' clean white clothing and the hygenic surroundings.*
(Opposite) Bottom: *Carnaval Blanca is the time when the Palmeros dress in white, tropical clothes and talcum powder is thrown over everyone, in a friendly manner!*

NINETEEN

Introducing La Palma

The pretty Island

La Palma (La Isla Bonita) is the most north-westerly and perhaps the most beautiful of all the Canary Islands, although each has its own special attractions. Seen from afar, whether from the air or the sea, this pear-shaped island is a mass of many shades of green. Tall dark forests of waving palm trees and thick banana plantations mingle with fields of broad-leafed tobacco and fruit orchards. The mountainsides are covered with dense vegetation, only the volcanic peaks are in sharp contrast.

San Miguel de la Palma (to give the island its full name) has an area of 726 sq km. In the centre lies the world's largest volcanic crater called the **Caldera de Taburiente**, now declared a National Park. The crater has a circumference of almost 27 km, with the base of the crater descending to a depth of 763m. The island's highest peaks encircle the crater: **Roque de los Muchachos** (2423m), **Pico de la Cruz** (2351m), **Pico de la Nieve** (2230m) and **La Cumbrecita** (1883m). All are thickly forested and very beautiful.

(Opposite) *The winding roads of La Palma mean that travel is slower than expected, but the views of mountains and valleys are impressive. This is near El Time.*

LA PALMA

Scale 1:365 000

0   5   10 km

The population of La Palma is 80,000 and it is among the few places in the world where there is no real poverty. A large proportion of the inhabitants own land and have plenty of work, and no one is in real need. It is noticeable how well-built and sturdy are all the buildings in both town and countryside. People are well dressed, neat and tidy, quiet of manner and friendly towards visitors. Yet it is a well-known fact that they owe their wealth and ease to the high incomes derived from their thriving export markets, and many of them see little need to expand the tourist trade.

Indeed, although only six hours by sea from Tenerife (which lies to the south-east) the island is not on the usual itinerary for tourists and, until recently, there has been little accommodation for visitors. High-rise apartments and hotels are being built along the coast at **Playa de Cancajo**, where there are pleasant sandy coves suitable for tourists, the black sands and lava rock are impressively different. Bars and restaurants are being opened at inland beauty spots, with scenic routes signposted.

However, for the moment La Palma is still a haven of peace and quiet, delightfully green, with vivid contrasts of scenery, few beaches and shops, but quiet coves and small bars; wonderful panoramic views, impressive volcanic craters, terraces of abundant crops and a warmth that is almost constant the year round.

La Palma is easily reached by air and by a ferry that takes cars and caravans though it is not recommended that the latter are used for touring, because of the steep terrain and the poor surface of some of the country roads. Particularly careful driving is required at all times because of the tortuous nature of most of the roads.

History

Although little is certain concerning Guanche history, it is known that the Spanish had a hard time conquering La Palma. It is said that de Lugo managed to lure the Guanches out of their natural fortress, the volcanic crater of **Caldera Taburiente**, by inviting them to a peace conference; but the Spanish then slaughtered many and enslaved the rest. Tanausú, King of Acero, an unsubmissive Guanche chief, preferred to starve himself to death rather than submit to the conquerors but he was finally captured in the Barranco del Riachuelo (Ravine of the Stream).

The conquest of La Palma by the Spanish finally took place in 1492, when it was incorporated into the Crown of Castile. The

following year Alonso Fernandez de Lugo returned to confirm the
submission of the native Guanches; disembarking at the port on 3rd
May 1493 he named the town **Santa Cruz** (Holy Cross).

From the sixteenth century, Santa Cruz welcomed a great number
of Spaniards from every region. Flemings, French and Italians settled
there, and traces of these ethnic origins can be observed in the local
people today. Although attacked repeatedly by European and Berber
pirates, the port of Santa Cruz flourished. In 1585 Sir Francis Drake
was repelled and his flagship sunk.

La Palma with its rich soil and profitable exports of sugar, bananas,
tobacco and Malmsey wine became a place where merchants built
grand houses, some of which still remain. Fine churches were
adorned with gold, silver and jewels brought back from Mexico and
Chile; and with so much timber and water available ship-building
became of prime importance. Today, La Palma is prosperous with a
modern airport that opens the island to the outside world. Most
Palmeros are involved in agriculture and fishing, while cigar making,
basket work and embroidery add to the island's stable economy.

La Bajada de La Virgen

In La Palma this most important fiesta is held every five years in June.
The last occasion was in 1990, the next occurs in 1995. If you wish to
visit La Palma in the year of the Bajada, book early as many
emigrants from Central America return for the festivities.

The Palmeros are often dressed in traditional folk costume. The
women wear long, full skirts, sometimes with lace aprons and
beautifully embroidered white blouses, white head scarves are topped
by small straw hats with coloured ribbons. The men have white shirts
with black and red waistcoats, their short black trousers have
cummerbunds and thick long white socks are worn with soft suede
shoes. Unique black and red caps have ear flaps and hang down at the
back of the neck.

The Descent of the Virgin, the Bajada, is a month long fiesta
starting with the tiny Holy Image being taken from the Church of El
Salvador in Santa Cruz. During the month there are parades, bands
playing and dancing in the streets. Canary wrestling takes place and
the Dialogue between the Castile and the Ship involves the replica of
the Santa Maria.

A great attraction is the Dance of the Dwarfs, when normal sized
men disguise their height by wearing mock naval uniform and outsize
admirals cocked hats. At another event men on stilts dress as giants
with large heads. These celebrations always end with a huge firework
display.

Calendar of festivals and fiestas

Jan 17   Fiesta de San Antonio (Fuencaliente)
Feb 02   Fiesta de San Blas (Mazo)
Feb   Winter Festival (Santa Cruz de la Palma)
Mar 03   Fiesta de San Vincente (Garafia)
Mar 19   Fiesta del Patriarch San José (Fuencaliente and Breña
           Baja)
May/Jun   Corpus Christi, everywhere (especially Mazo and
           Santa Cruz de la Palma)
Jun   (every fifth year) La Bajada de la Virgen (Santa Cruz),
           the descent of the Virgin.
Aug/Sep   Fiesta de la Virgen de las Nieves (Santa Cruz de la
           Palma)

Climate

La Palma is affected by the moisture-carrying trade winds. Rain falls plentifully from November to the end of March, but the variation of temperature is slight. Sea temperature makes it possible to swim all the year round.

The annual average temperature is 20°C, in summer it can reach 28°C, while in winter it goes no lower than 14°C, except on the high peaks.

What to wear

Summer-weight clothes and beachwear are required, but take something warmer for the evenings and for excursions to the mountains, a wind-proof jacket and sturdy shoes. During the winter, raincoat and umbrella could be useful, as La Palma has the highest amount of rainfall in all the Canaries. The local *Palmeros* can be seen wearing winter clothing during January and February.

Some places of interest in La Palma

Barlovento (38 km) Very small quiet farming village in the north. Scenic narrow road mainly along coast, can be reached by bus or car. Views, bar, restaurant.

Breña Alta, Breña Baja (8 km) These 'high' and 'low' twin towns are inland. Command splendid views over green agricultural land and the coast. Tobacco factory can be visited at Breña Alta.

Caldera Taburiente (33 km) National Park in the centre, with one of the largest volcanic craters in the world. Huge pine forests, ferns, craggy mountains. Roque de los Muchachos 2423 m. Spectacular view points, good roads from Los Llanos and Santa Cruz.

El Paso (31 km) Prosperous town in the centre of island, good views surrounding mountains and forests.

Fuencaliente (33 km) The most southerly village, in pine forests. Vineyards, which produce Malmsey wine.

Garafia (53 km) Remote northern village difficult to reach due to poor roads. Cattle area.

Las Nieves (3 km) Tiny village, beautiful seventeenth-century church. Sanctuary of La Virgen de la Nieves (Our Lady of the Snows). Orange and lemon groves.

Los Llanos de Aridane (32 km) The second most important town. Busy market, good shopping. Impressive views of mountains above the flat agricultural plain which surrounds the town. Sixteenth-century church, almond, fig and banana cultivation.

Los Sauces (30 km) A region of hamlets and woods in the north east. A narrow road winds through valleys, hills and sugar cane plantations. The town has an imposing church in a central square.

Mazo (17 km) School of Craftsmanship open to the public. Nearby is the Cueva de Balmaco, which has famous prehistoric inscriptions.

Playa de Cancajo (5 km) On the east coast near to Santa Cruz, series of black sandy coves, black lava rocks, good swimming, beach café and restaurant. Parking and apartments.

Puerto Naos (42 km) A small tourist village on the west coast with the best beach of black sand.

Puntagorda (59 km) Northwest village with not too well surfaced roads. Among almond and pine trees, white houses, heather, peaceful rural atmosphere.

Puntallana (8 km) Tiny village near coast northeast of Santa Cruz. Scattered houses, green fields and woods. Sea views, narrow winding road.

Santa Cruz (Capital) Dignified busy port. Historic old buildings. Canarian wooden balconies, church, *parador*, hotels, restaurants, market, souvenirs, narrow streets, pebble beach.
Tazacorte (36 km) Small town, centre of island's banana production on west coast. Tiny fishing harbour.
Volcan San Antonio, Volcan Teneguia (33 km) In extreme south, amazing volcanic cones and wastelands. Teneguia erupted 1971. Lava and rocks still retain heat. Spectacular.

Beaches

The coast line of La Palma is mostly rugged with steep cliffs and few beaches, none of which are golden sands. Once one gets used to the idea of sitting on a black sand beach it can be just as enjoyable as any other colour. However it may be wise not to wear a white swim suit as the particles may cling and make it look grubby.

The most accessible beaches are at Playa Cancajo, Playa Charco, Puerto Naos, Playa Tazacorte and Playa Zamora.

Getting about

Some of the roads on the island are well engineered but can nevertheless be difficult, owing to the steep terrain. In the north the surface can be very rough, with potholes; however, road improvements are steadily making touring less arduous.

Taxi
A day tour of the island, by arrangement with the driver, could cost about 8,000 pesetas. A taxi to the airport from Santa Cruz is 400 pesetas.

Buses
Buses leave Santa Cruz de la Palma from Avenida Maritima and Avenida Blas Perez Gonzalez for Los Sauces, Barlovento and Garafia, Los Llanos de Aridane and Fuencaliente. These run to most areas, but to the more remote places there is only one bus a day. To Los Sauces and Barlovento there is an almost hourly service. The single fare from Santa Cruz to Barlovento, in the north, is 220 pesetas.

Coach
A coach tour of the southern part of the island (8 hours) includes lunch and visits volcanoes, a tobacco factory and wine caves; the cost is 2,400 pesetas. Book through Viajes Insular (travel agents) in Plaza de España 2, Santa Cruz de la Palma, Tel. 41 11 10. Plaza España, Los Llanos de Aridane. Tel: 46 04 59.

Self drive car hire
This is an island that can be enjoyed with the use of a rented car. There are numerous car firms, including Avis, with all types of vehicles and the usual hire procedure.

A selection of accommodation

Accommodation is not easy to find in La Palma, where they are only just beginning to accept tourists. Playa Cancajo, close to Santa Cruz de la Palma, is now being developed as a tourist *urbanizacion*, aimed predominantly at the German market with apartments being booked in Germany. One British tour operator, Paloma, use the Parador. Classic Collection feature five hotels in La Palma.

Santa Cruz de la Palma
Maritimo * Hotel. Avenida Maritimo 80. Santa Cruz de la Palma. Tel: 41 63 40. A newly erected modern style hotel run by Canarians. It has 69 rooms, nicely furnished with bathroom and terrace, some with a sea view. Minibar, telephone, TV, video. A restaurant, coffee room and small lounge make this a pleasant place as a base for touring La Palma.
San Miguel * Hotel. Avenida Puente 33. Tel: 41 12 43. 72 rooms are furnished in simple Spanish style, with bathrooms. An old type of hotel, the staff speak little English. The ground floor bar is busy with Palmeros.
Parador Nacional de Santa Cruz de la Palma * Hotel. Avenida Blas Perez Gonzalez, Santa Cruz. Tel: 41 23 40. 32 rooms, TV, telephone. Old Canarian building with attractive wooden balconies, on Santa Cruz seafront. Pebble beach. Price for double room per night 6500 pesetas. The interior is not disappointing, for furniture, paintings and carpets are of the high quality that is associated with these national tourist hotels. Its large reception has an imposing carved staircase; upstairs there are twenty-eight bedrooms, all comfortably furnished and with telephones. Those facing the sea

have their own balconies. There is, of course, a bar, and services include a lift and foreign currency exchange. The manager speaks English and his friendly manner makes guests feel very welcome. Service is polite and attentive.

Aparthotel Castillete *** Hotel Apartments. Avenida Maritima 75. Tel: 42 08 40. Fax: 42 00 67. 36 Studio apartments, 3 double rooms all with sea view, solarium, pool, jacuzzi, minibar, laundry facilities. Cafeteria open to the public. Functional base for touring.

Barlovento

Romantica, **** Hotel. Barlovento. Here is a hotel ideal for honeymooners and anyone who wishes for first class accommodation which is situated in an isolated and elevated position in the north east of La Palma. Recently built in traditional Canarian casa style with pine balconies and wood floors. Log fires make a tranquil and romantic atmosphere. The 34 rooms and 5 suites are pleasantly furnished with views overlooking the green countryside. Amongst the facilities is an astronomical observatory with the latest equipment for star gazing under La Palma's clear skies. A modern gymnasium, indoor and outdoor swimming pools, tennis and an automatic bowling alley makes this hotel attractive for all age groups. An excellent restaurant has attentive staff and pleasing decor. Because this hotel is at 500m it is suggested that you take some warm clothing for cooler evenings.

Cancajo

Hacienda San Jorge Tel: 41 30 71. Fax: 43 45 28. Although recently built these 164 architect designed apartments are constructed in a colourful way to represent the old style Canarian houses with wooden balconies. In the centre of the modern complex is a large swimming pool cum lake with lush tropical garden surrounds and sun terraces. A la carte restaurant, video TV room, solarium, jacuzzis, children's play park, laundry service.

Garafia

San Antonio Pension. Vila de Garafia. Tel: 40 00 15. In the rural north of La Palma, this tiny pension offers basic rooms with a restaurant and a bar. Canarian cooking. In winter the roads may be impassable.

Los Llanos de Aridane

Valle Aridane *** Hotel. Tel: 46 26 00. Fax: 46 25 71. 42 rooms with full bathroom, TV, telephone and safe. This small friendly hotel is situated in a central situation close to the market. Breakfast room, TV lounge, solarium. Restaurants are short walk. The owner speaks good English and is helpful.

Eden * Hotel Residencia. Angel 1. Tel: 46 01 04. 15 rooms, some with bath, situated in centre of the town. No restaurant but bars and cafés nearby.

Puerto Naos

Sol La Palma **** Hotel. Punta del Pozo. Tel: 48 04 00. Fax: 48 09 04. 308 rooms with balconies and colour TV. Also three blocks of apartments. In a pleasant position directly in front of the sea by the sandy beach of Puerto Naos. This modern hotel is similar to other Sol hotels which are noted for their wide range of sports and entertainments for all age groups. Meals are buffet style except in the à la carte restaurant. Cafeteria bar by the swimming pool and sun terraces. Hairdresser, shopping centre, supermarket, gymnasium, bowling alley and tennis courts. 35 km from airport.

Camping

There are two places on La Palma which are official picnic and camping sites. There is no need to have permission to use these if you are only there for a picnic. Should you wish to camp you are advised to get a permit by either writing or telephoning to Unidad Insular de la Vice Consejeria de Medio Ambiente (Environment Agency), Plaza de La Constitucion, Santa Cruz de La Palma. Tel: 41 15 83.

If you are on the island you can apply direct to the Casa Forestal at El Paso for the El Pilar Camp or the Casa Forestal at Barlovento for La Laguna Camp.

The site at **El Pilar** is high up amongst a forest of pine trees and near to a volcanic crater, a region that is used for organised walks. It can be reached by taking the road from Santa Cruz de La Palma toward El Paso and Los Llanos de Aridane. Soon after you have been through the long tunnel look out for a left turn marked Refugio El Pilar. This is quite a steep way up a dirt track leading along the slopes of the Cumbria Vieja. On the right can be seen the lava from the 1585 eruption; Volcan San Juan still has little vegetation. Continue uphill through the forest trees until you reach the campsite. Here in an open area you will find camping, picnic tables, barbecues with ready chopped wood, toilets, cold showers, water taps and a children's playground. It is well to remember that it can be quite cool here at night being over 1,400m high. This camp can also be reached from Breña Alta and San Isidro.

Quite a different sort of picnic and camping park is at **La Laguna**, near Barlovento, where an open space by the side of a large reservoir, with views over the green countryside and to the coast 702m below, has been enclosed. Here are modern toilet blocks, water taps, barbecues, picnic tables and a marked camping area. In summer there is a bar. It is a notable place for bird watching and walking.

Both these parks have some level ground suitable for motorcaravans. At present no charge is made for camping at either of these recreational parks (*parques recreativos*).

Shopping

La Palma has no large department stores. There are supermarkets, with a *mercado* (fresh food market) in the bigger towns. All normal requirements can be met in main centres, and in villages small shops have a wonderful assortment of commodities. Specialities are: beautifully made basket work, embroideries including locally-produced silk, hand rolled cigars (*puros*) made from locally-grown tobacco and of high repute; almond cheese (*queso de almendra*); almond biscuits; almond honey; *rapaduras* (a sweet made from *golfio* and honey). Malvasia wine, available sweet or dry, is light and pleasant and suitable as an aperitif. A unique kind of gilded pottery is hand-made on the island. This may be seen at the School of Handicrafts Centre in **Mazo**, which is 17 km from Santa Cruz de la Palma. Visitors welcome.

Nightlife and leisure pursuits

For your entertainment in La Palma you will mainly depend on going for a meal at a restaurant, unless your visit coincides with a *fiesta*, when you can enjoy processions and folk dancing. The larger hotels and bars have TV and at the Sol La Palma Hotel in Puerto Naos, live entertainment is presented several nights a week.

The island has some ideal areas for walking, especially in the ancient forest of Los Tilos and the Cumbrecitas of the Caldera, but it is wise to go with a group. The Viajes Insular, travel agent, in Santa Cruz de la Palma organise walking tours.

Restaurants

Santa Cruz de la Palma

Bar Canarias Avenida Maritima. Tel: 41 10 00. Close to the port, local dishes and snacks.

Bistro La Placeta Situated in a picturesque plaza, amongst old buildings. Specialities beef stroganoff, roast meats and local puddings.

El Chino Calle Pedro Poggio 7. Tel: 41 67 24. A Korean family-run clean restaurant, which is easily located uphill behind Plaza El Salvador. Canarian and Chinese dishes.

El Faro Avenida Maritima 27. Tel: 41 28 90. Founded in 1936, this small bar and tiny restaurant is always popular. The cooking is very good and prices moderate.

El Parral Calle del Castillete 7. Tel: 41 39 15. This pizzeria is in front of the Castillo de Santa Catalina. The cuisine is Italian and there are Chinese type dishes.

Out of town

Parrilla Chipi-Chipi Between Los Nieves and La Concepcion. Tel: 41 10 24. An attractive patio and bar, in the mountains above Santa Cruz. Serves delicious grilled chicken and pork. Sometimes the local folk group sing here, which makes a wonderful cheerful evening.

La Fontana Near the beach at Cancajo. Tel: 43 42 50. Here you can enjoy international dishes that include salmon, seafoods and pastas.

Parrilla Las Nieves Tel: 41 76 00. Close to the church, this grill house serves up very good meat dishes, especially pork and goat.

Barlovento

Romantica Barlovento. Tel: 45 08 21. An attractive restaurant in this delightful hotel offers an international menu, with friendly polite service.

Breña Bajo

Casa Pancho La Polvacer, by cross roads Hoyo de Mazo. Tel: 43 48 34. Specialities local cuisine and fish dishes.

Las Chozas By Cross of St. Antony. Tel: 43 41 53. This is the place to enjoy grilled pork, rabbit, tripe and fish.

El Paso

Las Piedras Near the road to La Cumbrecita. Noted for Venezuelan cuisine and grilled meats. This large restaurant is used by coach excursions and for local weddings. Night club.

Bar Nao At km 6 on the road to Puerto Naos. Tel: 46 35 92. Fresh fish and fried *calamares* (squid) prepared daily.

Garafia

Santo Domingo Tel: 40 00 15. If you reach as far north as this *tipico* small restaurant, you will really have seen a lot of this beautiful island. The menu will depend on when you arrive and what is in the pot!

Jedey

Casa Evangelina Tel: 46 16 05. On the main C832 from Fuencaliente to Las Manchas. Family run, *tipico* Canarian menu, used by coach tours, good value and friendly.

Los Llanos de Aridane

San Petronio Signposted before the town. Tel: 46 24 03. This pizzeria is reputed to be one of the best Italian cuisines on La Palma. Also noted for fine desserts prepared by an expert Italian chef.

Puerto Espindola

Meson del Mar The fish is freshly cooked at this simple restaurant by the sea.

Puerto Naos

Sol La Palma Punta del Pozo. Tel: 48 04 00. Hot and cold buffet lunch and dinner. Hotel à la carte restaurant with international specialities.

TWENTY

Santa Cruz de la Palma

A striking sight as one enters the harbour of Santa Cruz de la Palma are the huge, green, forest-clad ravines, to the north, deeply indented and stretching down the very edge of the town in a uniform pattern, as if fashioned by hand rather than by nature. The white buildings, too, seem to be ranged neatly together in a tidy pattern, giving the impression that they are modern, even newly-built. But, as one discovers later when exploring the town, there are here many fine old buildings of historic interest and great architectural beauty with steep, narrow roads running between them.

La Palma's capital and main port of Santa Cruz (population 80,000) is in fact, a town of considerable dignity and calm, a restful place which never seems crowded or noisy.

Town tour 1

Avenida Maritima – Parador Nacional – Castillo de Santa Catalina – Barco de la Virgén – Iglesia de San Francisco: about 2 hours, walking

Leaving the port, turn right into the **Avenida Maritima**, which follows the seafront the full length of the town. On the left is the tall building of the **Cabildo Insular**, the council offices. A little further along are some striking examples of Canarian architecture: old houses in ornate style, with beautifully carved balconies, decorated in various patterns and colours. These are carved from native laurel and pine, and have stood the test of time. It is hoped that they will be preserved for many years.

Along here the sea comes close to the road and there is a beach of large pebbles, but no attempt has been made to improve it for swimming. There is a large car park, dusty and uneven. Several small shops, bars and offices mingle along the sea front, and there are cafés with tables and chairs on the pavement, where it is pleasant to take a drink in the shade of the oleander trees.

Halfway along the Avenida Maritima is La Palma's National Tourist Inn, the Parador, which has been carefully constructed to blend in with the older buildings. The brown and white façade has a series of balconies supported on a lower level by wide rectangular windows.

Los Indianos, Carnaval Blanca

The origin of the Carnaval Blanca goes back to the time when the poor people of La Palma emigrated and went to Mexico, Chile, Venezuela and the West Indies to seek their fortune. Some were successful and returned later dressed in fine clothes, many bringing black servants with them. Naturally the resident Palmeros were envious, so it was decided that at the time of the Carnaval everyone would dress up in clothes suggesting that they, too, were the returning wealthy. The most popular garb is a panama straw hat and white suit or full long white frock, and carrying a suitcase. Some like to black their faces and dress as servants.

Added to this an extra feature now is the use of talcum powder on the face to denote their wealthy status. This has now developed into the prime feature of the Carnaval Blanca, because everyone sprinkles talcum powder all over each other as an uproarious joke. The air is filled with it and the ground becomes white and slippery, all in harmless good fun.

Further along on the seafront is the **Castillo de Santa Catalina**, a seventeenth-century fortress and national monument. Beyond, at the end of Avenida Maritima, the road curves round into the **Avenida de las Nieves** (the road to the north) and just past the **Cuartel de la Policia Armada** (naval headquarters) one is confronted with an impressive sight – a full size replica of Christopher Columbus's ship, the **Santa Maria**, looking with its tall masts and rigging, amazingly real. Yet it is made out of concrete and now houses a naval museum with scale models of Christopher Columbus's ships, marine artefacts, maps, old flags and documents of naval interest. The **Barco de la Virgén**, as it is called locally, features prominently in the island's main fiesta during August and September – the fiesta of the Virgen de las Nieves – when it is dressed overall with flags and flowers. The Ship is open from 1000 to 1300 and 1600 to 1900 hrs daily. Entrance costs 100 pesetas.

The nearby **Church of San Francisco** is in a square which is paved and cool with leafy trees and tall palms – just the place for a shady rest after sightseeing.

Town tour 2

Avenida de Alvarez – Calle O'Daly – Plaza de España – Iglesia de San Salvador – Market: about 2 hours walking

Returning to the quay (*muelle*) by way of **Avenida de Alvarez**, and across the road at the beginning of the **Carretera General al Sur** (the road to the south) is the very grand old post office building, **Correos y Telegrafos**. Further along the General al Sur is a yacht club (**Servicio Náutico**) which is used by yachts, both large and small, for provisioning and overhaul before they set off into the vast Atlantic and for the Americas.

Calle O'Daly (named after an Irish businessman who came to the island in the early days) commences near the post office and runs parallel with Avenida de Alvarez and the seafront. It is one of the most important and attractive streets in Santa Cruz de la Palma for commerce, shopping, and sightseeing and it is the town's social centre. It is narrow, cobbled and lined with splendid houses built by some of the island's wealthy merchants a very long time ago. Many have little carved wooden balconies and huge doors embellished with heavy locks and knockers. When these are open it is possible to get a fleeting glimpse of a bygone age – inner courtyards bright with colour and cool with glazed tiles, fountains and green foliage.

Amongst the interesting small shops on the south side of Calle O' Daly (sometimes referred to as Calle Real), look for Artesania Tamanca at No. 29. You may like to purchase some shirts or blouses imported from Guatemala, the colours are very bright, the design and embroidery interesting.

At the time of writing The Tourist Information Office is located next to the Banco Santander: you may have to look hard to see the brass plaque. On the opposite side of the road is the Cafeteria La Palma.

To the north end of Calle O'Daly is the heart of the town, the **Plaza de España**, an elegant setting for the parish church of San Salvador and the impressive *Ayuntamiento* (town hall) built 1563, and the Real Convento de la Immaculada Concepción, with a statue of Philip II in whose reign it was built. This tiny square is a tourist's delight, especially for the keen photographer and historian.

Stone steps lead to the lovely Renaissance portal of the **Church of San Salvador**. The bell tower is very tall. Inside a *Mudejar* (Moorish) style carved ceiling draws the eyes upward. There is a carved altar piece of great beauty and a sacristy with Gothic vaulting. The interior is a sanctuary of peace and quietness and the many fine paintings and images make this church a treasury as well as a place of worship.

Outside in the small square is a stone fountain built in 1776 and tall palm trees stand erect in front of the delightful arcade of arches that house the town hall.

The **Casa Consistoriates, Ayuntamiento**, was built in the middle of the sixteenth century, during the reign of Phillip II of Spain. On the façade of the building is the coat-of-arms of the island of San Miguel de la Palma and an image of King Phillip II. Inside the building lavish woodwork adorns the walls, ceiling and central staircase. Several frescos are by Cossio. Upstairs, in the Banqueting Hall and Mayor's Chambers the great arched windows look out over the Plaza España and the San Salvador church.

Next door to the town hall are the offices of the shipping company, Trasmediterranea. Across the square are fine ancestral houses of Palmero families, whose coats-of-arms adorn the white façades. The **convent** is of the Order of St Francis and contains an imposing collection of religious imagery in a museum. Before leaving the square you may wish to visit the Agencia de Viajes Insular office, and book a day-trip by coach around the island.

This street now becomes Calle Real. It is still narrow and cobbled and on either side there are splendid eighteenth-century mansions, many with wrought iron balconies and coats-of-arms carved on the stonework.

It is but a short walk eastwards to Avenida el Puente where you will see the **market** (mercado). A daily supply of fresh vegetables, fruit, flowers, eggs, cheese and meat are sold in a cheerful atmosphere. Try some white goat's cheese (about £1 per pound) sustaining and delicious when eaten with a crusty roll of bread. The exotic flowers of the Canaries will be on sale: great bucketfuls of sweetly perfumed carnations; poinsettias whose red leaves we always associate with Christmas; roses of all colours, their tight buds giving a delicate fragrance and an air of sophistication; and, of course, strelitzia, this amazing waxen like flower that so strongly resembles a bird of paradise, and which lasts for at least three weeks in water.

TWENTY ONE

Touring La Palma

Island tour 1

Santa Cruz de la Palma – Playa de Cancajo – Breña Alta – Breña Baja – Mazo – Cueva de Belmaco – Fuencaliente – the San Antonio and Teneguia volcanoes: about 33 km; half day by car or taxi

There is a good road to the south of Santa Cruz de la Palma leading, eventually, to Fuencaliente. It is signposted at a junction just outside the town on the south road. After half a kilometre there is another junction, with a turning off for **Playa de Cancajo**. This beach with its series of volcanic coves is growing into a tourist resort. Fine black sands and sheltered pools make it pleasant for swimming and sunbathing. Two beach restaurants are at hand for refreshments. Modern apartments and hotels for holidaymakers are there already, and more are being built. It is undoubtedly a place that will develop quickly, being so close to the airport.

Returning to the main Fuencaliente road, the route passes through the village of **Breña Baja**. A parallel road leads to **Breña Alta**, the higher of these two villages, and it is on the higher road that the coach tours stop to visit a tobacco factory. In fact it is just a small room where six people sit at a large table rolling cigars by hand. Their nimbleness and skill is something to be appreciated in these days of automation. The cigars are of high repute, comparable to Havanas, and quite inexpensive considering the quality.

Just south of Breña Baja is the **Aeropuerto de La Palma**, which is capable of taking modern jets. The climatic conditions make it one of the safest airports in the region. There is plenty of parking space and a useful restaurant. Luggage trollies are available, there is a lift, toilets and facilities for the disabled, also a First Aid room. A well stocked news kiosk has some English paperbacks and newspapers. A gift shop sells local honey, piquant *mojo* sauce and the excellent La Palma goat cheese.

Telephones, post box and car rental firms are open when aircraft arrive and depart.

From the airport you can take a minor road signposted Mazo. This runs parallel with the C832 main road running south through Mazo (Santa Cruz 12km). On this road you will come to a small dip and bend where to your right you will see the famous **Cueva de Belmaco** (not easy for parking) with its prehistoric inscriptions of spiral and geometrical signs. To reach the cave you will have a short walk. Do not expect to see much here for the site is much neglected, as is a similar cave at Zarza, near Garafia in the north. But some important archaeological finds have been discovered. No one is quite sure of the origin or meaning of these ancient messages.

Along the same route going south you will reach El Molino (the windmill), which is a School of Craftsmanship. Visitors can see pupils at work and purchases can be made at the Craft Shop. The little baskets woven from palm leaves and exquisitely embroidered tablecloths are examples of the patience and skill of the local people. These make decorative and lasting souvenirs. It is in Mazo at the feast of Corpus Christi (May/June) that the sides of the streets are decorated with floral carpets and elaborate arches made from vegetables and greenery. Just past Tigalate this road joins with the

---

Silk, ceramics and crafts

Spain's Museum of Art and Popular Traditions made a study of silk-making. They found that the only place in Spain where silk is still hand made is in La Palma (in Murcia they work in silk but use modern machinery).

In the village of El Paso the tradition of handmade silk is being kept alive. The secret recipes for their dyes date back to the eighteenth century. Two natural dyes called orchillo and cochinillo are used. Orchillo is a lichen found on rocks near the coast: it is beaten and left to soak for at least fifteen days; by leaving the silk in the dye longer it becomes darker. Cochinillo is collected from the opuntia (prickly pear), toasted until the seeds are dry, then ground and soaked in water. A further natural dye is made from almond shells which turns the silk a beige colour. Some items of this work may be on sale at the Craft Centre El Molino, near Mazo.

At this same Centre you can watch Carmen Etelina and Ramon Barreto, both from Venezuela, who are making authentic pottery copied from original Guanche designs found at burial sites in La Palma. They have made ceramics for the Spanish Royal family and are very happy to be re-creating the old craft form of earthenware.

C832, going past Monte de Luna and Las Caletas, two small villages that cling to the mountain side.

Fine views are to be had as the road carries on south. Tobacco fields mingle with banana plantations and tomatoes, potatoes and green vegetables all grown extensively. Much water is available from the mountains, often contained in underground storage tanks. The volcanic soil retains the moisture from the air and the warm sun helps to make the crops plentiful.

Fuencaliente, 33 km from Santa Cruz, is the most southerly village on the island. It is surrounded by pine forests and vineyards that produce the famous *Malvasia* (Malmsey) wine. In the centre of the village are two bars and several small shops. The coach tour stops at one of the bars where tourists are given a sample of the local almond biscuits. Similar to macaroons, they are crunchy but soft inside, well flavoured with ground almonds. You can buy six biscuits for 300 pesetas. Almond cheese and honey are also for sale. Little cone shaped sweets called *Rapaduras*, which are made of *golfio* (a type of maize flour) and honey cost 50 pesetas.

It is in Fuencaliente that one turns off the main road to visit the volcanoes of **San Antonio** and **Teneguia** at the southern tip of La Palma. These are spectacular sights well worth a visit.

The San Antonio Volcano

It was on 13 November 1677 that earthquakes started, shuddering and growing in intensity. On 17 November the earth split and smoke, fire and lava poured forth. In less than a quarter of an hour eighteen different holes appeared. By 24 November, the river of fire and stones poured down to the sea, sending up smoke in the form of huge, white clouds. The outburst continued until 21 January 1678, when it suddenly ceased. One of the consequences of the volcanic eruption was that the famous Fuente Santa (Holy Spring), a source of thermal healing waters, disappeared, never to be found again. Today the volcano is a huge deep crater of dusty ash where, in places, forest and vines grow freely.

Close to the San Antonio volcano is **Roque Teneguia**, which was known to the Guanches as Tiniguiga and worshipped as a divine symbol. This majestic rock, a landmark for mariners and walkers, rises in the middle of sandy ground surrounded by volcanic cones. Recently a very rare plant called *Centaurea Junoniana* has been discovered here, growing in the cracks of the rocks, having survived the volcanic outbursts.

The Teneguia Volcano

This source of the island's most recent eruption became active on 26 October 1971. After several days of seismic movement, the volcano burst and vomited lava from twenty-six mouths of fire. Gradually these came together to form one enormous cone which continued to erupt until 22 November of the same year. This volcanic eruption was the shortest in the history of the island. Fortunately, vulcanologists are now able to predict such events and the villagers had warning and were able to move from the area, so no loss of life was suffered. But the volcano still has heat. Its smoke holes make this obvious. Tourists are allowed to walk amongst the ashes and lava rock, putting their hands into the fissures and feeling the heat below. It is an awe-inspiring experience and much photographed.

If you wish you can drive down to Punta Fuencaliente to see the old and new lighthouses. The small beach here is stony.

Island tour 2

Fuencaliente – Las Manchas – Los Llanos de Aridane – Puerto Naos – Tazacorte – Tijarafe – Puntagorda: about 51 km; 2 hrs by car or taxi

At the southern point of the island, a side road leads down to **Las Indias**, where the banana plantations stretch down to the sea's edge. The main road continues inland amongst pine woods and vineyards that thrive on the volcanic lava. About 2 km north of El Charco the little church of Santa Cecilia, built of lava stones, stands on a hill.

This is a country drive with constant sea views. The pine trees and wild flowers make the air sweet and the lack of traffic makes driving pleasant. At Jedey look for the restaurant Jedey on the inland side of the road. Here you can have genuine Canary cooking. Tasty vegetable soup, grilled pork chops or chicken, with local *papas arrugadas*, little potatoes cooked in salt water until their skins wrinkle. A friendly family establishment, you may be able to purchase some delicious home made almond biscuits from the ample woman who presides over the restaurant. She will always remember you and with a beaming smile saying *hasta luego*, see you again.

At **Las Manchas** the old Bodega Tamanca has been enlarged for the benefit of coach parties and tourists. Now visitors are invited to have a free sample of the *Malvasia* wine which is stored in the dark caves. Tasting the sweet and dry wines makes one hungry, so it is a good idea to have a *jamón boccadillo*, a large ham roll, to sustain you on your journey. Of course you may also purchase some wine at about 350 pesetas a litre.

From that high vantage point a clear view of **Puerto Naos** can be seen. Some consider this to be the best beach on the island and it is being developed into a seaside resort. Fine black sand and clear calm water make it pleasant for swimming but to reach it one has to continue north into **Los Llanos de Aridane**, then drive back south a distance of ten kilometres.

Puerto Naos

A detour of the main southern route can be made to visit Puerto Naos, which most consider to have La Palma's finest beach. Leaving Los Llanos de Aridane or El Paso (for there are two routes leading to Puerto Naos) you drive past many small villas ablaze with colour from their tidy gardens. All Palmeros love their flowers. Down by the coast acres of bananas, their tightly packed leaves waving in the breeze, are enclosed by walls built of breeze blocks and deep ditches. If you walk alongside the plantations in the evening the croaking of the marsh frogs, who live in the water channels, vies with the singing of the crickets.

Puerto Naos lies amongst these banana plantations. It is a designated area for tourist development and what was once a small port for fishing and banana boats has now become a seaside holiday resort. Restaurants and bars provide refreshment for holiday makers from the apartments and hotels. A small promenade has steps leading to the beach which is fine black sand. The Hotel Sol La Palma provides good quality accommodation including self catering apartments and two swimming pools.

One can drive about a further four kilometres past the hotel to reach Charco Verde and San Remo. The former has a nice quiet beach with a small roadside café. At San Remo (the end of the road) there is just a gathering of fishermen's houses amongst the bananas. Do not swim on this coast when a red flag is flying.

Close to Manchas is the small community called **San Nicolás**, victim of a volcanic eruption in 1949, when the Nambroque volcano cut the village in two, leaving just the tiny church and a few metres of soil untouched. The landscape is still scarred and the clinker-like lava rocks are much in evidence.

Approaching the town of Los Llanos de Aridane one realises that the area is a highly fertile plain. Avocados, bananas, figs and almonds grow well here to make it lush and cultivated. Tobacco, with its huge leaves, and fruit trees add colour especially in spring time. The houses are well built, many have patios and verandahs which are a blaze of exotic bloom. Hibiscus, poinsettia and bougainvillea mix with the striking white Angel's Trumpet (*Floripondio*) or Lady of the Night, a poisonous plant of the *belladonna* family. The Fire Bignonia spreads its bunches of orange-yellow and tubular blossoms over trellis and walls. Rubber trees, palms, and junipers add to the mixture that make La Palma a botanist's delight.

Los Llanos, an ancient and important town for commerce and agriculture, is the second largest on the island of La Palma. It rests in a beautiful setting with the high mountains as a powerful background. In the Plaza España a typical Canarian church houses a shrine for the image of Our Lady of the Remedies, a Flemish carving of the sixteenth century. Outside, the square is cool and peaceful under the hundred-year-old laurel trees.

The market (*mercado*) has a prominent place at the west end of the town, set in a plaza; here fruit and vegetables are piled high in a colourful display. Remember to buy some of the little Canarian new potatoes. Only two inches in circumference, they need only to be washed and boiled gently in their skins. Rolled in plenty of salt and eaten when cool they are delicious, particularly with Canarian *mojo picon*, a piquant red, hot sauce made from red peppers, oil, vinegar, salt and, sometimes, garlic. A milder version of this sauce is *mojo verde*, which is green and flavoured with coriander. It is often served with fish.

Nearby **Tazacorte**, 3 km to the west of Los Llanos, possesses the two qualities that define the island's economy: the cultivation of bananas and fishing. From the very beginning these have been a contributing factor to the stability of La Palma. This was one of the first Spanish settlements for it was near here, on 29 September 1492, that Alonso Fernandez de Lugo landed and took the island for Castile, Spain. A large breakwater has been built to protect the harbour but strong westerly winds can make it difficult for yachts to enter. A pleasant beach here has restaurants, bars and cafés. Some days coach excursions stop here for lunch. The main part of the village is two kilometres up a steep hill.

A little north of Los Llanos, there is a look-out point close to **El Time** (1,900 ft, 579m) from which you can view a remarkable panorama of the Aridane plain, **Barranco de Las Angustias** and the blue Atlantic. To reach there you have a steep and winding road, not too difficult unless you are behind a heavily laden banana lorry that belches diesel fumes and goes very slowly.

The road from the mirador (where there is a large restaurant) now winds its way north crossing many deep gorges, and passing through small villages. The road has recently been widened and most of the time one can see the Atlantic. **Tijarafe** has about 2,700 inhabitants and its well built houses are spread on either side of the main road. It is noted for its fine basket work. The Church of Candeleria has a sixteenth-century altar piece attributed to Antonio de Orbaran. In spring the countryside is particularly beautiful with pink and white almond blossom.

Just before you reach **Puntagorda** (which can be bypassed) you can stop to admire the view at a newly built Mirador. Puntagorda is noted for its picturesque landscape, where small white cottages, pine trees and heather woods add much to the peaceful countryside; at present there is no tourist accommodation in Puntagorda.

Island tour 3

Puntagorda – Santo Domingo de Garafia – Llano Negro – Roque Faro – Barlovento 26 km

This route is partially on unmade roads that can become rutted and flooded during the rainy season from November to March making it impassable for tourist cars. There are few bars or restaurants and only one petrol station at Santo Domingo de Garafia. Work is in hand to make this northern route link up with the rest of the road system that goes around the island but because of the precipitous *barrancos* it is likely to be some time before it is finished. In fine weather this is a pleasurable drive in a lovely remote part of the Canary Islands.

From **Puntagorda** the road is tarmac all the way to Llana Negro, the junction where you turn off north for the coast at Garafia (you will pass a turning to Roque de Los Muchachos). Quite different from the rest of the island, this region of Garafia is very green with meadows full of sheep and pastures where black and white cows munch the white spartocystus bushes. In the past the Palmeros who dwelt here were a community apart, for only mules could traverse the rough terrain. Until quite recently the bus came weekly, even now it is only once a day. The locals seem to enjoy their quiet existence and peaceful way of living off the land. Fruit trees and vegetable plots, chickens and pigs scratching in the soil, fields being ploughed by hand or with a donkey, the pace is unhurried.

As you drive by a wave of your hand will be met with a delighted look of pleasure, the response is warm hearted.

As you drop down to **Santo Domingo de Garafia** which lies a few metres above its port, turn right at the T-junction and shortly you will come to a small plaza with a very large church. Not much parking space but usually there are few visitors. Opposite the church is a simple hostal, restaurant bar San Antonio, where you are likely to be offered Canarian stew (*estafado*). However, if you arrive at the same time as one of the occasional excursion mini buses, all the tables could be booked, so it is wise to have some emergency rations with you. Be careful if you walk near the cliffs as the soil is soft, down below the waves crash on jagged rocks; it is reported that osprey nest on this coast.

Returning uphill from Garafia back up to the Llano Negro crossroads, should you feel like exploring then nearby is Fuente Secreta, the secret fountain or spring where you can look for some rock engravings. Should you not locate these you still have a chance to see some prehistoric inscriptions at **Cueva de la Zarza** (also called Feunte de la Zarza). It may be a bit of a treasure hunt to find them, you will have to park your car near Roque Faro and take a footpath. We hope there is now a sign showing the way. The engravings are on the side of a large rock face, a narrow ledge with railings leads to the site. Imagination can dwell on the mystery of why these markings are here and what is their meaning. Once an ancient people lived in this remote wilderness, now only wild flowers, butterflies and blackbirds remain.

Roque Faro is a small village which is a centre of goat rearing. You are likely to hear their bells as they move so nimbly along the mountain ridges. It is about here that the new road is being made, so be prepared for some diversions that will send you along rough rutted tracks. If you see a sign 'Vino de Tea', you may like to taste this wine which is laid up in pinewood casks; it has an unusual resin flavour. The main road goes through some dense pinewoods and is 1000m high, signed are turnoffs to the coast down deep *barrancos* to Tabalado, Franceses and Gallegos. At Mimbreras there is a picnic site with drinking water, tables and barbecues. Along here you will notice the abundance of *aeonium*, the green rock roses that cling to the shaded rock faces.

When you are approaching Barlovento look for a turning right signposted La Laguna de Barlovento. This lane leads to a reservoir and a picnic and camping site (see Chapter Nineteen, Camping). Should you wish for something more sophisticated then make a stop at the Restaurant Hotel La Palma Romantica, one of our favourite places. It is at a height of 600m with good views of the sea and mountains and has an observatory for star gazing.

A ten-minute drive from this hotel brings you to the centre of **Barlovento**, a sprawling, mostly modern, village, with a few shops, restaurants and a seventeenth-century church Nuestra Señora del Rosario.

Island tour 4

Barlovento – Los Sauces – San Andrés – Puerto Espindola – Bosque de Los Tilos – Puntallana – Roque de las Muchachos – Santa Cruz de La Palma: 48km. (This tour can be made by bus from Santa Cruz to Barlovento, return in one day; about six hours with a one-hour stop in Barlovento for lunch.)

Barlovento is a quiet, tidy village set high above the coast, so when you drive south you start descending and get closer to the sea. The C830 follows the coastline in a winding route. The road surface has been much improved and apart from a few sharp and blind corners in the valleys, driving is not difficult. It is a pictorial route with many views over banana plantations that are close to the cliffs.

After you leave Barlovento you start to descend, passing a side road leading to Punta Complida, signposted to Faro, a narrow road winding its way through the plantations. The lighthouse stands out on a point from which sailors take their bearings before crossing the mightly Atlantic. **Los Sauces** and **San Andrés** are places worth making a stop, the former having the very fine and imposing church Nuestra Señora de Monserrat, built in the sixteenth century. Inside, above the Flemish altar piece is a beautiful seventeenth-century Image of the Virgin. Across from the church and close to the bus stop is a cafeteria where you can have a snack (there are clean toilets, too). The surrounding region is lush with sweet potatoes, tomatoes and vines; sugar cane, too, for making rum.

San Andrés, close to the sea is surrounded by the green leaves of bananas, and white houses with red roofs and the tall palm trees give it a tropical look.

Down by the sea at Puerto Espindola fishing boats are seen in a tiny harbour. It is not really suitable for swimming here but you may care to take a dip at nearby Charco Azul where a man-made sea water pool is washed with each incoming tide.

Back on the main C830, still progressing south, the winding road goes round many deep *barrancos*, whose sides of volcanic rock are covered with thick vegetation. In places it has been necessary to bore a tunnel where it was not possible to widen the road. The Barranco del Agua has the famous **Bosque de Los Tilos** in its upper reaches. Part of this forest is under the protection of UNESCO. It is a luxuriant, great ancient forest, with giant ferns; the limes and laurel trees are dense and shiny green. Fungi and wild flowers delight the botanists. Organised walking tours go into the depths to show visitors species of endemic plants and rare flora. It is one of La Palma's unique treasures.

Astrophysical Centre, Roque de los Muchachos

The La Palma Observatory was inaugurated in 1985 and it contains the third largest telescope in the world. Astronomers from all over the world visit La Palma which has an exceptional clarity of air. Visitors must have permission to enter the Observatory, but if you wish to see the location you can drive there.

From Santa Cruz on the C830 before reaching Puntallana, look on the left for the road signed to Miranda and Roque de los Muchachos. You will drive for 36 km climbing all the time constantly turning and twisting, to a height of almost 2,426m. It is most scenic, passing through thick sweet smelling pine forests, waterfalls and many wild flowers, with virtually no traffic. As you climb higher the air becomes more pure and the only sound is birdsong. At Fuente de Olen there is parking and picnic tables. Almost at the top the landscape becomes strikingly barren and quite awesome, with occasional glimpses of villages and sea below. If it has been windy beware of rocks on the road. The observatory buildings come into view as huge white domes, very modernistic and space like. A barrier is across the road leading into the Centre.

Continuing on you have a choice of route, either going on 8 kms to Briestas, northwest then south to Puntagorda, or you can travel northeast to Barlovento. It must be stressed that the drive up and down is hard and it can be dangerous to travel fast; there have been many accidents on this road, particularly when coming down hill, some caused by brake failure.

At San Bartolome there is a mirador where you can stop and enjoy the clear air and admire the mountains and coastal scenery; there is a track nearby that leads to the summit of Montana de la Galga. Gradually you will start to descend as you approach the town of **Puntallana** with 2,400 inhabitants, its houses spread out in an easy going manner. Many have rainbow coloured gardens, brilliant with geraniums, lilies and trailing plants. Small roads lead through farmed fields to the low cliffs. A wide modern road continues down to the sea and the capital, Santa Cruz. Allow plenty of time for this drive as it is likely to take longer than expected because of the many undulations and bends.

Island tour 5

Los Llanos de Aridane – El Paso – La Caldera de Taburiente – La Cumbrecita – Las Nieves – Santa Cruz de la Palma: about 57 km; 1 day tour by car or taxi

A good road leads from Los Llanos de Aridane by banana plantations and pretty villas with colourful gardens, up into the higher region of El Paso, where silk worms are still reared and silk is produced. The **Parque Nacional Caldera de Taburiente**, one of the largest volcanic craters in the world, is a real wonder of nature. Reached by a good road either from Santa Cruz de la Palma or from Los Llanos, it is signposted to **La Cumbrecita** (little summit). A narrow road winds gradually deeper and higher into the pine forest, twisting and turning in a breathtaking climb to 1833m where a splendid *mirador* (view point) allows one to look at the imposing grandeur.

La Caldera de Taburiente is in the centre of the island. It is huge – circumference almost 27 km, maximum height 2439m, depth reaching 762m – the world's largest volcanic crater. The details are hard to grasp and when one sees it in reality it is even more amazing. The vastness and majesty of the place, the beauty that is now contained in the enormous crater, fills one with awe. Lined with pine trees, craggy lava and thick vegetation, La Caldera is now an international meeting place for mountaineers, geographers, geologists, vulcanologists and botanists making studies of the area. At **Roque de los Muchachos**, the highest point of the crater and in La Palma, an **astrophysical centre** has been built. Several European nations have joined together in this important international complex. Standing out from a jagged stone spine is a small rocky spike, the **Idafe Rock**, once sacred to the Guanches, the rose coloured rock dappled with light and shade. The blue sky gleams overhead and white clouds hang low over the tops of the peaks; below in the deep ravines there is a symphony of green and brown: this is nature at its most impressive.

Returning from La Cumbrecita to the main highway and taking the direction for Santa Cruz one will come to a popular restaurant, Las

One of the mighty volcanic peaks of La Caldera de Taburiente: this one amongst the pine trees can be easily seen from the viewpoint at La Cumbrecita.

Piedras, where nicely cooked food is promptly served. There is disco music in the bar and an attractive decor. The adjacent night club, Tana, is much used by young people from Los Llanos.

Going through the longest tunnel on the island (450m) one arrives at **Breña Alta**. There is a vantage point, **Mirador la Concepción**, with a particularly fine view of Santa Cruz and the harbour below.

Take the road that winds to the north behind Santa Cruz, to find the tiny peaceful village of **Las Nieves**. This place has significance for all *Palmerios*, for there in the centre of the square stands the church where the Patroness of La Palma, Nuestra Señora de Las Nieves (Our Lady of the Snows) is venerated. Overshadowed by the Pico de Las Nieves (Snow Peak) the seventeenth century church is guarded by great laurel trees. Inside the stillness is compelling. On the high altar the little terracotta image (origin unknown) is dressed in magnificient robes, surrounded by ornate and intricate gold and silver adornments. It is said that the 18 kilograms of silver in the altar came from Mexico in 1620.

During eleven months of the year Our Lady of the Snows remains in the Church, but in August she is carried into Santa Cruz for the fiesta, La Virgen de las Nieves. Every five years a more important fiesta is held, called La Bajada de la Virgen, when the figure is led in procession down to the boat built in her honour, the Barco de la Virgen, in Santa Cruz.

Traditions are preserved on the island of La Palma. At fiesta time each town presents programmes which have survived over the centuries, folklore and culture are being carefully handed down to each generation. Fourteen regional costumes are still worn. The contented people of La Palma are looking after their heritage. It is hoped that this will prevail with the coming of more tourists to the green island of La Palma, La Isla Bonita.

TWENTY TWO

Introducing La Gomera

Island of Sincerity

La Gomera (Isla de Cordialidad), roughly circular in shape, is the second smallest of the Canaries, with an area of about 378 sq km and a population of 24,500. It is a rugged country of deep ravines, green valleys with steeply terraced slopes, and dense dark forests that grow around the almost central **Mount Garajonay** (1487m), now designated a National Park.

La Gomera is just the place for anyone who wants a very quiet and restful holiday. It has been the only island without an airport, so it is still very much in the early stages of tourist development. It can only be a matter of time before the airport is built and then the naturally relaxed and peaceful atmosphere may well be replaced by an awareness of the commercial aspects of tourism, as has happened on the larger islands. But at present there are few hotels, little entertainment, only small beaches, and a way of life that goes on very slowly and simply. The *Gomeros* are friendly and cheerful, having a natural desire to communicate with visitors. However, English is not generally spoken, since the majority of tourists are Germans.

To reach La Gomera one has to take a ferry from Los Cristianos in the south of Tenerife. The Gomera ferry takes cars, trailers and caravans, but the Transmediterranean hydrofoil takes foot passengers only. Gomera's roads are being improved and it is now possible to tour most of the island. It must be emphasised, however, that owing to the difficult terrain there are few straight stretches of road. Because of the hills, twists and hairpin bends, travel is always slow and very careful driving is required.

Unique to the island of Gomera is the special whistle language used by the *Silbadores* (the Spanish word *silbo* means whistle). In the past, because of the lack of good roads and the difficult terrain, communication was made by a phonetic whistle that could carry for a

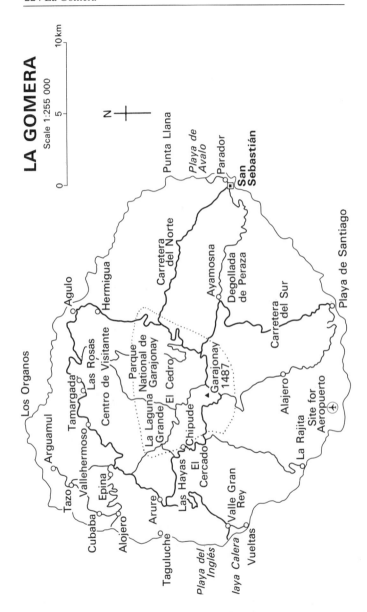

LA GOMERA

Scale 1:255 000

0   5   10 km

distance of two miles or more. By using various combinations of fingers in the mouth a great range of notes was produced which enabled people to 'speak' at a great distance. It has been said that the whistle language was created when the original inhabitants, the Guanches, had their tongues cut out by the Conquistadores, and began using their fingers to articulate different sounds. Later, shepherds and villagers continued to use the language.

Today, with telephone and radios, these skills are less necessary. Fortunately tourists are fascinated by this unusual method of communication, and quick-witted restaurant owners are ensuring that the language is not lost. Demonstrations are laid on for coach parties and visitors. Astute taxi drivers will whistle to their friends as they drive from village to village. It seems that this unique skill will be preserved after all, one of the better effects of tourism.

Yet another unusual feature of Gomera, and almost as famous as the whistle language, is the *astia* – a kind of pole used by the peasants to speed their walk about the mountains. With the aid of the *astia*, they are able to descend at almost breakneck speed, vaulting like acrobats from rock to rock.

History

La Gomera has had an eventful history, being invaded by the Moors, Portuguese and the Spanish. The Guanches fought hard here as on the other Canary Islands. It is said that Jean de Bethancourt conquered the island in 1404 but that fighting went on sporadically. The island became one of the seignorial islands, ruled over by the Condes (Counts) de Gomera. The first Count was Fernan Peraza, who built the fortress of which the keep or tower still stands today. Now used as a museum, the stone tower is situated close to the sea front.

In 1492 Christopher Columbus sailed into the natural deep water harbour at San Sebastián. It was already a busy port and he was glad to get livestock, water, provisions and to overhaul his ships before his departure for the Indies. Later he returned and it is reputed he was attracted by the charms of Beatriz de Bobadillo, a beautiful widow of that time. Beatriz de Bobadillo had been present at the court of Castile during the time when Columbus visited Queen Isabella of Spain. He called in three times to La Gomera, but found, on his third voyage, that Beatriz had married Alonso de Lugo, the Governor, and was living in Tenerife. Rather conspicuously Columbus avoided La Gomera on his fourth and last voyage in 1502. To this day, the 6th

September is celebrated as the start of Columbus week – a fiesta. Folk dancing, singing, football matches and eating and drinking are enjoyed day and night.

By the mid-sixteenth century the chief sources of wealth were timber and sugarcane. San Sebastián was a useful harbour for Spanish ships sailing to the West Indies. However the port suffered from repeated pirate attacks, so few settlers remained and many islanders emigrated to South America. The difficulty of transport over the rugged terrain led to La Gomera becoming the poor sister of the other islands. Now, although only 27 kms from the island of Tenerife, the inhabitants of La Gomera lead a rural life which appears to the visitor to be an almost idyllic existence. Most of the Gomeros own both houses and land and, with the fairly fertile soil, they maintain a degree of prosperity.

Calendar of festivals and fiestas

Jan 06	Valle Gran Rey, Santos Reyes
Jan 20	San Sebastián, Fiesta de San Sebastián
Feb or	
Mar	San Sebastián Carnival
Apr 25	Agulo, Fiesta San Marcos
Jun 25	Vallehermosa, Fiesta San Juan
Aug 15	Chipude, Fiesta de Candelaria
Sept 01 – 06	San Sebastián, Seman Colombina (Columbus week)
Sept 15	Alajero, Virgen del Buen Paso
Oct 03	Puntallana, Virgen de Guadalupe (Patron Saint of the island)

Climate

The climate of Gomera is similar to the rest of the Canary Islands. Rainfall is moderate, with moist winds blowing softly to condense on the high ground. In winter the temperature remains amazingly constant without abrupt changes. The sea is warm enough for swimming even in January and February.

The island is a place to wear comfortable rather than smart attire. Lightweight casual summer clothes and a sunhat are required and perhaps a cardigan or an anorak if a mist comes down over the mountains. Sturdy shoes are needed for walking in the forest.

The Virgin of Guadalupe

Situated on the remote promontory of Punta Llana, beyond San Sebastián and north of Playa de Avalo, lies the tiny chapel Ermita Nuestra Señora de Guadalupe. Inside is housed the image of the Patron Saint of La Gomera, La Virgen de Guadalupe.

Every five years and during the month of October the image of the Virgin is taken in procession from the sanctuary to a boat and then by sea to San Sebastián. This is an important religious festival, and many Gomerians from abroad return to the island for the event.

The climax is always celebrated with much rejoicing, fireworks, Canary wrestling, and folk dancing, the two best known folkloric groups being Groupo de Dantas de Hermigua y Agulo and Los Nagos de Chipude.

What to wear

Your holiday clothes for Gomera can be very casual, unless you plan to stay at the Parador or the Hotel Tecina, where you will require smarter clothes for the evenings. Take lightweight clothes with a good windproof jacket, hat and stout footwear for the mountains, where it can be cool in the mist. There are few clothes shops on the island.

Places of interest in Gomera

Approximate distances are given from San Sebastián (capital).

Centro Visitante (38 km) Above Agulo. Information Centre with well laid out exhibition rooms, videos and botanical garden, workshops for pottery, weaving, spinning and basket work. Open 0900 to 1630 hrs. Closed Sunday and Monday. Tel: 80 09 93.

Chipude (40 km) Remote pottery village in central high mountains. Simple pots made from local clay, traditional Guanche design. Woollen blankets and bags.

El Bosque del Cedro (27 km) Beautiful cedar forest, part of the National Park. Off the main San Sebastián to Hermigua road. Unmade roads can make forests difficult in wet weather. Walking/ nature trails.

Garajonay National Park (32 km) Alto de Garajonay 1487m.

Central ancient forest with lichen clad laurels, pines, heathers, many wild flowers. Craggy rocks, deep ravines.

Hermigua (22 km) Fertile area in north, bananas, palm trees, quiet town, souvenirs, local woollen rugs, basket work from banana leaves.

La Laguna Grande (35 km) In Garajonay National Park, picnic area in heart of thick forest. Children's playground, café, toilets, car park, barbecue ovens.

Las Rosas (38 km) Roadside restaurant high in northern mountains overlooking terraced valley. On Hermigua to Vallehermoso road. Unique setting, demonstrations of dancing and Gomera whistling.

Playa Calera (64 km) On west coast, remote small seaside resort reached from Valle Gran Rey, winding narrow approach. Sand and pebble beach, swimming. Beach bars, local fish, apartments, supermarket, banana plantations, palm trees.

Playa de Santiago (30 km) Fishing village in south of island, large harbour suitable for yachts. Pebble beach, supermarket, petrol, hostel, bananas.

San Sebastián Capital. Main port in picturesque natural harbour. Steep cliffs and mountain views. Hotel, supermarkets, restaurants, ancient monument, church, local market. *Parador* above the town.

Valle Gran Rey (64 km) Beautiful valley steeply terraced and intensively cultivated. Many palm trees, small white houses, wild flowers, cactus. Narrow winding roads need careful driving, panoramic views.

Vallehermoso (44 km) Village lies in valley surrounded by huge craggy mountains. Busy agricultural centre. Supermarket, petrol. Fertile area, fruit trees, plums and bananas.

Beaches

There are few accessible beaches around Gomera. Most are of pebble and some are difficult to reach, or have dangerous under currents. The best places to take children for a swim are the beaches by Valle Gran Rey.

Getting about

At present there are no coach tours of Gomera that commence in the island. However, coaches from Tenerife tour the main areas of the island in a day, though it requires an experienced and careful driver to make it an enjoyable drive. The journey is not for the nervous traveller who dislikes heights or narrow roads with unguarded edges; many roads have sheer drops to deep ravines below. But the scenery is spectacularly beautiful with high craggy mountains and forests which make the effort of travel worthwhile.

A day tour of the island (not possible by bus) should start at San Sebastián and travel anti-clockwise round the island. This way the more arduous driving is done at the beginning.

The Tourist Information Office in San Sebastián is located in Calle Medio 4. Tel: 87 05 04. It is just two minutes walk from the seafront, Plaza de America. Free leaflets and maps giving information about the Parque Nacional de Garajonay and tours of the island are available, with limited supplies of editions in English.

Buses

Main buses run from San Sebastián to Hermigua, Vallehermoso, Valle Gran Rey and Playa de Santiago. Services are infrequent, generally once a day. The bus to Valle Gran Rey departs from San Sebastián at 12.00 hrs and 1700 hrs. The single fare from San Sebastián to Valle Gran Rey is 350 pesetas.

Self drive car hire

There are several car hire firms in San Sebastián, one being 'Cabello', Ruiz de Padron 12. It costs about 3,250 pesetas to hire a car for the day; this includes insurance but not petrol. Other companies are: Avis (Tel: 87 04 61. Fax: 87 10 54), Hertz (Tel: 87 04 39), Auto Garajonay (Tel: 87 13 62). There is also Rent-a-Bike at Valle Gran Rey and Playa de Santiago.

Taxi

Hire is by arrangement with the driver, who should have a written tariff. A day tour of the island, from San Sebastián to Vallehermoso, Valle Gran Rey, Playa de Santiago and return, taking about eight hours, costs 5,000 pesetas; a tour from San Sebastián to Playa de Santiago, 2,200 pesetas. A recommended taxi driver is David Diaz Herrera, taxi number TF3272V, San Sebastián, telephone 870045 or 870524. Be prepared for him to play taped Canarian folk music and he will probably join in with a song himself!

A selection of accommodation

Accommodation in Gomera has always been sparse until recently when some tourist development has begun with the opening of a large hotel close to Playa de Santiago. Already one British tour operator, Thomson Holidays, is offering package holidays there. This must be with the thin end of the wedge, for with the widening of the roads and the projected airport the situation for accommodation will be improved. It is suggested that prebooking is sensible, especially at Christmas and Carnival time (February) and during school holidays, July and August, when many Gomerians return, bringing friends with them and tourists from the Spanish mainland. Village rooms are cheap and average about £10 per night for a double room. Apartments are from £10 to £20. The town hall in San Sebastián has a list of 41 pensions or apartments to let but these can be expected to vary from year to year.

San Sebastián de la Gomera

Parador Nacional de la Gomera **** Hotel. Tel: 87 11 00. San Sebastián. 42 rooms, TV, telephone, swimming pool, gardens. High situation overlooking San Sebastián with fishing and sailing. Delightful old-style building with cool interior patio, antiques and attractive gardens. Price for double room per night – 10,000 pesetas.

Hotel Garajonay ** Hotel. 17 Ruiz de Padron. Tel: 87 05 50. A small friendly hotel, accommodation only, 30 rooms, no restaurant or bar. It is very quiet and simple with clean rooms – some with private bath or shower – and comfortable beds. There is a small lounge. It is a convenient, low cost place, useful as a base for touring the island.

Canarias * Hotel Residencia. Ruiz de Padron 3. Tel: 87 03 55. Unpretentious and small, in the centre of town. 19 rooms, some have a bath. There is no restaurant. Open all year, the high season is from October to the end of March.

Colombina * Hotel Residencia. Ruiz de Padron 81. Tel: 87 12 57. 25 rooms have bath. This accommodation is available from November to the end of April. Adjoining is a small restaurant serving all meals at up market prices.

Villa Gomera ** Pension. Ruiz de Padron 68. Tel: 87 00 20. 16 double rooms with bath, TV, sitting room. In town centre.

Casanova * Pension. Avenida Maritima 6. Tel: 89 50 02. Double rooms and an apartment.

El Carmen * Pension. Avenida Maritima 18. Tel: 89 50 28. 4 double rooms.

El Pajar * Pension. Del Medio 23. Tel: 87 11 02. This 7 room pension is open all year and situated near the pebble beach. Bar restaurant open from 1000 hrs to midnight.

Gomera * Pension. Del Medio 33. Tel: 87 04 17. 6 rooms without bath. No restaurant.

Hesperides * Pension. Ruiz de Padron 32. 9 rooms, some with bath. No restaurant. Open all year.

Orquidea ** Apartamentos. Avenida de Colon 22. Tel: 87 14 88. In town centre. Clean simple furnishings.

Emilio Negrin * Apartamentos. Marichal. Avenida Maritima. Tel: 89 50 62. 2 double apartments.

D. Ramon Padilla * Apartamentos. Padilla Las Trincheras. Tel: 89 50 57. 6 apartments.

Ramon Arteaga * Apartamentos. Calle Fragairibarne 9. Tel: 87 00 89. 12 apartments with two and four bedrooms. Open all year.

Agulo

La Montaneta Apartamentos. Tel: 88 09 29 (ask for Carmita). 4 apartments.

Hermigua

El Piloto Pension. Playa Santa Catalina. Tel: 88 02 14. 8 beds, no meals.

De Angel Curbelo Clemente Pension. Lomo San Pedro. Tel: 88 02 29. 6 beds. No meals.

Los Telares Apartamentos. Calle General del Norte. Tel: 88 07 81. 22 studios. Half board available.

Playa de Santiago

Tecina **** Hotel. La Lomo de Tecina. Tel: 89 50 50. Situated in a high position overlooking Playa de Santiago. A large hotel built in attractive Canarian low style, with patios and balconies. 330 rooms are placed in chalets close to the main public rooms and restaurants. The decor is in good taste. Pine floors have colourful carpets and the floral arrangements and tropical plants make it very pleasant. All the facilities of a four-star hotel are here and the service is attentive and friendly, ideal for a quiet holiday. A lift to the beach below is being constructed. The manager is German.

Pension Casanova Avenida Maritima 5. Tel: 89 50 57. Rooms with bath. Situated by sea front.

Pension La Gaviota Avenida Maritima 34. Tel: 89 51 35. Modern building with simple double rooms, clean. Breakfast only. Situated by pebble beach.

Apartamentos Noda La Laguna de Santiago. Tel: 80 50 87. For two or four persons. Situated on hillside above the port.

Apartamentos Tapauga Avenida Maritima. Tel: 80 51 59. Apartments for two persons with sea view. By the port.

Valle Gran Rey

There are no hotels yet in Valle Gran Rey village or at the playa: however apartments and rooms are becoming more plentiful. The Tourist Information Office there has a list of accommodation and will make a reservation, or your taxi driver will take you to his relations! Prices range from 2,000 to 4,000 pesetas, per person, per night. Some places stipulate a minimum stay of two nights. There is a predominance of German visitors.

Vallehermoso

El Paso * Hotel Residencia. Tel: 80 00 73. 7 rooms. Simple and clean without bath, old fashioned beds. Bar restaurant next door. Quiet town with lovely mountain views.

Camping

The only official camping ground in Gomera is at El Cedro in the National Park, where a large area deep in the forest has been cleared. The setting is beautifully remote and peaceful, except for the young campers about you.

Facilities are basic but there are level terraced places for tents, toilets, cold showers and some dormitory accommodation. This camp is used mainly by students and walkers during the summer months. Occasionally a motorcaravan will venture two kilometres down the very steep, narrow and badly rutted track to the camp. We do not recommend taking a caravan. Further details can be had from the Tourist Information Office in San Sebastián.

At Playa de Avalo a rough camp ground is used by backpackers and naturists; permission to camp must be obtained from the farmer who owns the land.

Shopping

Shopping presents no problem for normal requirements of food. There is a good local market in San Sebastián, and lovely crusty bread from the *panaderia* (bakery). Try the little almond cakes, 15 pesetas each, similar to macaroons. Small supermarket type shops are found down many side streets; look into the dark interiors or you may miss them, as few have front windows displaying goods. In the country villages a few *artesania* (craft shops) are now being opened and taxi drivers will be glad to stop there.

Good buys are locally made straw baskets and goods made from woven dried banana leaves; attractive dolls; dishes; ornaments; jewellery boxes; colourful, handwoven rugs; woollen ponchos; attractive embroidered tablecloths and mats; pottery.

Sports, pastimes and entertainments

The prime pastime of the island, apart from touring by vehicle, is walking. The Visitors Centre at Juego de Bolas has maps and a guided walks booklet for sale (further information can be had from the Tourist Office in San Sebastián).

Mountain bicycles can be rented in Playa de Santiago and Valle Gran Rey. The Tecina Hotel in Playa de Santiago has a disco open to non-residents.

Restaurants

Your choice for eating out in La Gomera is small. You have the very good restaurants in the Parador and the Hotel Tecina (in Santiago) with international cuisine, or you will use the few village restaurants as you tour the island. In most the food is always freshly cooked and tasty, the service will be simple and clean, with plastic table covers and basic cutlery. At Playa de Santiago and Valle Gran Rey you should be able to have good fresh fish meals.

San Sebastián
Casa del Mar Calle del Medio 61. Tel: 87 12 19. A roomy bar restaurant by the seafront and near the bus stop. Snacks and Canarian meals.

El Pajar Calle Ruiz de Padron 44. Tel: 87 11 02. A popular bar restaurant with the locals. Low ceilings and quite a lot of atmosphere and reasonable prices.

La Cabana Barranco de la Villa. Tel: 87 02 59. Take your car or taxi from town (five kilometres) to get to this rustic wooden house. Used by locals, the food is entirely Canarian.

Hermigua

El Silbo Tel: 88 03 04. Used by coach tours. Closed Tuesdays.

La Laguna Grande Parque Nacional de Garajonay. Tel: 89 54 45. In the centre of the National Park by the picnic area. This small bar restaurant serves Canarian dishes during daytime.

Las Rosas

Las Rosas On edge of village of the same name. Modern restaurant caters for coach parties. Sometimes demonstrations of *silbo* (whistling). Splendid view.

Playa de Santiago

Bodegon Del Mar Tel: 89 51 35. Unpretentious Canarian restaurant. On seafront.

Banana plantations abound in the Canary Islands. Some are protected behind walls, but others are open for tourists to see those green fingers that seem to grow upside-down.

TWENTY THREE

San Sebastián

On arrival at San Sebastián, the capital of Gomera and its main port, one sees a small town of mainly white flat-topped buildings set in a natural harbour, against a backcloth of high mountains.

The tall palm trees add to its attractive appearance, yachts are moored in the sheltered bay, small fishing boats and nets line the stony beach, children dart in and out of the sea.

The thrice daily arrival of the large Gomera ferry m/v *Benchijiguia* and the Trasmediterranea Hydrofoil, bring the town to life. A recently built Estacion Maritima has booking office for the Trasmediterranea and Gomera ferries. Here you will find telephones, toilets, Avis Rent-a-Car office, a shop selling newspapers, postcards, souvenirs and a photocopy service. On the first floor is a cafeteria and bar. Taxis meet the ferries. Close to this port a small tunnel in the high cliff leads to a tiny beach, while above it the National parador is built on the promontory. A short walk from the port, past a petrol station, travel agent and shipping offices brings you to Plaza de America. An indifferent beach of pebbles shelves quite steeply into the bay that once sheltered Christopher Columbus and his ships, the Pinta, the Nina and the Santa Maria.

In the central square a small garden has exotic trees and shrubs. On one side the newly-built Canarian style Town Hall (*Ayuntamiento*) has a clock tower whose chime is delightfully mellow. To the west a newly built cafeteria and restaurant bar, Ramon Kiosco, provides refreshments, toilets and telephones – a good place to rest before catching the ferry.

The town has few streets: the two main ones, **Calle del Medio** and **Calle Ruiz de Padron**, run parallel and are partially one-way for traffic.

M/v Benchijiguia, *the Gomera ferry, berthed at San Sebastián; the headland behind is where the Parador commands fine views of the town and across the sea to Mount Teide.*

Town tour 1

Pozo de la Aguada – Iglesia Nuestra Señora de la Asunción – Casa de Colón – Mercado – Torre de Conde: a 2 hour walk

Walking from the Plaza de America rowards Calle del Medio (Middle Street) on the right hand corner you will see a low and ancient building. Its doorway faces the Plaza, where there are huge old Indian laurel trees. On the outside wall are the arms of the family of the Counts of Gomera, the Perazas. This single storey building, built before the seventeenth century has a pitched roof of Moorish tiles. Inside is a cool patio with many urns full of ferns, also a well with a stone parapet. Known as **Pozo de la Aguada** (The House of the Watering Place) this well is said to be where Christopher Columbus took water before his voyage to the New World. It is also known locally as the Customs House because it was used this century for that purpose. This house is now incorporated with the **Oficina de Turismo**, Tourist Information Office in Calle del Medio, open Monday – Friday 8am–3pm. Tel: 89 50 87.

Further up on the right is the fifteenth-century church **Nuestra Señora de la Asunción**. Built by the order of Count Fernan Peraza, it is reputed that Columbus prayed here with his crews before setting off on his first voyage. Outside the imposing façade has three entrance doors, whilst the interior is predominantly Gothic, with three naves. The framework of beams is rich in ornamentation. On the wall is a faded painting dated 1760 depicting a naval attack made on the island by the British Navy.

The next place of historic interest is also along this streeet. The recently restored **Casa de Colón** is past the church on the right, an ancient two storey, white and brown house. Once lived in by Christopher Columbus it now belongs to the Cabildo Insular (Island Council) and is open to the public as a museum. Another ancient church is the tiny fifteenth-century **Ermita de San Sebastián**, said to be the first chapel to be built on the island. Should you need a **Post Office** it is a short distance further north on the same street.

By crossing the road and going along Calle San Sebastián you can turn left into Calle Ruis de Padron, which runs south straight down to the seafront. On this street you will find Libreria Castilla selling English books.

The **market** (*mercado*) is open in the mornings in Avenida de Colón. Good fresh vegetables, fruit, flowers, meat, fish, eggs, bread and cheese are all laid out with care. Here, no one will try to sell you anything that you do not want, and you will be given help if you request it. Look for some local palm honey.

One of the dominant features in San Sebastián is the **Torre de Conde** – all that remains of the fortress built between 1447 and 1450 by Fernan Peraza. It is a tall square tower, with five foot thick walls and slits for arrows. Once it held the treasures brought back by the Spanish Conquistadores. Now a Spanish National Monument, it holds a collection of weapons and native artefacts. The ground around Torre de Conde is currently being cleared and developed as a recreational park and gardens with seats.

A huge statue of Christ on the hill overlooking the bay stands out strikingly against the backcloth of rugged rocky mountain peaks that lie to the north. Called the **Sagrado Corazon de Jesus** it is seven metres high. A dirt track road will take you to the site where you have a fine view of the town, harbour, sea and the island of Tenerife. It is especially beautiful at sunset.

Town tour 2

Parador Nacional – Hermitage of Our Lady of Guadalupe: by car or taxi, about 2 hours

Perched high on a northern cliff top overlooking the town and harbour, on the so-called **Lomo de Horca** (Ridge of Gallows) is the **National Parador Conde de La Gomera**. The attractive long low building has an entrance that is a perfect replica of the one built five centuries ago, and still preserved, at the Hermitage of San Sebastián.

The Parador is a fine example of an old aristocratic mansion. The interior has beautiful wood panelling and is furnished with antiques. Huge paintings adorn the broad staircase which has a fine carved handrail. An impressive formal drawing room is full of *objets d'art*, including a large model sailing ship. The dining room is air-conditioned, the service quiet and efficient. A small lounge has colour TV and there is a modern bar.

Perhaps the most delightful part of the Parador is the indoor patio garden, where climbing plants and ferns cover the pillars and balconies, giving it a cool and tropical atmosphere. The chatter of song birds makes it a happy place to take *desayuno* (breakfast) of coffee and cakes. Incidentally, the breakfast served in the dining room consists of toasted rolls, butter, jam, cake, cold meats, fresh fruit and tea or coffee.

In the grounds are many important species of native shrubs and plants including some enormous cacti. The large swimming pool has a sunbathing patio, with changing rooms and showers. Most days there are clear views of Mount Teide, across the sea on Tenerife. Non-residents are welcome for meals, which can be served by the pool.

Past the Parador a turning leads to Punta Llana and the **Hermitage of Our Lady of Guadalupe**, where the island's patroness is enshrined. A pilgrimage and festival to her honour is held in October each year, out at the tiny chapel.

TWENTY FOUR

Tours around La Gomera

Island tour 1

San Sebastián – Hermigua – Agulo – Las Rosas – Centro de Visitantes (Juego de Bolas) – Vallehermoso: 65 km

Head north on the Carretera de Norte, along the north side of the Barranco de la Ville, with good views of the central mountains. After driving through a 450m tunnel you have sight of the picturesque green valley of **Hermigua**. The road winds down steep cultivated slopes passing terraces of vines, potatoes and cereal. A large dam here helps to conserve the water supply.

This is one of the most flourishing banana zones on the island, and the banana leaves make a waving sea of green foliage. White-washed, red-roofed houses have palm trees, bright bougainvillea and geraniums outside the doors; with few people about, it is a quiet, colourful scene. It is here that you will find an *artesania*, Los Telares, a craft centre where young girls work with hand and foot at the looms making multi-coloured floor rugs. Upstairs an assortment of souvenirs is laid out to tempt the tourist. A drink on the shady patio is welcome. Almost opposite is an old Dominican convent which can be visited; it contains some fine Moorish woodwork.

Driving on one sees huge hands of bananas, some weighing 25 to 50 kilos, lying by the roadside awaiting collection by the big banana lorries that pound up and down the valleys. Never does one see a yellow banana, for they are always cut when hard and green.

Just past **La Castellana** is a fine view-point where you can take splendid photographs of the beach below, with the turquoise blue sea and distant Mount Teide on Tenerife to complete the picture. Watch your foothold as it is a sheer cliff without any railings.

Agulo has a spectacular setting by the coast, a spread out place which is dominated by the round dome of the San Marcos church. As one climbs up beyond the town there is a clear view across the sea to

Tenerife and the peak of Mount Teide, weather permitting. After going through a tunnel the road goes inland, twisting and turning. The air here is clean and crisp. Beyond Agulo is another *artesania*, should one feel like more tourist shopping. The craggy mountain tops vie with one another for splendour, the outlines clear against the blue skies. It is important not to choose one of the rare, cloudy days for this spectacular drive.

At **Las Rosas** there is a roadside restaurant prettily perched at the side of the green valley. It is much used by coach tours from Tenerife, and the food is recommended. Sometimes there are demonstrations of Gomerian music and dancing, also exhibitions of the *silbo* (whistle) language. The smell of the pine log fires is wonderful and one has a great feeling of being somewhere remote and different.

You should leave the main road near Las Rosas to follow the sign for **Juego de Bolas** where the Garajonay National Park Information Centre is located, a most worthwhile stop. It is open 0900–1400 hrs, closed on Tuesdays. Tel: 80 09 93. The centre is very well laid out with attractive Canarian gardens surrounding the buildings. Videos in several languages, an exhibition room, a number of workshops for arts and crafts (only opened when coach parties arrive), and a room depicting an old cottage, these are just some of the things you can enjoy here.

If you wish to be adventurous, there is a rough track from the Information Centre to Los Acevinous and El Cedro. It should only be attempted by car in dry weather or on foot provided you are suitably equipped. It is a wonderful experience walking through this ancient dense forest where the trees are so old they are dripping with fluffy, soft green lichen; tall primitive laurels and eucalyptus trees which are hundreds of years old make it seem like a scene from a fairy tale.

(Opposite) *Scattered hamlets nestle amongst the mountains and green countryside, where palm trees and cactus vie for space.*

Down amongst all this vegetation is the tiny Ermita de Nuestra Señora de Lourdes, where an important religious festival takes place in August. The chapel was built in 1964 with a donation from an Englishwoman, Elizabeth Parry. Near here is a picnic and camping centre with drinking water, toilets, barbecues and chalet accommodation. It is a wonderfully peaceful setting, but not easy to reach if rain has made the track rutted and slippery.

Back on the main road from Agulo and Las Rosas, going past **Tamargada** we take the high route to Vallehermoso, passing on the way a Mirador which allows extensive viewing over the dense forest below.

Vallehermoso, with a population larger than San Sebastián, is a busy commercial town. *Hermoso* means beautiful, which indeed this valley is, with the huge volcanic rock formation called **El Cano** standing high above. Anyone travelling by motorhome and requiring camping Gaz, will find an ironmonger (*ferreteria*) in the main street; there is also one of the few petrol stations on the island providing drinking water.

If you are interested in country made souvenirs, then you are likely to find some attractive gifts and mementos made from the stems of the banana plants; little figures, flowers and baskets are reasonably priced and it is good to help keep the local crafts alive. Although Vallehermoso is commercially important, for tourists it has a sleepy, peaceful atmosphere and the air is gloriously pure. To the north of the town is a tiny beach, **Playa de Vallehermoso**, where in calm weather you can take a boat trip to see Los Organos, a collection of basalt pillars or cliffs 80m high and 200m wide. Do not expect to swim here as the undertow and surf make it dangerous.

(Opposite) *A catch of* Bonita *being unloaded at the fishing port of Playa de Santiago, where you can join a sea excursion and go fishing too.*

The Wines of La Gomera

Although the Canary Islands export little wine it can be a pleasant pastime to seek out the local products. The history of Canary wine dates back some five hundred years and during this time its equality became renowned in the European Courts. Famous British writers, like Shakespeare and Sir Walter Scott, extolled its virtues.

Vineyards cover ten per cent of the total farm land in the islands, most of the grapes being grown for making wine. The Province of Tenerife has vineyards covering over ten thousand hectares. The soil in which all the vines are grown is of volcanic origin. In La Gomera the land is extremely mountainous and the vineyards lie on steep hillsides, where the small terraces are protected by dry stone walls and most of the ground is tilled by hand. The biggest production is in the regions of Agulo, Valle Gran Rey and Vallehermoso.

The Forastera Gomera variety dominates together with the Listan Blanco and Marmajuelo, the most important being the white wines. Those produced on the hillsides around Vallehermoso are golden straw coloured with a pleasant bouquet, mild and light with usually an alcoholic strength nearing fifteen degrees; they should be served chilled.

The red wine made to mark the fifth centenary of the discovery of America is called Don Juan (*vino de mesa*) and produced by Espinosa Ayala Cia. Hermigua. Ruby red in colour with a fruity and somewhat rough flavour when young, it ages well.

The cultivation of vine is on the increase in the Canary Islands and it is said that in the countryside there is no house without a wine cellar – 'Salud'.

Island tour 2

Vallehermoso – Epina – Alojero – Arguamul – Arure – Valley Gran Rey: 60 km

From Vallehermoso you take the road south through the Barranco Macayo, on a good but twisting route to a junction, with a turning north to **Epina**. Look out for the Fuente de Epina, it is said whoever drinks this water will return to La Gomera! Now you are on a secondary road which winds its way down a narrow route to the small village of **Alojera** in the northwest. This is a place that few visitors have time to see, but the authorities hope the region will be developed by tourism. The main produce here is tomatoes and the palm honey (*meil de palma*). The date palm trees are tapped for the sap (*guarapo*) which is then boiled until it forms a black sweet syrup like honey. If you see a ladder leaning against a palm tree, you will know it is probably being used to collect the sap to make the palm honey.

The small beach near the village has black sands. From there you can continue to Cubaba and Tazo on a dirt track road to **Arguamul**, a really isolated village, cut off from the rest of the island by its remote position. Because of the abundance of pure water the Gomerians are able to live off the land by farming mainly goats and sheep. At present it is not possible to travel up the mountain except by a footpath, or a track only suitable for donkeys. So we must retrace our way back to Epina, leaving behind a world almost untouched by the passage of time. Note that these country roads may be impassable in wet weather.

The route down to Valle Gran Rey goes through the village of **Arure** where you can make a stop at the Mirador Ermita El Santo. You will have to park your vehicle and walk a short way down a track and under a small bridge. Here you can look down over a huge spread of land, mostly undeveloped, and reaching to the remote village of Taguluche. For refreshments there is Bar Conchita.

Even though the route to Valle Gran Rey is being widened, care is required by the driver who will be tempted by the spectacular vistas to take his eyes off the road. On the way there is another newly built Mirador, designed by Cesar Manrique of Lanzarote fame, which allows everyone to have a stunning bird's eye view of the deeply cultivated *barranco* and the high escarpment behind. The many palm trees and lush greenery are reminiscent of the West Indies.

It is only within the last few years that the road to Valle Gran Rey has been passable for tourists. The narrow, poorly surfaced road is being replaced and widened. The **Barranco del Valle Gran Rey** (Valley of the Great King) is the most spectacular and most photographed ravine on the island – an area of vegetation, steeply terraced on both sides, very neatly patterned with little white houses, date palms and cultivated fields. Potatoes, vines, cereals and bananas, grow in well tilled soil. This is a little paradise tucked away in the sheltered south of La Gomera.

The steep and winding road leads right to the seashore, where a beach that is a mixture of greyish sand and pebbles forms a series of bays. At one end is found the *puerto*, where fishing boats unload and a few visiting yachts anchor. There are no hotels but plenty of apartments, suitable for tourists who are content with clean but simple furnishings. The easiest way to find accommodation is to ask one of the taxi drivers in San Sebastián: he probably has a relative in Valle Gran Rey.

Looking at a map of La Gomera, you will see that **Playa del Ingles**, **Playa Calera**, **Playa de Valle Gran Rey** and **Vueltas** all join one another. The same road runs from one to the other. Do not expect many tourist developments or tourist shops. Walking up the main street you will see one garage with a toilet and drinking water, four or five small village shops selling a little of everything, and a post office. One supermarket is tucked away behind some houses up a steep hill. There you will find a good selection of German type foods, including dark brown bread. The little sweet bananas grown locally are almost given away. It is interesting that one can telephone the UK and get a clear line quickly from so remote a place!

If you are the 'get away from it all' type, and adventurous, then Valle Gran Rey will provide a tranquillity that grows on you the longer you stay. There is absolutely no entertainment. The people seem to blend well, yet they are a strange mixture of Gomerians and visitors – mainly German tourists – some of the 'hippy' type including young girls and babies and others retired couples, happy to take a swim or walk along the dusty roads amongst the banana plantations. From the harbour there are boat trips to view **Los Organos**, an imposing line of cliffs 200m long and over 80m high, made up of large basalt columns at different levels, so resembling organ pipes; these can only be seen from the sea.

You can be assured of really freshly-caught fish every day at the restaurants along the newly built promenade by the beach. Try Meson El Pejin, Calle Colin. A typical meal consists of Canarian soup which usually has potatoes, meat and chopped egg in it; a generous salad; fresh crusty bread; fried or stewed fish served with Canarian potatoes and *mojo* sauce; and a caramel pudding or fresh fruit. Carafe table wine included, the meal for two should cost about 2000 pesetas. I doubt if there is better value, or more atmosphere, in any other place in the Canaries, for an easy-going few days holiday.

Island tour 3

Valle Gran Rey – Garajonay National Park – Chipude – El Cercado – La Laguna Grande – Playa de Santiago – San Sebastián: 80 km

At Valle Gran Rey, only one road leads in and out, and only one bus runs each day. To continue the tour of the island one has to drive back almost to the centre of the island, where new smooth tarmac roads run through the **Garajonay National Park** and within 2 km of **Mount Garajonay**. A very steep road runs down to **La Rajita** on the coast, which is more easily reached by boat. There is a sad legend about how the mountain, Garajonay, was named. It seems two young lovers used to secretly walk in the mountains, until one day they were discovered by their families and forbidden to meet again. The heartbroken lovers did go once more to the mountain where they fitted two sharp stakes between themselves. In a final embrace their hearts were pierced. The lovers' names were Garon and Jonay.

Garajonay National Park

Garajonay National Park was declared a World Heritage Site in 1981 and richly deserves the designation. Spread across the tiny island of La Gomera, this mass of dense forest contains some of the world's most ancient examples of laurel (*laurisilva*) forest.

Ever since the park was created the forest has been protected with some parts being closed to the public so that nature can remain undisturbed. Nevertheless other areas have been adapted to tourism and used as nature walks by those who appreciate its unique quality. Great ravines and aged volcanic rocks are thickly covered with woodlands. The basic climate of the forest is mist, which is condensation of the moist air of the trade winds meeting the hot air from the Sahara Desert. The result is a damp humid atmosphere with little light, so that moss and lichen cling to the twisted trees and in places on the ground where ferns and grasses grow.

Some four hundred species of flora, some endemic, thrive here. Although mostly silent this great forest contains a number of birds such as the buzzard, hawk, chiffchaff, blackbird and blue tit. The dark tailed and white tailed pigeons are endemic. There are a vast number of insects, spiders and molluscs. After the winter rain great waterfalls (*cascada*) create streams that flow through the undergrowth keeping the ground moist all the year.

Garajonay National Park allows everyone to see the wonders of nature unspoilt by mankind.

The villages of **Chipude** and **El Cercado** near the centre of the island are known as the potter's *pueblos*, where the distinctive, deep red, earthenware replicas of Guanche pots are fashioned by hand and then baked in a clay oven. If you purchase any for presents and souvenirs treat them carefully. To the south of Chipude you have a clear view of La Fortaleza (the Fortress). This is a large, basalt rock 124m high, that has an enormous flat surface on top. It can be seen from a great distance and it is said to have been a Guanche holy place. Now visitors can take photographs from a terrace there.

Some time should be allowed to enjoy the National Park, a dense wilderness of crags, rocks and gorges, where some of the oldest trees in the world are to be found. The trunks and branches of the trees are covered with lichen and moss so that they have an unreal, 'Sleeping Beauty' quality. Song birds are heard and the air is fragrant with sweet herbs, wild forget-me-nots, marigolds, violets and much other flora. It is a place of perfect peace, forests of undisturbed natural beauty with an aura of timelessness.

Should you wish to have a picnic visit **La Laguna Grande** where, in a large forest clearing, you will find a car park, toilets, café-bar and a splendid playground for children, made from logs. Everyone enjoys having their photograph taken on life-size donkeys cleverly carved from wood. There are ready-made stone barbecue ovens, even piles of nicely chopped wood for visitors' use. The picnic place is clearly signposted on the main road through the forest.

There is one more place of interest to visit before the tour of the island is complete. The road to Playa de Santiago is a comparatively easy drive, and the only village of any size that one passes is **Alajero**, with narrow streets and a Moorish-style church with a cool tree-lined patio. As we passed the cemetery, our taxi driver made us smile when he said '*hotel finale*'! The Canarians love a joke. Just before reaching the port, as you descend in sweeping bends of the road, you will see on your left the entrance to the four star Tecina Hotel. Its situation is outstanding and the architecture and style of the place is worthy of a visit. It is open to non-residents.

It is here on the high ground above Playa de Santiago that the projected airport is being built, as this part of the island is very dry and unsuitable for cultivation.

Down in **Playa de Santiago** you will see a small deep water harbour, used by fishing boats and a few visiting yachts. The beach is stony and the main road runs along the shore. Bananas grow down by the beach. A garage, post office, a few tiny shops and market make up the little village. The tuna canning factory has recently been closed down. Small guesthouses provide limited accommodation but are often full, so phone in advance if you wish to stay there. Listen for the bullfrogs croaking, especially in the evening.

A walk along the quay could give you a chance to see fishing boats unloading their catch; usually it is *bonita*, ot tunny. In good weather the m/v *Alcajuma* takes visitors on boat trips to discover La Gomera from the sea, sailing around the coast past the high cliffs of Los Organos to Valley Gran Rey. It also goes to San Sebastián and takes fishing parties, which include swimming and food. These excursions can also be joined from San Sebastián, details from Transmar Gomera, Calle Republica Chile 11, San Sebastián. Tel: 87 09 21.

There is nothing of significance to see on the return journey to San Sebastián except the incredible rocky mountains and different strata which make up this remote island. Do allow time if you plan to catch the evening ferry, for the distance is very deceptive and driving can be slow if caught behind a fish or banana lorry.

You will join the main road to San Sebastián at Ayamosna and drive past the Degollada de Peraza, which is where Count Fernan Peraza was ambushed by two Guanche chiefs and thrown off the mountain. To the left of this junction are the spectacular lava rocks of Ojila, Agando and La Zarcita. We turn east and make our way down towards San Sebastián, which from a distance looks snug and tidy in the bay below.

La Gomera is well worth a visit. The grandeur of its mountains, steep valleys and thick forests impresses even the experienced traveller. The friendly Gomerians will give you an open smile of welcome and burst into song at any excuse. It is indeed a happy island full of spectacular landscapes, clear light and mountain peaks. Go soon while the island remains unspoilt.

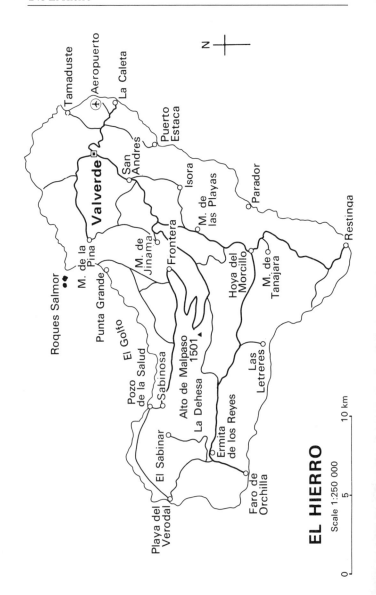

N

Tamaduste
Aeropuerto
La Caleta
Puerto Estaca
Isora
Parador
San Andres
Valverde
M. de las Playas
M. de la Pina
M. de Jinama
Frontera
Hoya del Morcillo
M. de Tanajara
Restinga
Roques Salmor
Punta Grande
El Golfo
Pozo de la Salud
Sabinosa
Alto de Malpaso 1501
La Dehesa
Las Letreres
El Sabinar
Ermita de los Reyes
Faro de Orchilla
Playa del Verodal

EL HIERRO

Scale 1:250 000

10 km

5

0

TWENTY FIVE

Introducing El Hierro

The Peaceful Island

Tranquilo is an evocative Spanish word which seems to fit Hierro (Isla de Tranquilidad) perfectly. This is not an island for anyone who wants bright lights and lively entertainments but an island for nature lovers, ideal for those who wish for a truly quiet holiday in a setting that remains completely natural and beautiful. It can offer few places suitable for bathing, and little accommodation.

Hierro is the most westerly and the smallest of the seven main islands of the Canarian archipelago, lying 52 kms south-west of Gomera. Looking at it on a map, it seems to resemble a small boot; seen from the air or from a distant ship, it appears as a dark green mass of mountains and steep cliffs. At one time considered to be remote, El Hierro is now becoming more accessible to tourists. It has a modern airport, suitable for the medium-sized aircraft that fly in three times a day (a 30-minute flight) from Tenerife. A passenger and car ferry operates three times a week from Santa Cruz de Tenerife to **Puerto de la Estaca**, which is the main port of Hierro, and the sea crossing takes about sixteen hours.

The island is small – only about 278 sq km – with a population of some 7,600 inhabitants known as *Herreños*, who speak a very pure Castilian. The central plateau reaches 1501m at its highest point, **Alto de Malpaso**. The coastline rises steeply from the sea, except at **El Golfo** where a deep bay some thirteen kilometres wide edges a fertile plain. The high rocks behind are the walls of an ancient volcanic crater. Because of this steep coastline, El Hierro lacks good sandy beaches. Where it is possible to reach the sea, lava rocks and pebbles make swimming difficult, though not impossible. In spite of having no rivers and a negligible rainfall, there are subterranean water reserves and fertile soil, allowing various crops and fruits, including figs, to be grown. On the high slopes, pines and beech form a thick forest. These obtain moisture from the mists which often cloak the higher levels, surviving well enough to give the island a green appearance.

In scattered villages on agricultural land and at the very edge of the pine groves, the inhabitants go about their daily life quietly. Crops include tobacco, potatoes, tomatoes, grapes, figs, apples, almonds and cereals. Recently bananas and pineapples have been grown successfully in the El Golfo region.

An excellent local cheese is produced at Isora from a blend of goat, cow and sheep's milk, and exported to Tenerife, where it doubles in price and is much sought after. A little fishing helps the island's economy.

On this unique and peaceful island, most of the inhabitants live by farming. In the north is a high plateau where the green fields are enclosed by grey stone walls with plenty of grazing for the black and white cows and long haired sheep. When the grey mists swirl, the landscape is reminiscent of the fells in Yorkshire. In marked contrast the south of El Hierro is dry and the volcanic strata are impressive and equally as notable as those seen in Lanzarote. The windswept north-west has the unique gnarled sabine trees (a form of juniper) which are the emblem of the island.

El Hierro is the only one of the Canary Islands whose capital is not a sea port: Valverde (pop. 1,400) is perched 600 m high above Puerto de la Estaca, and about 10 km from the coast. Perhaps, in the past, frequent invasions by pirates drove the inhabitants inland to seek protection.

History

Owing to the fact that the National Library in Valverde has been burnt down three times, much of the past history of the island has been lost forever. Remote caves in the west of the island have obscure symbols and alphabet-like inscriptions which no one has yet been able to decipher. Ancient Arab and European geographers set O degrees longitude, the zero meridian line, at **Punta Orchilla**, the western end of El Hierro. However, in 1884, Greenwich in London was chosen as the prime meridian of the world.

Early records of the history of the Canary Islands seem vague as to the exact date when Hierro was conquered, varying between 1402 and 1405. During that time Jean de Bethancourt settled one hundred and twenty Norman colonists there in an effort to subdue the original inhabitants. It was only by using treachery that he finally overcame all resistance. This was done by inviting the Guanche leader and his chiefs to peace talks, but instead of an armistice Bethancourt imprisoned them and later sold them into slavery.

These prehistoric inscriptions on the volcanic rock face are cause for much speculation amongst historians, who are still trying to decipher the meaning of the ancient writings. They can be seen at various places in La Palma and El Hierro.

When conquered by the Spanish Conquistadores, El Hierro had nothing in the way of safe harbours, and little was built or developed. Jean de Bethancourt made an early invasion of the island; later it was inherited by the Counts of Gomera, Fernan Peraza and his descendants. It is thought the name of the island derives from one of the early counts whose name was Herrera (*hero* or *ercero* means strong).

In Valverde a few surviving houses can be seen, but elsewhere the buildings are simple. Over the years the population has been depleted by emigration, especially to South America. Some have returned with families and there is a distinct likeness in a number of today's *Herreños*, both in character and features, to South American Indians, though they are mainly of Spanish descent.

Fiestas

Feb	02	La Virgen de La Candeleria, Los Lanillos, Golfo
Feb/Mar		Carnavales Entierro de la Sardina, Valverde
Apr	24	Las Pastores. La Virgen de Los Reyes, Cueves del Caracol
May	15	Santa Misa, San Isidro, Valverde
June	24	San Juan, Tamaduste
Jul first weekend		La Bajada de La Virgen de los Reyes (every fourth year – see Box)
Aug		Fiestas Patronales del Tamaduste
Sept	14	Fiesta San Telmo
Oct	28	Fiesta del San Simeon, Sabinosa
Nov	30	Fiesta San Andrés
Dec	08	Virgen de La Concepción Patronata de Valverde

Bajada de la Virgen de los Reyes

Every four years, on either the first or second Saturday in July, this the most important fiesta in El Hierro takes place. The next occasions will be 1993, 1997, etc.

Taken very seriously by all the inhabitants, the event is a combination of a deeply religious nature and a joyous festive occasion. The legend of Nuestra Señora de los Reyes, Our Lady of the Kings, the island's spiritual patroness, tells of a French ship which was becalmed off El Julan for many weeks; its crew would have starved had it not been for the food given them by the islanders. Having no money to repay this kindness the ship's captain gave them a statue of the Virgin Mary. It was 6 January 1577, the Day of the Kings. Now housed in a small white walled and wooden beamed chapel, set on a remote hillside, the tiny Madonna is much revered by the Herreños.

The Bajada is when the Madonna 'descends' and is taken in solemn procession over the hills for thirty four kilometres to Valverde, a long and arduous walk. Dressed in their colourful national costume and beautiful headresses, the islanders respect this ancient tradition. Lunch is taken near Malpaso at Cruz de Los Reyes, then the journey continues to wend its way to Valverde.

Toward the end of the month Our Lady is returned to the Ermita. This time the occasion is more festive, with dancing and singing from happy crowds.

Climate

Being so small, about 50km long and 20km wide, and the most south westerly of the Canary Islands, El Hierro is much affected by the north west winds, especially along the east and west coasts; the lee of the island, called Mar de las Calmas (calm sea), is protected from these winds by the central mountains which rise to 1501m.

On the hills in the northwest at El Sabinar, trees are blown so hard by the buffeting winds that they grow bent over and have now become the emblem of El Hierro. Another feature of the climate is the swirling white mist that can come down unexpectedly in the north and central regions, changing a sunny day into a moist and cool atmosphere. Fortunately the mist can blow away as quickly as it appears.

Like the other Canary Islands the temperatures along the coast can be 22 to 25°C and cloudless blue skies may make it necessary to seek shade in the middle of the day. Generally speaking it is a healthy and invigorating climate.

What to wear

Basic holiday clothes should include lightweight casuals for summer wear and a windproof jacket. During the winter woollen jumpers, windproof skirts and trousers are required, also light rainwear. At all times stout footwear is useful. Both a sunhat and a wool cap could be required. Formal clothes can be worn at the Parador.

Places of special interest

Approximate distances are given from Valverde, the capital.
Alto de Malpaso (26 km) The highest mountain, 1500m, in a central high plateau. Mirador de Jiname (viewpoint) gives magnificent vista over the west and El Golfo. Good roads.
Candeleria (32 km) Overlooking El Golfo, eighteenth-century church, separate bell tower on huge volcanic mound. Pension and bars nearby.
El Golfo (30 km) Wide north-western bay, submerged basin of ancient crater, slopes, dense forest, low plateau, cultivated, bananas, vegetables. Coast is black, rocky lava, some pools suitable for careful swimming.

Ermita de los Reyes (34km) Tiny chapel containing image of Patron Saint of Hierro. In remote region reached by dirt road. Nearby are interesting caves.

Faro de Orchillo (46km) Most south-westerly lighthouse in Spain. Important navigation point. Noted for being on original zero meridian line.

Frontera (33km) Wine producing town, north-west plateau, small agricultural and commercial centre. Scattered houses, pension, bars, supermarket.

Hoya del Morcillo (20km) Large area for picnics, barbecues, camping and playground in pinewoods.

La Caleta (7km) Tiny village by sea with man-made swimming pool and sun terraces. Ancient inscriptions on rock face.

Las Puntas (19km) Flat fertile area by north-west coast. Bananas, vines. Interesting modern restaurant and hotel by the sea at Punta Grande.

Puerto de la Estaca (10km) Tiny port for cargo passenger ships, car ferry, yachts, small bar and cafeteria. Very steep climb on road out of port.

Restinga (34km) Most southerly point. Fishing village, harbour suitable for yachts. Apartments, fish restaurants, underwater swimming, fishing, newly developed.

Sabinosa (41km) Tiny remote westerly village beneath high cliff. Quaint, donkeys, basket work, honey. Nearby is Pozo de Salud (well of health), a notable medicinal spa. Pension.

Taibique (20km) Second largest town in central area. Beautiful pine forest. Local wool hand-made bags called *talegas*, handicrafts, supermarket, bars, petrol. New Mirador de Tanajara.

Tamaduste (10km) Modern seaside development in north east. Natural inlet of seawater, calm for swimming, impressive rocks. No shops, one bar.

Tinor (5km) Hamlet in centre of plain, green fields, pyramids of volcanic ash, wild flowers, peaceful.

Valverde (Capital) Spread out town on steep hill 571m. Church, supermarkets, souvenirs, cheese, narrow streets, simple restaurants, bars, pension, guesthouse, petrol, taxis, buses, hospital, school.

Beaches

None of the beaches surrounding El Hierro have golden sands and all are very small. Because of rough seas and the great Atlantic rollers, swimming is dangerous for most of the year. However, man-made bathing pools amongst the lava rocks can be enjoyed.

Places where it may be possible to swim are Arenas Blanca, Charcos Manso, Hoya de Tacoran, La Caleta, La Restinga, Playa Verdal, Pozo de las Calcosas, Tamaduste and Tijimiraque.

Tourism in El Hierro

With about five hundred tourists coming to the island each year tourism is increasing very slowly. The Patronato de Turismo, working on a very slim budget, is aware that it will help the island's economy to develop tourism. To this end dramatic viewpoints (miradors) are being constructed, also Casas de Cultural (museums) are being erected in several districts. These cleverly built reconstructions of old manor houses will hold replicas of olden times, local costumes, ancient artefacts and historical objects of interest to visitors. Most tourists are Spanish, the rest mainly Germans and small groups of walkers. The tourist office is keen to increase the number of British visitors to El Hierro.

Getting about

For a small island to have such good wide roads is a pleasant surprise. Much effort is being made to create tourist picnic places, and road signs are attractively carved in local pinewood.

It is possible to tour the whole island by car or taxi in one day, but in some instances it is necessary to retrace one's route to get to another part of the island. Of course it is preferable to allow much longer to enjoy the quiet and varied landscapes of El Hierro.

There are no organised excursions from Valverde.

Buses

Four buses a day leave the capital, Valverde, travelling to the major villages. The bus service is very limited and subject to alterations. Buses generally leave Valverde early in the morning and return from other parts of the island the following day. Timetables can be obtained from the Tourist Office in Valverde. A small bus from Valverde attends each ferry at Puerto de la Estaca and also aircraft arrivals and departures, the fare in each case is 100 pesetas. The single fare from Valverde to Frontera is 175 pesetas, Sabinosa 225 pesetas and La Restinga 200 pesetas.

Car hire, taxis and tours

Cars may be rented at the airport and in Valverde. Taxis meet all aircraft and ferries. The taxi office in Valverde is at the corner of Calle Constitucion and Calle San Francisco and there are several along these streets. Car hire is approximately 3000 pesetas per day, this includes insurance. Taxi drivers will arrange to take you on half or full day excursions. A full day tour of the island would cost 8,000 pesetas. For example a taxi one way from Valverde to Tigaday costs 2,000 pesetas.

A selection of accommodation

El Hierro has approximately 400 beds, located in one Parador, three hotels, eleven pensions and thirteen apartment blocks. These are open all the year and are especially busy during July and August with visitors from Tenerife and Gran Canaria.

Parador de Turismo El Hierro *** Hotel. Las Playas. Tel: 922 55 80 36. 47 rooms with TV. Set in isolated position by pebble beach, modern building, well appointed. Outdoor pool and terrace. Table tennis. Double room with bath 10,000 pesetas, includes breakfast. Lunch or dinner 3,000 pesetas.

Boomerang ** Hotel. Calle Dr Gost 1, Valverde. Tel: 55 02 00. 19 rooms. In the centre of the capital with views of countryside. Modern, simple hotel which makes a convenient centre for touring.

Puntagrande ** Hotel. Las Puntas, Frontera. Tel: 55 90 81. 4 rooms. Famous for being the smallest hotel in the world (Guinness Book of Records). Once a banana packing station. By the sea and now furnished in nautical style. Restaurant specialises in fresh fish. other accommodation available in apartments nearby.

(Opposite) Top: *This twisted old sabina tree is native to El Hierro. Its fascinating growth is caused by the strong winds.*
(Opposite) Bottom: *The important Faro de Orchilla is the most southwestern point of Spain, once on the zero meridian. Its beam shines out across the Atlantic Ocean.*

Casanas * Hotel. Calle San Francisco 9, Valverde. Tel: 55 02 54. 11 rooms, simple, clean but without food. Double room 2,200 pesetas.

Casa Rosa * Pension. Pozo de Salud. Tel: 55 90 22. 6 rooms. Close to seashore. The well is said to have medicinal waters. Attractive isolated position.

Kai Marino * Pension. Puerto de la Restinga. Tel: 55 80 34. 8 rooms. Close to harbour, well established, German cliental, restaurant.

Bar Restaurant Tamaduste El Tamaduste. Tel: 55 01 77. Clean rooms above bar, 3,000 pesetas. Close to harbour and natural swimming pool.

Camping

The tourist authority tell us that because of the small number of campers who visit the island there is no restriction as to where they camp, provided they have the permission of the owner of the land.

Towards the centre of the island at **Hoya del Morcillo** a large area in the pine forest has been developed into a fine picnic and camp site, with water taps, cold showers and toilets, also picnic tables. Stone barbecues have an ample supply of firewood making this a pleasant place for a short holiday. Notable too, is the children's adventure playground. It has some cleverly made animals created from logs.

Shopping

All the main necessities are available on El Hierro but the selection of goods is limited. Fresh vegetables, milk, eggs, cheese and bread are

(Opposite) *This Well of Health is thought to contain natural spring water that is a helpful cure for many ailments. Nowadays there is a sanitorium close by for treatment.*

easily obtainable. Most shops have a variety of commodities but often the tinned stock is old and dusty and one has to seek out certain items. In **Valverde**, the capital, there are signs that shopkeepers are becoming aware of tourist requirements; postcards and small souvenirs can be found. Best buys for taking home are the local cheeses stamped *queso herreño* which, if kept cool, will travel well. Amongst the island's specialities are the rich cheese cakes in light pastry, called *quesadilla*: they are very tasty. Simple wooden ornaments, national costume dolls and basket work can be purchased. Look for a hand-made bag unique to El Hierro, called a *talega* and often for sale in the streets of Taibique. This is used by the shepherds, but is excellent for people who like to go walking as it can be worn over the shoulder or round the neck. Very strongly woven, usually in natural or grey shades of wool, these bags fetch a high price as so few are made now. The local wine is bottled and found in the supermarkets.

Sports and pastimes

In the usual tourist sense there is little organised entertainment on the island; so it is left to the visitor to find enjoyment in the natural landscape and the simple way of life of the Herreños. Much pleasure can be had from walking. The Tourist Office has suggested routes. Picnics, fishing, swimming and snorkelling are also offered as outdoor activities. Amongst the Herreños football matches and Canary wrestling (*lucha Canaria*) are popular.

No English newspapers are sent to El Hierro, so you need to take your own reading material with you.

Two folklore groups, Grupo Tejeguate and Grupo Sabinosa are well known. You are most likely to see them at fiesta time. Details are on posters in Valverde and the Tourist Office. Most bars and restaurants have TV, relaying Spanish programmes or showing videos. At the time of writing there is no cinema.

Restaurants

The few scattered restaurants in El Hierro are much used by the locals. They are simple, cheerful places to eat, with a Canarian menu. If you wish for a more sophisticated meal you must drive out to the Parador. The taxi drivers know the best eating places, some of which are mentioned in the tours.

TWENTY SIX

Exploring El Hierro

Valverde, the capital

Above the plaza winds Valverde's sinuous main street which today allows only one-way traffic from the Cepsa petrol station. Incidentally should you require Camping Gaz 907 this is where you exchange your cylinder for 350 pesetas.

A small private museum, **Casa Museo**, is a short walk downhill from the petrol station. Juan Padron the owner has a splendidly odd collection of curios and Canarian memorabilia. Knock on the door if it is closed.

Continuing along Calle Constitución you will find two parking areas. We suggest that you do not look for parking in the centre of town. The main **post office** (*correos*) is on the southern side of the road. It is interesting to know that once a day a large post office van complete with counter travels round the island giving service, collecting and delivering mail.

Car rent firms, small shops, including a chemist, banks and the Cabildo Insular (council offices) are located each side of the narrow street. Suddenly one comes to a sharp left hand bend. It is here that you are in the centre of town and the taxi rank.

To reach the **Oficina de Turismo**, the main tourist office, you go past the taxi rank and take a short walk up hill. The office is on the left and opens 0800 to 1500 hrs Monday to Friday, Saturday till 1300 hrs. The staff understand English and are most helpful. Some excellent brochures, well illustrated and informative, are given freely.

Continuing along the main street of Valverde, past the small hotel Casanas and bar restaurant Zabagu, the road winds uphill to the south of town and the area known as San Juan. It is here you will find the bus station, the football stadium, a large supermarket and a butcher's shop (*carnerceria*).

Turning right, this is still a one-way road which is called Dacio

Darias. It winds its way above and around the back of the town passing the police station (Guardia Civil), Government Offices (Delegacion de Gobierno), the Tax Office (Delegacion de Hacienda) and the Court of Justice (Juzgados), finally joining the Carretera General Norte and two-way traffic. By turning to your right in 100m you will see ahead the Cepsa petrol station.

If you are tired of the noise and bustle of the big cities this sleepy town will seem a delightful place, for here all seems peaceful. The only noise comes from the giggling young students who gather in the bars for coffee and a gossip. This hill top town set so safely away from the sea looks over green meadows and folding hills. Here you can relax and rest awhile amongst the friendly *Herreños*.

Island tour 1

Parador del Hierro – Tijimiraque – Puerto de la Estaca – Aeropuerto de Hierro – La Caleta – Tamaduste: about 45 km

The setting for the **Parador Nacional Isla del Hierro**, opened in 1981, is remote and wild. It is situated 19 kms from Valverde, along the coastal road south of Puerto de la Estaca at Las Playas. Built right at the edge of the sea, this modern building has the usual high standard of furnishings found in all Paradors, and patios, landscaped gardens and a large swimming pool. But it is the setting that makes it a one-in-a-million type of place to stay. Behind the Parador rises a huge escarpment of volcanic rock, immensely impressive in its size and variation of colour. With only three very small houses further along the bay, the quietness and isolation of the place reach one immediately. This is an hotel for the independent spirit and a perfect place to relax, if you do not wish for organised entertainment.

From the Parador the narrow tarmac road winds its way towards Valverde, along the edge of a shallow ridge of volcanic land close to the sea. The black volcanic lava with the passing of time has become covered with many plants of the cactus family and in springtime colourful wild flowers grow in profusion. Isolated houses often without fences are mostly holiday homes and they hardly notice in this wildly beautiful landscape. Here one really does feel on a very small island in the Atlantic with nothing to the west but sea and far off America.

Fifteen kilometres from Valverde out at sea but close inshore is the striking sight of **Roque de Bonanza**. This strange upthrust of volcanic rock seen from the road can in certain lights resemble the face of a lizard; at other times it may look like a bear leaning on a rock. It makes a splendid photograph and if you are cleverly positioned you can get a picture of the Parador framed through a hole in the rock. Incidentally, the headland by this rock, **Punta Bonanza**, is supposedly so named by ancient mariners who, seeing the rock, knew they were at last sighting land and calmer seas.

Here new tunnels have had to be bored into the cliffs to take the road further inland because the rough seas were washing away the old road. At **Tijimiraque**, ten kilometres from Valverde a smattering of houses lie close to a tiny sandy beach. When the weather is calm it is possible to swim, but notices warn visitors about the dangerous undercurrent. It is a nice place to sunbathe and picnic, there are benches and tables. Nearby a modern bar restaurant provides refreshments.

Shortly you will pass (on the left) the UNELCO electric power station and DISA gas and petrol installations. Notice behind them that the rock face has a number of huge natural caves. Soon the road comes to a sharp T-junction when it meets the Valverde–Puerto de la Estaca road. Watch carefully for big tanker lorries and heavily laden trucks climbing up the steep road from the port.

Puerto de la Estaca, seen from incoming ships, is just a tiny quay with a few houses built into the cliffs. This very small port is used by the cargo and passenger ferries as well as a number of private yachts seeking shelter for a few days, before continuing their respective voyages. Shabby shipping offices line the quayside. One small bar provides drinks and sandwiches for the lorry drivers or passing traveller. About thirty small houses are built in terraced disarray up the steep cliffside; canaries in cages, hens scuttling about, dogs barking and the laughter of children makes one realise that a small community lives there.

Only when the Trasmediterranea Ferry arrives and departs three times a week from Tenerife (via La Palma) does this little port with shipping offices and one small cafeteria (good for an inexpensive meal) become a scene of activity. Taxis and a bus meet the ship, relatives of returning Herreños crowd by the ferry gangplank calling excitedly to their families. Vehicles with foreign number plates are looked at with interested curiosity as they disembark. If you are amongst them it could be a good idea to park awhile at the port and give way to the huge trucks that fill the very winding nine kilometre road from the port to Valverde which is 571 metres high above the harbour.

While in this part of the island we suggest that you turn off right at a junction from the main road to Valverde to the Aeropuerto de Hierro and Tamaduste just four kilometres from the port.

The airport, **Aeropuerto de Hierro** is built right on the coast with aircraft arriving and departing out over the sea. The short runway has now been extended to take the seventy-seater aircraft operated by Binter to and from Tenerife three times a day, less frequently between Gran Canaria. Inside the small modern airport building are an information desk and two check-in counters. Toilets, including for the disabled, telephone, first aid, money change facility and a small *artisania* souvenir shop, selling products made on the island, are all on the ground floor; there is also a small bar and waiting room. There is no restaurant but ice cream *(helado)* and sandwiches *(bocadillos)* are available. There is plenty of car parking space and taxis and a bus attend flight arrivals and departures. Cruz Alta, car rental firm (Tel: 55 03 49) can arrange to meet you with a car. Avis (Tel: 55 01 92) have an office in Valverde as do four other car rental *(coches de alquiler)* firms.

Returning on the main road from the airport, in about five hundred metres at a T-junction, you will see a sign to the left for La Caleta (Valverde to the right).

La Caleta is a tiny quiet hamlet on the coast, consisting mainly of holiday houses, one bar and public telephone. The main road ends by the sea where amongst the lava rocks a man-made swimming pool is swept clean by the incoming tide. Steps wind down to a small terrace and a tiny bridge over the waters leads past a green gorge to a vantage point where La Caleta's claim to fame can be viewed: difficult to locate unless one knows the exact position and what one is seeking. Here on the north-east coast of Hierro are prehistoric inscriptions carved into the vertical dark basalt rock. As yet undeciphered, this short message, similar to other writings at Los Letreros in the south, remains a mystery yet to be solved.

The next place to visit is **Tamaduste**, which is reached by returning to the Valverde road from La Caleta (past the turning to the airport) and in under a kilometre a turning right is sign-posted Tamaduste. One has a good view of the airport runway along this road which skirts round a volcanic hill covered with green euphorbias and other cactus type flora. Finally, round a sharp and narrow corner, into view comes the deep sea inlet and sheltered bay of Tamaduste, ten kilometres from Valverde. Black volcanic soil surrounds the village buildings, terraces of vines make an unusual landscape beneath the rim of what once was a volcanic crater. Much of the lava remains petrified into weird and wonderful shapes, which can be dangerous if you try to walk on it. Attractively set on the coast, the small natural deep water inlet of sea is calm and safe for swimming. Diving boards have been erected – there are no sandy beaches.

Modern holiday homes are being built by local *Herreños* and one small bar is open. In the summer the resort is busy with islanders who regularly come down from Valverde to enjoy its refreshing waters.

At one part of the rocky coast there are spectacular volcanic rocks which reach out to the sea. The waves come lashing in with great cascades of spray and foam – a myriad of colours in the sunlight, the water pouring through holes and crevices in angry urgency only to recede for a moment, leaving a turquoise pool of clear water.

Island tour 2

Valverde – Echedo – Charco Manso – Pozo de las Calcos – Mocanal – Guarazoca – Mirador de la Peña – Las Montanetas – San Andrés – Tiñor – Valverde: 40 kms.

Start this tour from the Cepsa petrol station in Valverde. Going past the hospital, on the left is a main road signed to Echedo. This is a scenic route with views over Tamaduste and the airport. Drive through the little village of **Echedo** approximately 4km from Valverde; then if you wish take the road to **Charco Manso** where you can swim in a natural sea pool, provided it is calm.

Return to Echido and just after the main plaza turn right to join another dirt road to **Pozo de las Calcos**, an almost deserted village with a man-made swimming pool. Here a few lovingly restored thatched cottages are now holiday homes.

Back on the road to **Mocanal** this route will take you past fields of tomatoes and cereals, bounded by low stone walls. Here you may see donkeys drawing ploughs in the fields. Continue on the road through Erese. It is unlikely that you will see many inhabitants for they will be working in the fields, or have an occupation in Valverde. After **Guarazoca** follow the main road until you come to a bend and a sign to the right on a dirt track for the **Mirador de la Peña.** From here there is a wonderful view of the fertile plains below and the entire El Golfo region with the Atlantic rollers breaking over the Roques del Salmor which lie just off the shore.

The Mirador was designed by Cesar Manrique and created from natural stones. It has walkways with spectacular views and a modern restaurant offering a sophisticated menu and good service.

From here the country road curls back inland and in two kilometres you pass through the deserted village of Las Montanetas, one of the oldest on the island. It was abandoned because of the damp climate, where mist and clouds can swirl wildly.

A few owners have returned to modernise their houses for use as holiday homes. This is an area where shepherds graze flocks of long haired sheep and goats in the grassy fields. Stone walls mark the perimeters and when one sees them here in the stony lush meadowland it is reminiscent of the North Yorkshire Dales.

The road continues through **San Andrés**, a small scattered village bounded by dry stone walls. Between here and Valverde, ten kilometres, the road twists and turns past the almost deserted village of Tiñor, where neat fields of potatoes, vegetables, almonds and figs are carefully tended. You then arrive at the outskirts of Valverde.

Island tour 3

Valverde – San Andrés – Isora – Mirador Bermeja – El Pinar – Mirador de la Playas – Mirador de Tanajara – Taibique – Restinga: 30 km. Alternative return route: **Restinga – El Pinar – Hoya del Morcillo – Mercadel – Cruz de los Reyes – Malpaso – Valverde**: 40 km.

Leaving Valverde to drive south-west take the road to **San Andrés**, which passes neat fields and soft green hills, with wide views over pastureland. Hedges of *escoban* (broom) with its white blossom, and so enjoyed by the young goats, mix with *ericas* (heather) and banks of *vinagrera* (sorrel shrub). Lava rock walls mark the boundaries of the small fields. Potatoes, lettuce, cabbage and cereal crops are grown in well-tilled soil. This work is often done by hand or with the aid of a donkey. Sheep grazing on the higher slopes seem large because of their exceptionally long fleece.

Fig trees feature prominently on the island of El Hierro. They grow well and are a source of income to many families. Often the trees are encircled with low stone walls to mark the area which will be handed down from generation to generation as an important inheritance. Almonds grow in sheltered places and early in December their pale blossom is a joy to behold.

At San Andrés we turn left off the main road to visit another mirador. Look for a sign to *Isora* which is ten kilometres south of Valverde. Before the village you will see on the left the milk and cheese co-operative factory Ganadera. Once a home industry, now the cheese is made in three flavours: *blanco*, white, is mild; *alhumada* is smoked; and *curada* is mature. The latter is the most popular. These much sought after cheeses are exported to Tenerife where the price doubles on reaching there.

Drive through the old village of Isora where a new Casa Cultural is being built; a true replica stone house and museum of local handicrafts, ancient implements and historical relics. Look for the dirt track that in about 800m leads to the splendidly isolated **Mirador Bermeja** (770m) which overlooks Las Playas and the Parador (it is signposted), a vista that on a clear day is breathtaking. For the experienced walker there is a steep and rough track down to the hotel.

On leaving the mirador return along the dirt track to the road from Isora and continue westwards. This is a winding, narrow country route which eventually reaches the region of pinewoods called **El Pinar**. Another turning left is signed **Mirador de las Playas** (1,070m). This is a pleasant place for a picnic and another spectacular viewpoint from which there is a panorama towards the southern end of Hierro. Sometimes you will be able to see La Gomera and Mount Teide on Tenerife.

Back on the main road going towards Taibique you see in the distance El Pinar village on the hillside. Look out for a direction to yet another dramatic view at the **Mirador de Tanajara** (830m). You will drive for about 200m on a dirt road to reach this. On the way down from the **Mirador de Tanajara** you may care to stop at the small private Museo Panchillo; it is near Calle El Lager. As well as seeing a selection of curios you can buy country produce, figs and honey – both are particularly tasty. Nearby is the Artesania Ceramica, the place to buy pottery souvenirs.

The main road south winds itself around the hillside past Las Casas and El Pinar and through **Taibique**, which is the second largest town and a pleasant place to linger (Valverde 19km). It has several supermarkets, bars and restaurants, also a petrol station. You may be able to purchase a *talegas* (it means sack), which is a country person's coloured wool bag that can be worn like a rucksack or just looped over the head to hang in front of you. Craftsmen here carve wooden spoons, ladles and bowls. Nowadays these are sought after souvenirs and being handmade are expensive.

From here where the air has an aroma of the sweet eucalyptus, heathers and pine trees you travel south, gradually dropping down towards sea level. Soon you leave the forest region and as the road twists and turns the land becomes more arid and you notice vines and the ubiquitous fig trees growing in the volcanic soil. Eventually the black lava is too dense for any cultivation and only the *opuntia* (prickly pear cactus) and the white dwarf viper's bugloss cling to the *malpas* (waste land). These lava fields are quite varied and it is worthwhile to stop and note how some of this lava looks like coils of rope; yet in some places the molten flowing lava on cooling has created a wilderness of jagged rocks, even grottos and long tunnels. At first it is an awesome sight, then after a while one sees how nature is returning, if slowly, and in crevices and niches tiny plants and flowers are blooming again.

Cueva de Don Justo

Its concealed entrance lies two kilometres north of Restinga, leading to a labyrinth of tunnels formed beneath a volcanic cone. The tunnels are estimated to cover over 6,135m in total length, making the network the second largest in the Canary Islands (the first is the Cueva del Viento in Tenerife at 9,250m), and the sixth known largest in the world. The interior is completely dark and many of its stalagmites have been vandalised. Nevertheless there is a thought to make the cave into a tourist attraction. In the meantime visitors are strongly advised not to enter its claustrophobic maze without a guide.

Restinga, at the most southerly point of the island, is in a volcanic wasteland, but the approach road is good. A tiny fishing port, it is now being developed as a place for tourists, with the blessing of the local inhabitants who are keen on the tourist trade. Several apartment blocks, pensions and fish bars are being hastily erected. The deep harbour has a high wall that gives excellent shelter for visiting yachts, glad to rest and provision before going across the Atlantic. Fishing and underwater swimming are popular here as the clear waters and rocky depths provide the right conditions.

A fish meal in a bar-restaurant like the Refugio will cost approximately 1,300 pesetas per person, and you could expect to be served grilled tuna fish, Canarian boiled potatoes, *mojo* sauce, salad, caramel pudding, bread and local wine. It is possible that the man who serves you will have caught and cooked the fish himself and will be proud to tell you so. It will be eaten in a small room behind the main bar, plastic cloths on the table. If you go by taxi, the driver may sit down with you and enjoy the same food. He will not refuse when you offer to pay for his meal.

Away from it all

Beyond Restinga the south coast is steep, with only one recommended anchorage at Puerto Naos. It was here that in 1403 the Norman conquistador de Bethancourt first landed in his attempt to conquer the inhabitants. All is quiet now except for the soaring sea birds. Further along the coast in the region called Lajital, is Tacoron, reached by a dirt road, where several coves are suitable for snorkelling and small bays are pleasant for picnics and swimming. No sun beds, sunshades or timeshare touts here, just the blue sea, sometimes flecked with white foam but usually calm. This coast is called Mar de las Calmas.

Alternative return route

Should you wish to return to Valverde but would like to vary your route, go back to the main road, drive through El Pinar then on the northern side of the village turn left into the pinewoods. The next crossroads has a big signpost. If you turn left you will soon reach the picnic area of **Hoya del Morcillo**. Returning to the crossroads go straight across and in two kilometres take a dirt track on the left to **Mercadel** and its summit, 1,252 metres, another of the island's famous viewpoints. This one extends towards La Restinga, Tacoron and El Julan.

At the foot of the mountain another dirt road goes to the evergreen forest at **Cruz de Los Reyes**. Here the Forestry Commission has concreted the ground around an old sabine juniper tree to catch the water that condenses on its leaves from the mist that is unique to this island. This is an experiment to re-enact how the Guanches obtained their water supply. You may care to walk westwards to **Malpaso** (summit 1,501 m), the highest mountain on El Hierro, with extensive views over the whole of the island. From Cruz de Los Reyes follow the dirt road along the high ridge until it reaches the main road to Valverde.

Island tour 4

Valverde – San Andrés – Mirador de Jinama – Hoya del Morcillo – El Julán – Ermita de los Reyes – La Dehesa – Faro de Orchilla – Playa Verodal – Arenas Blancas – Sabinosa – Frontera: about 100 km.

This tour is a long and rather arduous drive as the middle part goes on dirt roads which in places may be rutted and there is a need for careful driving. Preferably it should be done with a four wheel drive vehicle, but ordinary hire cars and taxis make the journey safely. Certainly it is worth the experience as the scenery varies from thick pine forests to agricultural fields then turns into a weird volcanic landscape and finally impressive coastal scenery.

Leaving Valverde, drive south-west to San Andrés as in Tour 3. After San Andrés continue along a main road signposted Frontera and in about three kilometres you will see on your right a road leading to the **Mirador de Jinama** (1250m). From here you will have clear views over most parts of the island and beyond; to the south you will notice the distant mountains of Tenerife (1,417m) and Alto de Malpaso (1,501m).

About here the pines, laurels, beeches and *sabines* (evergreen shrubs that yield medicinal oil) cover the ground with a thick green forest. Look for the Hierro daisy (*Margarita Herrena*) which is endemic to the island. Villagers come to this area to gather edible mushrooms.

Continuing along the high ridge of what must be the rim of an extinct volcano, the air is scented with eucalyptus and pine. The road twists and turns giving glimpses of the fertile valley below, a panorama of little houses, palm trees, cultivated land and, beyond, the blue of the Atlantic. Slowly one descends like a god from heaven above to the mere mortals below. After passing a turning on the right marked Hoya de Fileba (1320m) keep a sharp watch for a direction on the left marked Hoya del Morcillo and El Pinar.

(At **Hoya del Morcillo** there is a fine picnic and camping ground, also a good area for walks). Follow this road and half a kilometre after the entrance for Hoya del Morcillo, turn right at the sign for El Julán and La Dehesa. it is here that you start driving on a dirt track. Provided the surface is dry you will enjoy the scenery, for the track leads west along the steep ridge of the wild southern slopes of El Julán. Deep valleys show where over the years water from the mountains has rushed down the slopes, creating these narrow *barrancos.* This is a beautiful wilderness where nature remains dominant.

It is here out on the rocky slopes that some early people left their own special marks. Known as Los Letreros, ancient enigmatic inscriptions carved into the lava rock have puzzled historians and antiquarians for years. Sadly, vandals have defiled these carvings, so much so that the Tourist Office has had to protect the site and allow only visitors with written authority to be admitted. But nature, too, has taken a hand and in a recent storm the road leading to Los Letreros was washed away with a landslide and became dangerous and unusable.

After nine kilometres on this track (34 km from Valverde), you will reach one of the most important places on El Hierro. It is the remote **Ermita de los Reyes**; enclosed by a low stone wall a small white church with a red tiled roof has a tiny tower with one bell. The door to the church is kept locked (the key is kept by the Town Hall in Valverde). This is because inside the church is housed the image of the patron saint of the island. Our Lady of the Kings is a beautiful Madonna dressed richly and sitting in a sedan chair, which is used to carry her in procession every four years to Valverde.

A short walk from behind the church leads across a flower-filled meadow to some primitive caves, used by shepherds and islanders when visiting the church on special saint's days.

Should you arrive here early in the day then consider driving north to **El Sabinar**, where another notable feature can be seen. For the strong north-east winds have bent low the *sabinas*, native juniper trees, into weird and wonderful stunted growths. So unusual are these trees that a photograph of them is used on much of the island's tourist literature and advertisements.

A little further ahead brings you to another of the island's spectacular vistas, the Mirador de Bascos. Here on a clear day you have a bird's eye view of El Golfo and sometimes in the far distance the islands of La Palma, La Gomera and Tenerife.

Returning by the same route to the Ermita, now you take a track signed **Faro de Orchilla**. You will drive through pasture land and are sure to see some of the many shaggy, long haired sheep and goats that graze the grassy meadows. How isolated are the small farmhouses here! You will have to open and close two sets of gates while you drive down to the famous lighthouse at Punta Orchilla. The name is derived from the orchil, a mosslike lichen which was found in the rocks and in ancient times much used as a purple or red dye.

The Orchillo lighthouse

The Faro de Orchilla has always been a notable landmark. In AD 150 Ptolemy placed his zero meridian line through El Hierro. Subsequent geographers agreed to this and it remained so until 1884 when it was transferred to Greenwich, London, England. To this day the tall lighthouse sends out its bright beam of light giving a hail or farewell to those who sail in these Atlantic waters.

Nowadays, any tourist who has reached this lighthouse may obtain, from the Tourist Office in Valverde, an impressive, sealed and numbered parchment to record and commemorate their visit.

The parchment states 'We certify that this person journeying to El Hierro, visited the lighthouse of Orchilla, the most western and most southern part of Spain, through which, from the times of Ptolemy until the end of the nineteenth century, passed the meridian.' The first Certifico No 1 was issued 25 April 1986. Our certificate is No 6135.

Close to the lighthouse the vegetation gives way to *malpas* or volcanic scree and the location of the lighthouse seems very desolate. Hopefully you will have taken some refreshment with you for there is nowhere to have a drink as you pause awhile. Nowadays the entrance to the lighthouse is kept locked.

Retracing your route back, and remembering to close the gates after you, take the dirt road signed Verodel. Again the way is narrow and rough in places and you need to watch for oncoming vehicles (not many, of course). This region of **La Dehesa** also has some *sabinas* trees, as well as colourful wild shrubs, flowers and cactus; the scenery is tremendous and solitary with nature in its wildest forms. Keep a look out for the beautiful *aguillas* (golden eagles).

Another stop can be made at **Playa del Verodal** where a red sandy beach allows you to have a swim. Now you have left the heights and are driving east near the sea along the northern coastline. Still amongst a volcanic landscape, note the contrast between the black weather beaten lava rocks and the lashing of the white foam that curls along the edge of the blue Atlantic. You are sure to photograph these tremendous rolling waves; in the background are enormous cliffs. Stop, too at **Arenas Blancas**, a small beach of white sands where shallow pools are fun for exploring. Suddenly you will be surprised to find you are on a tarmac road and you have left behind the most exciting part of the tour.

Shortly you will reach **Pozo de la Salud** (Well of Health), where a natural spring of sulphur and radium water is used for the treatment of various ailments. Here is a recently opened *balneario* (baths) and sanitorium, but it is far more interesting to look at the tiny well outside the pretty little Casa Rosa, a hostal and small restaurant.

Now it is necessary to climb up the great cliff on a breathtaking short, spiralling road past fields of vines, to **Sabinosa**, the most westerly village of all the Canary Islands. Its narrow streets cling perilously to the cliff side. A hostal and a good restaurant, with a few tiny shops, make up this community. Local wine and strong wicker baskets, used by the villagers as containers for their produce, make useful souvenirs.

A fast road past a few houses with pretty gardens soon brings you to Los Llanillos and the beginning of the agricultural region of El Golfo. Ten kilometres east of Sabinosa lies the sprawling town of **Frontera**. We suggest that you stay here a night in one of the small hostals or apartments to explore this interesting part of Hierro. (Or you can continue back to Valverde on Island tour 5.)

Island tour 5

Frontera – Las Puntas – Roques del Salmor – Tigaday – Valverde: 62 km

The Municipo de **La Frontera** extends along the cultivated valley of El Golfo. This is the vine growing region of the island. On either side of the main street houses are spread out, there are several national banks, some supermarketss, a chemist, post office also restaurants and bars. A road signed **Las Puntas** leads down to the sea from Frontera.

This flat, fertile area has been developed with banana plantations and more recently pineapples. Huge reservoirs hold the precious water so necessary for the successful cultivation of these crops. Vines are grown low on the volcanic sub-soil. The local wine is highly thought of by the *Herreños*, though to more sophisticated palates it may seem rather sweet and immature. In the last few years an increasing amount of *vino Herreño* has been bottled for export, and a widely available souvenir pack of red, white and rosé has become a popular buy for visitors leaving the island.

The road eventually comes to an end under the high cliff wall that is the ancient crater's edge. Far out at sea one can discern the jagged **Roques del Salmór**, reputed to be the home of the primeval lizard *Lacerta Simonyi*. This creature once grew to nine metres long and was thought to be extinct but in fact it still exists, though in a shorter version growing only to a meter or so. The story goes that a European visitor bribed a taxi driver to show him where the lizards could be found. Later, the same visitor was apprehended at the airport with one of these rare specimens. The taxi driver is now in prison and today no one dares tell of the exact hideaway of the precious lizards.

A small parking area leads to a narrow jetty on which one building stands all alone, looking rather like an abandoned warehouse. It is a great delight to find that inside is a splendid hotel and restaurant. Club Puntagrande at Las Puntas is reputed to be the smallest hotel in the world, having only four rooms, but there are some apartments nearby. The interior decor contains many antique articles related to the sea, including a complete diving suit and helmet of the 1940s era. All around the jetty the sea boils and lashes against the jagged volcanic rocks, the spume and roar of the foam creates an exciting and colourful sea picture. When the sea is calm you can swim. You may care to have a meal at a restaurant here called Noemi, the service is good and the fish fresh and tasty. Tel: 55 92 03. The four apartments by the restaurant have good sea views.

The agrilcutural zone of El Golfo has developed greatly in the past few years and much money and effort has been given to provide the *Herreños* with a source of income. Now fields of papayas, mangoes, bananas, strawberries and pineapples can be seen. Some farmers now use plastic to protect their valuable exports, which is practical but at the expense of the natural landscape,

Going back on the road towards Frontera you will pass the abandoned village of Guinea, one of the oldest on the island. Its remains are just stone walls covered with flowers and cacti. Around Frontera and **Tigaday**, fields of vines grow; the bars here will provide you with a glass of the local vintage and sell you a bottle as well.

Our route now takes you up out of this beautiful gulf in a winding godlike ascent. You are sure to notice the white Church of Nuestra Señora de Candelaria built 1818) that comes strikingly into view. When the church was completed the villagers found that the bell tower could not be seen from a distance, so it was demolished and rebuilt on a mound of volcanic ash thirty metres above the church. Now everyone is satisfied! Inside the large dark church a feeling of peace and quiet prevails: images look down serene in their glory, the altar glistens with adornments. On the opposite side of the road from the Church are two pleasant bars, simple and clean; one is also a pension.

The stadium by the church is not a football ground but is used for Canary wrestling *(lucha Canaria)*. The Herrio teams are well

Here on a tiny island in the Atlantic, at Las Puntas, is the smallest hotel in the world (according to the Guinness Book of Records). Once part of a banana packing station, it is now a sought after retreat.

renowned for their strength, skill, courage and team spirit. As you continue to climb nearly 1,000m with glimpses of the green valley below you will notice how clear the air is, made fragrant by the tall eucalyptus trees, heathers and pine trees. When you reach the top of the mountain ridge you will notice a change of scenery. The flatter land allows for fields of apple trees, almonds, potatoes and cereal crops, the dry stone walls being an unusual feature in the Canary Islands. You can return via Guarazoca, Erese and Mocanal or take the main road from San Andrés to reach Valverde.

Isla del Hierro, Iron Island (the literal translation), is a place of pleasant contrasts: green fertile hills, forests and immense volcanic escarpments. There are clusters of white houses, rich red soil, whirls of eroded lava, wild flowers, sheep, goats, donkeys, small dogs and a quiet people who go about their daily lives without giving much thought to the encroachment of the tourist industry. The smallest island is very beautiful, very peaceful.

Finale

The Canary Islands are easy to enjoy. Natural beauties abound, and the longer you stay the more you will have the opportunity to discover the delight in the vast variety. Whatever your age and interests it is probable that you will be able to indulge in your favourite pastime here. The majority of people visit the Canaries for warmth and sunshine. The fact that the tourist industry is ever increasing is a sure sign that visitors are not disappointed.

Mountain peaks, green valleys, busy cities, dusty deserts, restful beaches, palm trees and exotic flowers, entertainment, solitude, service and smiles, all are there in the enchanting Canary Islands. These 'Fortunate Islands' are truly a continent in miniature where the splendours of nature are combined with the modern conveniences that we have all come to accept as part of our lives.

For us, the Canary Islands will always be thought of as the Friendly Islands. We hope that this will be your happy experience too.

APPENDIX A: SPANISH-ENGLISH VOCABULARY

Public signs and notices

open	abierto
toilet	aseo
gentlemen	caballeros
closed	cerrado
push	empuje
entrance	entrada
free/vacant	libre
quay	muelle
engaged	ocupado
private	privado
depart/way out	salida
ladies	senoras
to rent	se alquilar
forbidden	se prohibe
toilet	servicio
for sale	se vende
no parking	se prohibe estacioner
no smoking	se prohibe fumar
pull	tire

Drinks

beer	cerveza
coffee/black	café solo
coffee/white	café con leche
gin	ginebra
ice	hielo
sherry	jerez
squash	zumo
tea	té
water	agua
wine dry	vino seco
wine red	vino tinto
wine sweet	vino dulce
wine white	vino blanco

Shops and places

baker	panaderia
butcher	carniceria
cake shop	pasteleria
chemist	farmacia
church	iglesia
cinema	cine
dairy	lecheria
fishmonger	pescaderia
grocer	alimentacion
ironmonger	ferreteria
library	biblioteca
market	mercado
post office	correos
shoe shop	zapateria
stationer	papelaria
theatre	teatro
town hall	ayuntamiento
view point	mirador

Restaurant

bill	cuenta
bottle	botella
breakfast	desayuno
cup	taza
dinner	cena
drink	bebida
fork	tenedor
glass	vaso
knife	cuchillo
lunch	almuerzo
plate	plato
sandwich	bocadillo
spoon	cuchara
table	mesa
tip	propina
waiter	camarero

Useful words

all	*todo*
before	*antes*
behind	*detras*
big	*grande*
cold	*frio*
everybody	*todos*
fast	*rapido*
food	*alimento*
good	*bueno*
here	*aqui*
high	*alto*
hot	*caliente*
how many?	*cuantos*
how much?	*cuanto*
left (direction)	*izquierda*
like	*como*
little (quantity)	*poco*
lost	*perdido*
many	*mas*
near	*cerca*
no	*no*
old	*viejo*
please	*por favor*
right (direction)	*derecha*
slow	*lento*
soon	*pronto*
too many	*demasiados*
too much	*demasiado*
under	*debajo*
up	*arriba*
very	*muy*
well	*bien*
when?	*cuando*
why?	*por que*
without	*sin*
with	*con*
yes	*si*

Days of the week

Sunday	*Domingo*
Monday	*Lunes*
Tuesday	*martes*
Wednesday	*Miercoles*
Thursday	*Jueves*
Friday	*Viernes*
Saturday	*Sabado*

Months

January	*Enero*
February	*Febrero*
March	*Marzo*
April	*Abril*
May	*Mayo*
June	*Junio*
July	*Julio*
August	*Agosto*
September	*Septiembre*
October	*Octubre*
November	*Noviembre*
December	*Diciembre*

Numbers

thank you	gracias
One	*Uno, una*
Two	*Dos*
Three	*Tres*
Four	*Cuatro*
Five	*Cinco*
Six	*Seis*
Seven	*Siete*
Eight	*Ocho*
Nine	*Nueve*
Ten	*Diez*

Food

apple	*manzana*	mushrooms	*setas*
banana	*platano*	mussels	*mehillones*
beef	*vaca*	mustard	*mostaza*
biscuit	*galleta*	oil	*aceite*
bread	*pan*	olives	*aceitunas*
butter	*mantequilla*	onions	*cebollas*
cabbage	*col*	orange	*naranja*
caramel pudding	*flan*	peach	*melocoton*
carrots	*zanorias*	pear	*pera*
cauliflower	*coliflor*	peas	*guisantes*
cheese	*queso*	pepper	*pimenta*
chicken	*pollo*	pork	*cerda*
chop	*chuleta*	potatoes	*patatas*
cream	*nata*	rice	*arroz*
cucumber	*pepino*	salad	*ensalada*
egg	*huevo*	salt	*sal*
fish	*pescado*	sauce	*salsa*
french beans	*judias verde*	sausages	*chorizo*
grapes	*uvas*	shrimps	*gambas*
ham	*jamon*	strawberries	*fresas*
ice cream	*helados*	suga	*azucar*
lamb	*cordero*	toast	*tostado*
lemon	*limon*	veal	*ternara*
lobster	*langosta*	vegetables	*verduras*
marmalade	*mermelada*	vinegar	*vinagre*

APPENDIX B: WIND FORCE: THE BEAUFORT SCALE*

B'Fort No.	Wind Descrip.	Effect on land	Effect on sea	Wind Speed knots	mph	kph	Wave height (m)†
0	Calm	Smoke rises vertically	Sea like a mirror	less than 1			-
1	Light air	Direction shown by smoke but not by wind vane	Ripples with appearance of scales; no foam crests	1-3	1-2		-
2	Light breeze	Wind felt on face; leaves rustle; wind vanes move	Small wavelets; crests do not break	4-6	4-7	6-11	0.15-0.30
3	Gentle breeze	Leaves and twigs in motion wind extends light flag	Large wavelets; crests begin to break; scattered white horses	7-10	8-12	13-19	0.60-1.00
4	Moderate breeze	Small branches move; dust and loose paper raised	Small waves becoming longer; fairly frequent white horses	11-16	13-18	21-29	1.00-1.50
5	Fresh breeze	Small trees in leaf begin to sway	Moderate waves; many white horses; chance of some spray	17-21	19-24	30-38	1.80-2.50
6	Strong breeze	Large branches in motion; telegraph wires whistle	Large waves begin to form; white crests extensive; some spray	22-27	25-31	40-50	3.00-4.00

Force	Description	Effects on land	Effects at sea				Wave height†
7	Near gale	Whole trees in motion; difficult to walk against wind	Sea heaps up: white foam from breaking waves begins to be blown in streaks	28-33	32-38	51-61	4.00-6.00
8	Gale	Twigs break off trees; progress impeded	Moderately high waves; foam blown in well-marked streaks	34-40	39-46	62-74	5.50-7.50
9	Strong gale	Chimney pots and slates blown off	High waves; dense streaks of foam; wave crests begin to roll over; heavy spray	41-47	47-54	75-86	7.00-9.75
10	Storm	Trees uprooted; considerable structural damage	Very high waves, overhanging crests; dense white foam streaks; sea takes on white appearance; visibility affected	48-56	55-63	87-100	9.00-12.50
11	Violent storm	Widespread damage, seldom experienced in England	Exceptionally high waves; dense patches of foam; wave crests blown into froth; visibility affected	57-65	64-75	101-110	11.30-16.00
12	Hurricane	Winds of this force encountered only in the tropics	Air filled with foam & spray; visibility seriously affected	65+	75+	110+	13.70+

* Introduced in 1805 by Sir Francis Beaufort (1774-1857), hydrographer to the Navy
† First figure indicates average height of waves; second figure indicates maximum height.

APPENDIX C: USEFUL CONVERSION TABLES

Distance/Height

feet	ft or m	metres
3.281	1	0.305
6.562	2	0.610
9.843	3	0.914
13.123	4	1.219
16.404	5	1.524
19.685	6	1.829
22.966	7	2.134
26.247	8	2.438
29.528	9	2.743
32.808	10	3.048
65.617	20	6.096
82.081	25	7.620
164.05	50	15.25
328.1	100	30.5
3281.	1000	305.

Weight

pounds	kg or lb	kilograms
2.205	1	0.454
4.409	2	0.907
8.819	4	1.814
13.228	6	2.722
17.637	8	3.629
22.046	10	4.536
44.093	20	9.072
55.116	25	11.340
110.231	50	22.680
220.462	100	45.359

Distance

miles	**km or ml**	kilometres
0.621	1	1.609
1.243	2	3.219
1.864	3	4.828
2.486	4	6.437
3.107	5	8.047
3.728	6	9.656
4.350	7	11.265
4.971	8	12.875
5.592	9	14.484
6.214	10	16.093
12.428	20	32.186
15.534	25	40.234
31.069	50	80.467
62.13	100	160.93
621.3	1000	1609.3

Liquids

gallons	gal or l	litres
0.220	1	4.546
0.440	2	9.092
0.880	4	18.184
1.320	6	27.276
1.760	8	36.368
2.200	10	45.460
4.400	20	90.919
5.500	25	113.649
10.999	50	227.298
21.998	100	454.596

Tyre pressure

lb per sq in	kg per sq cm
14	0.984
16	1.125
18	1.266
20	1.406
22	1.547
24	1.687
26	1.828
28	1.969
30	2.109
40	2.812

Temperature

centigrade	fahrenheit
0	32
5	41
10	50
20	68
30	86
40	104
50	122
60	140
70	158
80	176
90	194
100	212

Oven temperatures

Electric	Gas mark	Centigrade
225	1/4	110
250	1/2	130
275	1	140
300	2	150
325	3	170
350	4	180
375	5	190
400	6	200
425	7	220
450	8	230

Your weight in kilos

stones

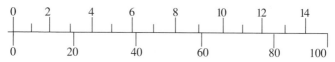

kilograms

Dress sizes

Size	bust/hip inches	bust/hip centimetres
8	30/32	76/81
10	32/34	81/86
12	34/36	86/91
14	36/38	91/97
16	38/40	97/102
18	40/42	102/107
20	42/44	107/112
22	44/46	112/117
24	46/48	117/122

Some handy equivalents for self caterers

1 oz	25 g	1 fluid ounce	25 ml
4 oz	125 g	1/4 pt. (1 gill)	142 ml
8 oz	250 g	1/2 pt.	284 ml
1 lb	500 g	3/4 pt.	426 ml
2.2 lb	1 kilo	1 pt.	568 ml
		1 3/4 pints	1 litre

APPENDIX D: BIBLIOGRAPHY

Myrtle and Phillip Ashmole *Natural History Excursions in Tenerife*, 1989. Kidston Mill Press, Peebles, Scotland. ISBN 0 9514544 0 4.

David and Zoe Bramwell *Wild Flowers of the Canary Islands*, 1974. Stanley Thornes, Cheltenham. ISBN 0 85950 227 9.

Canary Island Cruising Guide, 1991. World Cruising Publications, Alpine Press, Kings Langley, Herts. ISBN 0 9517486 0 2.

Isla de la Palma, 1981. Excmo. Cabildo Insular de la Palma, Santa Cruz de la Palma, Canary Islands.

John and Ann Mason *The Canary Islands*, 1976. Batsford, London.

Hubert Moeller *Flora of the Canary Islands*, 1981. Republished by Fred Kolbe Puerto de la Cruz, Tenerife.

Henry Myhill *The Canary Islands*, 1968. Faber and Faber, London.

Noel Rochford *Landscapes of Southern Tenerife and La Gomera*, 1988. Sunflower Books, London. ISBN 0 9485132 84

INDEX

Names of islands abbreviated as follows:
El Hierro: El H; La Gomera: La G; La Palma: La P; Tenerife: Ten